ADVANCE PRAISE FOR

Paul Tillich and Chu Hsi

"This is an exciting study in comparative theology and philosophy based on two major thinkers, Paul Tillich and Chu Hsi. Although Tillich and Chu lived in vastly different cultures, they articulate a strikingly similar view of human reality and its predicaments. This book makes use of a sophisticated hermeneutic based on three main analytic categories: unity, activity, and reunification. This work shows how Tillich and Chu diagnosed and then tried to heal the existential dilemmas that arise from finitude, ignorance, and error in the mundane world. Moreover, Kin Ming Au illuminates the religious dimension of Chu's thought and demonstrates how Chu becomes an effective dialogue partner for Christian theology. This book ably promotes the growing international and intercultural dialogue between and among Christians and Confucians in the modern world."

John H. Berthrong, School of Theology,
Boston University

"Kin Ming Au has written a pioneering study of the human predicament based on a sophisticated comparison of Paul Tillich and Chu Hsi. The sophistication in the method of comparison allows not only for two thinkers from very different cultures to be thought together, but also allows for an analysis of the human predicament more subtle than would be possible from either thinker alone. Au joins the ranks of careful comparativists who have moved beyond intellectual history to critical, normative philosophy and theology, faithful to the texts of the traditions they study but innovative and responsible to the normative issues."

Robert C. Neville, Dean, School of Theology,
Boston University

Paul Tillich and Chu Hsi

Asian Thought and Culture

Sandra A. Wawrytko
General Editor

Vol. 47

PETER LANG
New York • Washington, D.C./Baltimore • Bern
Frankfurt am Main • Berlin • Brussels • Vienna • Oxford

Kin Ming Au

Paul Tillich and Chu Hsi

A Comparison of Their Views of Human Condition

PETER LANG
New York • Washington, D.C./Baltimore • Bern
Frankfurt am Main • Berlin • Brussels • Vienna • Oxford

Library of Congress Cataloging-in-Publication Data

Au, Kin Ming.
Paul Tillich and Chu Hsi: a comparison of their views
of human condition / Kin Ming Au.
p. cm. — (Asian thought and culture; 47)
Includes bibliographical references.
1. Tillich, Paul, 1886—1965—Contributions in ontology. 2. Zhu, Xi,
1130—1200—Contributions in ontology. 3. Philosophy, Modern—
20th century. 4. Neo-Confucianism. I. Title. II. Series.
BX4827.T53 A92 233'.5'0922—dc21 2001046278
ISBN 0-8204-5147-9
ISSN 0893-6870

Die Deutsche Bibliothek-CIP-Einheitsaufnahme

Au, Kin Ming:
Paul Tillich and Chu Hsi: a comparison of their views
of human condition / Kin Ming Au.
–New York; Washington, D.C./Baltimore; Bern;
Frankfurt am Main; Berlin; Brussels; Vienna; Oxford: Lang.
(Asian thought and culture; Vol. 47)
ISBN 0-8204-5147-9

The paper in this book meets the guidelines for permanence and durability
of the Committee on Production Guidelines for Book Longevity
of the Council of Library Resources.

Printed in the United States of America

TABLE OF CONTENTS

Part One: The Thought of Paul Tillich

Part Two: The Thought of Chu Hsi

Part Three: A Confucian-Christian Dialogue

EDITOR'S PREFACE

At the onset of the twenty-first century, perhaps no term has resounded more pervasively, or garnered as much controversy, as "globalization." From news reports to market analyses, monographs to academic conferences, we are daily inundated by endless "insights" into the causes, trends, and consequences of globalization. While most commentators address the economic and political dimensions of globalization, one could equally explore its less obvious but more profound intellectual and cultural impacts.

Writing in 1964 (Ways of Thinking of Eastern Peoples) Japanese scholar Hajime Nakamura warned against two presumptuous presuppositions: "(1) the unity of Western culture, (2) the identity of Western culture with world culture." Dr. Nakamura would be both surprised and horrified to see that his warnings have gone largely unheeded, inasmuch as today's talk of globalization reiterates the same defective premises, supplying a new code word for the old notion of steam rolling westernization.

However, I believe Dr. Nakamura would take heart at the work of Au Kin Ming, who offers a unique form of interreligious dialogue spanning diverse cultures and times through informative case studies of outstanding representatives of two major world religions-the Neo-Confucianism of Song dynasty China and Protestant Christianity in twentieth century Germany. It constitutes a valuable addition to a growing list of works that explore the "globalization" of the Christian message as a creative inheritance that is multi-cultural in scope. What is required for Christianity to prosper in East Asian, Au argues, is "an East Asian theology" formed by an integration of Confucian and

Christian traditions. The specter of westernization is thus laid to rest, in line with Dr. Nakamura's own astute prediction that "with modesty and self-awareness a new culture may be formed through enlightened self-criticism." We are indebted to the author for this timely contribution to an authentic world culture, or globalization, now emerging.

S. A. Wawrytko
San Diego State University
San Diego, California , 2001

ACKNOWLEDGMENTS

I would like to express my gratitude to several people who helped me remain focused throughout this process. Thanks are offered to my former teachers at Boston University, Professor John H. Berthrong, who first directed my attention to Chu Hsi and has been extremely helpful to me during the process of completing this study, and Dean Robert C. Neville, who guided me in the comparative method of this book and has constantly encouraged my study. Thanks are also due to Professor Tu Wei-ming of Harvard University, who has enriched my understanding of Neo-Confucianism.

I would also like to thank my series editor, Dr. S. A. Wawrytko, for her insight and thoughtful comments regarding my text and her preface for this book.

Above all, to my wife for her help and support throughout the creation of this text. This book is dedicated with deep gratitude to her.

INTRODUCTION

As we approach the Third Millennium, we are aware that Christianity is rapidly expanding in East Asian countries. Demographically, Christianity has shifted gradually from the American and European regions to the East Asian region. In this respect, Christianity is no longer to be understood only from a Western perspective. Rather, it should be understood from a world perspective. Therefore, Christian theology today must become a world theology. Nonetheless, Christianity historically was exclusively a Western religion, at least from an East Asian perspective, because it has a long traditional history in the West and its system of thought is a part of Western culture.

Due to the fact that Christianity is not only planted in the soil of East Asia but also is flourishing in this region, an understanding of Christianity then must be sought from an East Asian perspective. Thus, the dialogue between East Asian religions and Christianity is unavoidable. Throughout the years since Christianity arrived in East Asia, the dialogue with other Asian religions and cultures has never ceased for a moment, at least in the daily life of every East Asian Christian. For example, East Asian Christians, whether they are Korean, Japanese, Vietnamese, or Chinese, are embedded in Confucian culture. Although East Asia is a diversified region, East Asian countries have much in common in terms of classical culture, including the original means by which Confucian thought was spread as a canon of commonly accepted texts. For Confucianism, the family, the educational system, and the state civil service examination system were the three traditional transmission points.[1] They are the characteristics of society in East Asia. For instance, the subordination of the individual to the family emerges from the humanistic Confucian tradition. Even though the original form and function of the examination system were abolished in China in 1905, there is still an analogous examination system for university admission in Mainland China, Taiwan, Hong Kong, Singapore, South Korea, and Japan. Based upon their Confucian tradition, East Asian Christians should take their own cultural tradition as well as their Christian faith seriously by enacting, re-enacting and transforming these two traditions in their mental and spiritual lives.

In modern times, many people anticipated the precipitous demise of the Confucian tradition. But at the end of the twentieth century the East Asian region is viewed as one of the three regions of rapid modernization in the world.[2] With their remarkable economic success, East Asian countries have called attention yet again to their common Confucian cultural roots. Although there are many East Asians professing to be Shintoists, Taoists, Buddhists, Muslims, or Christians, they cannot cease to be Confucians because Confucianism is their historical heritage.[3] That is to say, the primary mission of the East Asian Christian Church in general, or of the Chinese Church in particular, is now to develop its own theology through implicit or explicit dialogue with the Confucian tradition.

If Christianity continues to prosper in the East Asian region, an East Asian theology is needed for the church of East Asia. In order to establish an East Asian Christian theology, there must be an integration of both Confucian and Christian traditions. However, Confucianism and Christianity are two radically different traditions. Before integrating these two traditions, we need to find out their similarities and show that they are not incommensurable, or even incompatible.

This study attempts to show the similarity of Chu Hsi's (1130-1200) and Paul Tillich's (1886-1965) concepts of human nature. Although these two great thinkers came from two radically different religious traditions and cultures, they articulated similar views of the unity of human reality and the problem of human existence. Furthermore, they proposed remarkably parallel strategies to resolve the tensions of finite human existence in searching for a reunification of human nature with its root in divine reality. By analyzing similarities and differences between Chu's and Tillich's views on human nature, this study intends to facilitate the dialogue between Confucianism and Christianity as alternative expressions of major religious worldviews.

The comparative theological method employed here is derived from a close hermeneutical reading of Tillich. Furthermore, the fundamental perspective of the study is grounded in an ecumenical Christian reading of the human condition. Based on Tillich's systematic theology, three vague comparative terms are suggested for the task of comparison, namely unity, activity, and reunification.

The hypothesis to be tested is whether or not these three vague comparative categories for comparison, although generated from the fertile matrix of Tillich's thought, can address Chu's reflections on the problems of human nature as well as the resolution of this problem. Although the comparative categories are derived from the Christian theological tradition in their general contours, they are designed to deal with a problem and its resolution common to Confucianism as well. The common problem of humankind is that we know in our mind-hearts that we are not what we ought to be in relation to our primordial ground of being. Both *jen* and love, as ultimate principles, in the thought of Chu and Tillich respectively, share the same function of the resolution of the human problem.

I have deliberately chosen Chu Hsi and Paul Tillich because they are major intellectuals who well represent their respective traditions. Chu Hsi was the most influential thinker in Chinese history since Confucius and Mencius, the two most important of the classical Confucian thinkers.[4] His thought has been dominant in China for eight hundred years and has also influenced many phases of life throughout East Asia. He has been described as the "*chi ta-ch'eng,*" which is translated as "the one gathering into a great completion," the greatest synthesizer of Neo-Confucianism.[5] One of his major contributions to later generations was to group the *Analects*, *Mencius*, the *Great Learning*, and the *Doctrine of Means* together as the "Four Books." Ever since Chu Hsi completed his commentaries on these texts in 1190, the "Four Books" became the focus of Confucian thought and later the basic texts in civil service examinations and school education. Since 1313 his commentaries on the "Four Books" provided the orthodox interpretation and the basis for these examinations till 1905.[6] In this regard, Chu Hsi can be said to be the foremost Confucian of the Neo-Confucian movement[7] in China as well as East Asia.

The other interlocutor in this study, Paul Tillich, is considered by many as one of the pre-eminent Christian theologian of this century.[8] As

Langdon Gilkey indicates, almost every theologian nowadays must wrestle with Tillich's systematic theology, whether in critique or in agreement with it.[9] His influential thought also penetrates into related fields, such as philosophy and religion, philosophy of science, language, art criticism, psychology and therapy, cultural studies, and social theory. In addition, although the quantity of Tillich's writings that deal explicitly with the field of the inter-religious dialogue is relatively small and late in his career, Tillich's view of revelation and his sense of the immanent presence of Being-itself provide some possibilities for inter-religious dialogue.[10]

For the Confucian side of the comparison, the primary texts for this study are Chu Hsi's *Chu Tzu wen-chi* [Collection of Literary Works of Master Chu] and *Chu Tzu yü-lei* [Classified Conversations of Master Chu]. Among his voluminous writings, Chu His's *Jen-shou* [Treatise on Humanity] is one of the most important texts. This text has been preserved in chapter 67 of the *Chu Tzu wen-chi* and is universally regarded as an important source for understanding his notion of *jen*.

The primary texts for Tillich's theology are the three volumes of his systematic theology. His other main works, such as *Love, Power, and Justice* (1954), *Biblical Religion and the Search for Ultimate Reality* (1955), *Morality and Beyond* (1963), *Christianity and the Encounter of the World Religions* (1963), *The Future of Religions* (1966), *The Shaking of the Foundations* (1948), *The New Being* (1955), and *The Eternal Now* (1956) are also major sources for this study. The classroom exchanges, transcribed in *Ultimate Concern: Tillich in Dialog* (1965), is another major text that is useful in understanding Tillich's thought in general. Finally, some materials from the Tillich Archives are also included in this study.

This study consists of three parts: a Tillich section, a Chu section, and a comparative section. In the second chapter, I will elucidate Tillich's ontology, including the category of being, the ontological polarities, the meaning of human finitude through the relation of human finite being to nonbeing as well as to infinity, and human essential and existential nature. In the third chapter, I will examine the problematic structure of human existence. In the fourth chapter, I will discuss Tillich's idea of God as the answer to the problem of existence and also as the aim of human existence. And in the fifth chapter, I will analyze Tillich concept of love as the dynamic resolution of the problematic nature of human existence.

In the section on Chu, I will provide a brief introduction to Chu's thought in the sixth chapter. Then I will analyze Chu Hsi's ontological structure of principle (*li*) and vital energy (*ch'i*) in the seventh chapter. Based upon Chu Hsi's concept of principle and vital energy, I will expound Chu Hsi's concept of human nature in the eighth chapter. And in the ninth chapter, I will discuss Chu Hsi's concept of *jen*. By showing Chu Hsi's innovative Confucian concept of *jen*, I argue that Chu Hsi's concept of *jen* functioned to resolve human estrangement.

In the comparative section, instead of merely juxtaposing Tillich's and Chu's thoughts on human nature, I will develop three categories, namely, unity, activity, and reunification, in order to compare their thought in the ninth chapter. Then in the last three chapters, I will analyze similarities as well as differences between Chu's and Tillich's views on unity, activity, and reunification.

Finally, in the conclusion, I will review the thesis of this study and provide some implications for inter-religious dialogues in general and Confucian-Christian dialogue in particular for the Chinese Churches of East Asia. Dialogue becomes not only the basis for constructive theological formation, but also an ethical imperative for life in the global village of the modern world.

Notes

1. John H. Berthrong, *All Under Heaven: Transforming Paradigms in Confucian-Christian Dialogue* (Albany: State University of New York Press, 1994), 5.

2. Gilbert Rozman has divided modernization in the world into three types—the West, the "North" (the Russian tradition and the socialist path to modernization which grew out of it), and East Asia. See Gibert Rozman, ed., *The East Asian Region: Confucian Heritage and its Modern Adaptation* (Princeton: Princeton University Press, 1991), 14-23.

3. Tu Wei-ming, *Confucianism in a Historical Perspective* (Singapore: The Institute of East Asian Philosophies, 1989), 3.

4. Wing-tsit Chan, *Chu Hsi: New Studies* (Honolulu: University of Hawaii Press, 1989), vii.

5. Wing-tsit Chan, *Chu Hsi Life and Thought* (Hong Kong: Chinese University of Hong Kong Press, 1987), 38.

6. Ibid., 130.

7. Wm. Theodore de Bary defined neo-Confucianism as the most vital system of thought that links "modern China" and the rest of East Asia. It was the primary force in shaping a new common culture in East Asia. In contrast to the speculative and meditative learning of Buddhism and Taoism in the T'ang dynasty, a realistic group of Confucian scholars emerged in Sung dynasty. These scholars developed an inclusive humanist vision that integrated personal self-cultivation with social ethics and moral metaphysics into a holistic philosophy of life. They understood the classical Confucian thought as the establishment of the lineage of the "Learning of the Tao." This group of Confucians can be traced through a line of scholars from Chou Tun-i (1017-1073), via Chang Tsai (1020-1077), Ch'eng Hao (1032-1085), and Ch'eng I (1033-1107), to the great synthesizer, Chu Hsi (1130-1200). See Wm. Theodore de Bary, *East Asian Civilizations: A Dialogue in Five Stages* (Cambridge, MA: Harvard University Press, 1988), 43-66; Tu Wei-Ming, "Confucianism" in *Our Religions*, ed. Arvind Sharma (San Francisco: Harper Collins Publishers, 1993), 168.

8. Dean Liston Pope of Yale Divinity School sums up Tillich's contribution. "Perhaps no other recent theologian or philosopher has helped us so much and so courageously to face the meaning of our existence." Paul Tillich, "What is Man?—From the Viewpoint of A Theologian," (unpublished broadcast transcript) *Yale Christian Association*, 1/4/1957, 9pp., Tillich Archives: 407:016.

9. Langdon Gilkey, *Gilkey on Tillich* (New York: The Crossroads Publishing Company, 1990), 56.

10. Langdon Gilkey, "The Role of the Theologian in Contemporary Society" in *The Thought of Paul Tillich*, eds. James Luther Adams, Wilhelm Pauck, and Roger Shinn (San Francisco: Harper & Row, 1985), 349.

PART ONE
The Thought of Paul Tillich

In this part, we will basically elucidate the thought of Paul Tillich. In the initial chapter, we examine Tillich's structure of ontology, including the category of being, the four polarities of ontological concepts, the meaning of human finitude through the relation of human finite being to nonbeing as well as to infinity, and human essential and existential nature.

In the second chapter, we will discuss the problematic structure of human existence. Following his concept of human essential and existential nature, we will analyze what Tillich means by anxiety and despair. Due to this structure of anxiety and despair, we can see the problematic of human existence. And from this despairing circumstance, humans raise their ontological questions.

In the third chapter, Tillich's idea of God as the answer to the problem of existence and also as the aim of human existence will then be discussed. The concept of ultimate concern and faith will be addressed. And in the fourth chapter, Tillich concept of love as the dynamic resolution to the problematic nature of human existence will be analyzed. The forms of love and the relationship between love, power, and justice will be expounded. Furthermore, the concept of grace will also be discussed.

CHAPTER ONE
The Structure of Ontology

For Paul Tillich, ontology means metaphysics, and can be defined as the body of knowledge that concerns being. [1] "Epistemology, the 'knowledge' of knowing, is a part of ontology, the knowledge of being."[2] The Ontological question is "the question of being as being."[3] Further, Tillich says that ontology is "the knowledge of being,"[4] and the place to begin an "analysis of existence."[5] More specifically, Tillich claims that "the question of being is not the question of any special being, its existence and nature, but it is the question of what it means to be. It is the simplest, most profound, and absolutely inexhaustible question—the question of what it means to say that something is."[6] According to Tillich, the question of being is asked by philosophy. Philosophy is generally at a loss to answer this question fully. Tillich prefers to use the word ontology instead of philosophy, because "ontology derived from *logos* (the word) and *ontos* (being); that is, the word of being, the word which grasps being, makes its nature manifest, drives it out of its hiddenness into the light of knowledge. Ontology is the center of all philosophy"[7]

Paul Tillich asserts that ontology is at once simple, profound, and inexhaustible and indicates the difficulty of answering the question of being. The ontological question is of primary interest for him. This can be found throughout his writings.[8] The question of being, for Tillich, is a question that mainly had reference to the human beings, or to the human situation. As Tillich indicates, "The ontological question is the question: what makes man in distinction from all other beings? Or in a more sophisticated form: what is the kind of being that characterizes man within the whole of being? Every child has an unformulated answer to this question when he starts to treat his dog differently from his friend, but some philosophers have forgotten (what they knew as children and still practice in their own human relations) namely, to acknowledge a 'basic nature of man.'[9] Being then, for Tillich, "means the whole of human reality, the structure, the meaning, and the aim of existence."[10] Based upon this statement, the following is a presentation of Tillich's ontological structure.

The Whole of Human Reality

According to Tillich, no human reality can be apart from "being." Being is a category that penetrates below the distinction of object and subject, of matter and spirit, and of inorganic reality and organic and psychological reality. That is to say, Tillich uses being as a category with which to explicate this underlying and uniting ontological realm.[11] Since there is diversity within the universe and it causes a mutual strangeness, an inability to speak together and to comprehend one another, Tillich searched for unity on existential, cultural, and theoretical levels. For Tillich, this category is common to all aspects and fields.[12] Being refers, then, to the common structure and the common ground of subjects and objects, world and self; it transcends and includes impersonal, scientific ways of thought and "personal," spiritual ones.[13]

Tillich would agree that being is expressed in the human being as awareness in the form of self and world. Actually, every human being is a self.[14] As Tillich says, "A self is not a thing that may or may not exist; it is an original phenomenon which logically proceeds all questions of being."[15] There will be no question to be asked if we have no prior selves that are able to pose a question. Tillich tries to delineate the ontological status of the human beings. We can experience ourselves as having a world to which we belong,[16] and we alone occupy "a pre-eminent place in ontology . . . as that being who asks the ontological question and in whose self-awareness the ontological answer can be found."[17]

In order to be able to pose the question of the meaning of existence, humans must have at least a partial understanding of being. Otherwise, they would have no ground from which the question could be raised. And yet, on the other hand, they would not be asking the question if they possessed the understanding of being that they seek. In this respect, when humans ask the ontological question, it assumes that they both have and have not the being for which they ask.[18] As Tillich contends, "The ontological question presupposes the attitude of a man who has experienced the tremendous shock of the possibility that there is nothing or more practically speaking—who has looked into the threatening abyss of nothingness, such a man is called a philosopher."[19] Here, Tillich formulates the phenomenon of ontological or metaphysical "shock," namely, "the shock of non-being". This shock is expressed in the question: "Why is there something; why not nothing?"[20] This ontological question contends that when one is confronted with death, the most common and climactic shock, one will call one's being into question. What Tillich emphasizes here is that we belong to being and know its power in us but are also separated from it in our finitude.[21] This is the element of finitude. Due to our finiteness, we discover that our "power of being is limited,"[22] and thus we are a "mixture of being and nonbeing,"[23] or a mixture of potential and actual being. Therefore, as finite beings, we are "a mixture of being and nonbeing and [we are] aware of it."[24] Because of this structure, we necessarily raise the ontological question.

According to Tillich, as humans become self-conscious of their existence, they then will pose the ontological question, which is raised on an encounter with being and non-being. Simultaneously, when one becomes conscious of the self, one becomes aware of not-self. Tillich contends that the conditions for the ontological question imply that the self is part of not-self, and that the self is part of the world. To be a self means to be separated from everything else. Having everything else opposite one's self, one is able to look at it. At the same time, however, one's self is aware that a self belongs to that part of the world in which it lives. "Every self has an environment in which it lives, and ego-self has a world which it lives."[25]

In his *The Ontology of Paul Tillich*, Adrian Thatcher contends that Tillich is indebted, at least in part, to Martin Heidegger for the insight that the understanding of being is dependent on a "pre-understanding" of being. As Thatcher writes, "For Heidegger, the understanding of being which is present before the question of being is put is only a 'vague, average understanding'. For Tillich, the same understanding is sufficiently developed to tell us that we 'belong to being' (whatever that means). . . . His partial knowledge of what he asks about when he asks the question of being becomes a sufficient knowledge of his 'belonging' to being ('he knows . . . That he belongs to it'). This is to read too much into what it means to ask an ordinary question."[26] Tillich's argument, according to Thatcher, is that if a sufficient knowledge is the condition for asking the ontological question, then the question is actually answered before it is asked.

Although their pre-understanding of being may initially be "a vague understanding," the moment humans articulate the question of being is a reflection of their ontological state. In other words, instead of the question itself, humans find that existence itself leads to the question of meaning becoming meaningful.[27] Thus, this ontological question is a universal phenomenon for every human being. It is evident that we sometimes ask the ontological question, in some form or another, of ourselves and it is also clear that we participate in existence and our existence is a question for us.

Due to this universal phenomenon among human beings, the existential state of the human beings is one in which the self is separated from being in the world while at the same time belonging to it. "If a man is that being who asks the question of being, he has and has not the being for which he asks. He is separated from it while belonging to it."[28] Moreover, due to this belonging, humans have no choice in the asking of the ontological question. "Man can and must ask; he cannot avoid asking, because he belongs to power of being from which he is separated, and he knows both that he belongs to it and that he is separated from it."[29] This partial knowledge and belonging demonstrate the existential dilemma of the human situation that one necessarily finds oneself as a participant in the world. As Tillich says, "The misery of man lies in the fragmentary character of his life and knowledge; the greatness of man lies in his ability to know that his being is fragmentary and enigmatic."[30] This fragmentation anticipates the problematic structure of being that every human being encounters. It is a constituent part of the structure of existence and is composed of self and world.

The Structure of Existence

In his theology, Tillich seems to use the term "structure of being" in a more epistemological than ontological sense because this structure is already presupposed in any act of knowing. However, he argues that the structure of being is not only the structure of how we know but also of how things really are. Actually, this structure cannot be known prior to our experience. Instead, it determines the nature of experience and is present whenever something is experienced.[31] In Tillich's thought, there are four polarities of ontological concepts combined together to become the structure of being.[32] In addition to the basic ontological structure, the self/world polarity, there are three pairs of the ontological elements, namely, the polarities of individuality and participation, of dynamics and form, and of freedom and destiny.

Self and World

The polarity of self and world is the basic ontological structure.[33] In Tillich's understanding, the term "self" is more inclusive than the term "ego." It includes subconsciousness, unconsciousness, and ego consciousness on the basis of the total frame of self-consciousness. Tillich claims that "selfhood or self-centeredness must be attributed in some measure to all living beings and, in terms of analogy, to all individual *Gestalten* even in the inorganic realm."[34] But, humans alone are a fully developed and completely centered selves.[35] They have self-consciousness in the most complete sense.

As every being has an environment to which it belongs, we have a world in which we live. For Tillich, world and environment have to be distinguished. Environment is that limited space within which a being has an active interrelationship. World, on the other hand, "is the structural whole which includes and transcends all environments, not only those of beings which lack a fully developed self, but also the environments in which man partially lives."[36] For Tillich, "world is not the sum total of all beings," but rather it "is a structure or a unity of manifoldness,"[37] because regardless of our pluralistic interpretation of the world, its structure abides and underlies every process.

The self-world structure derives from the actualization of human self-consciousness and the resulting capacity or necessity of asking the question of being. According to Tillich, "This structure [self/world] enables man to encounter himself. Without its world the self would be an empty form. Self-consciousness would have no content, for every content, psychic as well as bodily, lives within the universe. There is no self-consciousness without world-consciousness, but the converse also is true. World-consciousness is possible only on the basis of a fully developed self-consciousness. Man must be completely separated from his world in order to look at it as a world."[38] Here Tillich refers to the subject-object structure of self-consciousness. On the one hand, "Man is a fully developed and completely centered self. He 'possesses' himself in the form of self-consciousness. He has an ego-self."[39] However, on the other hand, the self cannot stand alone by itself. We always experience ourselves as having a world to which we belong. That is to say, the self is empty without correlation with its world.[40] The self cannot be considered as an isolated being; rather it is always related to its world either dependently or independently. As there is no self without a world, so there is no world without a self. Therefore, as Tillich claims, "the interdependence of ego-self and world is the basic ontological structure and implies all the others."[41]

Tillich maintains, as Gilkey elaborates, that the world of experience is itself in part a construction of the self; and a world of things is always in correlation with an experiencing and knowing self. Thus "world" cannot be self-existent or self-sufficient. On the contrary, world is always a projection or construct of the self. "Man grasps and shapes his environment into a world," and hence, "world-consciousness is possible only on the basis of a fully developed self-consciousness."[42] For Tillich, we can know the "objective" structure of the world directly or immediately through our participation in that structure as existing and self-aware examples of being.[43]

Thus, "this self-world polarity is the basis of the subject-object structure of reason."[44] The structure of reason, which is manifest within the structure of being, is subject to the same fundamental determination as is the latter, namely, the self-world structure.[45] Reason is a key concept in Tillich's theology as indicated in the first volume of his *Systematic Theology*. Tillich emphasizes clearly the importance of using the term "reason" and distinguishes ontological reason from technical reason. Ontological reason, according to Tillich, "can be defined as the structure of the mind which enables it to grasp and shape reality."[46] However, technical reason is dependent on the subjective constructive powers of ontological reason and so "is adequate and meaningful only as an expression of ontological reason and its companion."[47] Reason, in the context of Tillich's ontology, is particularly meaningful in the self-world polarity. "Reason makes the self a self, namely, a centered structure; and reason makes the world a world, namely, a structured whole. Without reason, without the logos of being, being would be chaos, that is, it would not be being but only the possibility of it (*me on*). But where there is reason there is self and a world in independence."[48] The world, as Tillich depicts, is a structured whole, the logos structure of the grasped-and-shaped reality. Its structure is called objective reason. And the self is a structure of centeredness, the logos structure of the grasping-and-shaping mind. This is called subjective reason. In this regard, this self-world structure defines the subject-object structure of reason.

In Tillich's understanding, this dualistic structure is inherent in human consciousness. As Tillich claims, "The ontological question presupposes an asking subject and an object about which the question is asked; it presupposes the subject-object structure of being, which in turn presupposes the self-world structure as the basic articulation of being . . . Its analysis should be the first step in every ontological task."[49] Here Tillich contends that humans relate to the world through their subjective grasping of the world as an object; likewise they also find themselves as subjects in this world. Thus, humans remain in the configuration of subject and object. "Self-relatedness is implied in every experience. There is something that 'has' and something that is 'had', and the two are one. The question is not whether selves exist. The question is whether we are aware of self-relatedness. And this awareness can only be denied in a statement in which self-relatedness is implicitly affirmed for self-relatedness is experienced in acts of negation as well as in acts of affirmation."[50]

Therefore, the self-world structure is the starting point for ontological inquiry. In the relationship of the self to the world, we find ourselves in a world in which we belong to and participate in, and yet we simultaneously realize that we transcend the world. In regard to human ability to transcend the world, Tillich contends that as long as one is human, i.e., that one has not "fallen" from humanity, one is never bound completely to an environment. "One always transcends it by grasping and shaping it according to universal norms and ideas."[51] This human ability to transcend all environments involves the quality of freedom within a given destiny. We will discuss this polarity later. However, it is now necessary to comprehend the way that the self is able to integrate itself into its world. In volume three of his *Systematic Theology*, Tillich speaks of the relationship of the self to each polarity: self-integration (individualization/participation); self-creation (dynamics/form); and self-transcendence (freedom/destiny).

Individualization and Participation

Having discussed the basic ontological structure, Tillich turns to the other polarities, which are what Tillich calls the "ontological elements." A basic manifestation of the structure of subject and object in human existence is the relationship between the individual and the group. In Tillich's idea, "Individualization is not a characteristic of a special sphere of beings; it is an ontological element and therefore a quality of everything. It is implied in and constitutive of every being."[52] In this regard, the human being is not the only being to which the term "individual" applies. Other beings may be termed "individual." But the basic difference between the individuality of human beings and of other beings is that humans experience their individuality. That is to say, humans are aware that they are separate entities apart from other beings. "For this is just what participation means: being a part of something from which one is, at the same time, separated."[53] Humans are "completely self-centered" and in them "the world is present not only indirectly and unconsciously but directly and in a conscious encounter."[54]

In order to understand Tillich's position on the uniqueness of human nature, there are two points to be clarified, namely, what he means by the analogous individuality of other beings, and what he means by stating that a human being is "completely self-centered." In volume three of his *Systematic Theology*, Tillich argues that there is potential self-awareness in animals. "Here, again, the distinction of the potential from the actual provides the solution: potentially, self-awareness is present in every dimension; actually it can appear only under the dimension of animal being."[55] However, this self-awareness is quit a different from that of the human being. "Under special conditions the dimension of inner awareness, or the psychological realm, actualizes within itself another dimension, that of the personal-communal or the 'spirit.' Within reach of present human experience, this has happened only in man."[56] This dimension of personal communal awareness is elaborated on Tillich's discussion of centeredness.

As Tillich asserts, "Centeredness is a quality of individualization, in so far as the indivisible thing is the centered thing." [57] Also, "centeredness is a universal phenomenon."[58] By universal, he means all organic and inorganic being potentially is centered. He includes atoms, stars, and crystals, and states that because of this potential they have "a kind of individuality."[59] Continually, Tillich makes a clear demarcation between the centeredness of a star and that of a human being.

According to Tillich, centeredness "does not imply integrated *Gestalt*, or 'whole,' but only processes going out from and returning to a point which cannot be localized in a special place in the whole but which is the point of direction of the two basic movements of all life processes." [60] Although this definition is rather confusing, the phenomenon Tillich is alluding to is simple. All beings encounter reality. In the encounter all beings either accept or reject the aspect of reality they encounter. Accordingly, there are two basic movements of all life, namely, integration and disintegration. In reality all beings experience integration or disintegration. Integration serves as an affirmation of being, while disintegration serves as an affirmation of non-being. "The process of self-integration is constitutive for life, but it is so in continuous struggle with disintegration, and integrating and disintegrating tendencies are ambiguously mixed in any given moment."[61] This will be made clearer by discussing the centeredness of the human being.

The difference between the centeredness of the human beings and that of other beings, for Tillich, is that humans are "the highest living being." However, Tillich reminds us that "one should not confuse the 'highest' with the 'most perfect.' Perfection means actualization of one's potentialities; therefore, a lower being can be more perfect than a higher one if it is actually what it is potentially."[62] The criteria of the higher or lower being are "the definiteness of the center, on the one hand, and the amount of content united by it, on the other."[63] The definiteness of center and the united content decide that humans are the highest living being because their centers are definite and the structure of their content is all embracing. Instead of relegated to operating in an environment as other beings do, humans have a world which is "the structured unity of all possible contents."[64]

In the connection between centeredness and self-awareness, Tillich contends that humans are capable of a "centered awareness" which "implies a center which is definite, and at the same time, it implies a more embracing content than in even the most developed preconscious being."[65] This centered awareness can also be understood as a "psychological self." This self, as Tillich claims, means "the point to which all contents of awareness are related, in so far as 'I' am aware of them."[66] In accordance with Tillich's distinction between essence and existence, this self remains potential until coming into existence. What Tillich argues is basically that all beings have centeredness but that their centeredness remains potential, or in the case of certain "higher" animals, is not fully actualized. Because of their power of self-awareness, humans are bestowed with a more definite center. And also because of this awareness, their selves are able to incorporate their environment, or world, more completely.

Based on the above discussion of the polarity of self-world, the existential situation of the human being and the constituent configuration of subject and object within human consciousness show that the individual is not isolated. Without the interaction of the self with other selves, there will be no self-actualization. That is to say, participation is correlative with individualization. "Man becomes man in personal encounters. Only by meeting a 'thou' does man realize that he is an 'ego'. No natural object within the whole universe can do this to him."[67] Every human being is a potential person. Only by participating with another person, can a human being be termed a person. Moreover, through encounter with other persons, we discover the ego-ego dynamic that characterizes all human existence. This dynamic means that each ego necessarily tries to objectify everything, or everyone, it encounters.

By attempting to objectify another human person, one comes up against the battle with another ego. As Tillich says, "There is one limit to man's attempt to draw all contents into himself—the other self."[68] This objectification of one's subjectivity is being resisted. "Everything resists the fate of being considered or treated as a mere thing, as an object which has no subjectivity."[69] But if one persists in objectifying another human person, there are two possible outcomes. The first is that one ego is surrendered to the other and thus destroyed, and the second is the incorporation of one ego into the other, thus resulting in the destruction of the incorporated ego.[70] However, according to Tillich, there is a third alternative, communion.

> The person as the fully developed individual self is impossible without other fully developed selves. If he did not meet the resistance of other selves, every self would try to make himself absolute. But the resistance of other selves is unconditional. One individual can conquer the entire world of objects, but he cannot conquer another person without destroying him as a person. The individual discovers himself through this resistance. If he does not want to destroy the other person, he must enter into communion with him. In the resistance of the other person, the person is born. Therefore, there is no person without an encounter with other persons. Persons can grow only in the communion of personal encounter.[71]

Through this dynamic of ego-ego confrontation, humans realize their selfhood, themselves as individuals. But, on the other hand, in this communion with another, humans begin to associate with and participate in the structure of their world.

Dynamics and Form

According to Tillich, "'being something' means having a form."[72] Closely linked with Aristotle, Tillich contends that "form should not be contrasted with content. The form, which makes a thing what it is, is its content, its *essentia*, and its definite power of being. The form of a tree is what makes it a tree, what gives it the general character of treehood as well as the special and unique form of an individual tree."[73] But form is not a static concept. "Every form forms something. The question is what is this 'something'? We have called it 'dynamics.'"[74] Adrian Thatcher contends that "of dynamics, one can neither say that it is nor that it is not; rather it is a concept that cannot be understood conceptually."[75]

For Tillich, form can be understood as the static side of being and dynamics is "the *me on*, the potentiality of being, which is nonbeing in contrast to things that have a form, and the power of being in contrast to pure non-being."[76] That is to say, Tillich does not consider dynamics "as something that is;" rather it is the "not yet" of being, something about-to-be.[77] In other words, form is being and dynamics is the becoming of being and the passing away of being.[78] Thatcher rightly believes that the polarity of form and dynamics mirrors the polarity of being and non-being, that is, on the "lower ontological level of essence prior to existence, and the basic dialectic as creatures actually participate in it."[79]

By using the concept of potentiality to designate both dynamics and form, Donald R. Ferrell points out that "the general form (e.g. treehood), . . . is potential being and as such it is a power of being. . . . Dynamics is also the potentiality of being, which as sheer potentiality has no form (it is nonbeing in contrast to things that have form), but which, in contrast to pure nonbeing, is the power of being. . . . Dynamics represents 'potentiality-in-general' within the structure of being, since it is not subject to any particular form, while the potentiality of the general form is potentiality within the limits of that form, 'delimited potentiality' perhaps."[80] In order to understand the dynamic-form polarity more clearly, Tillich discusses further human experience as the polar structure of vitality and intentionality.[81]

Vitality is the power in a living being that maintains and enhances its life through growth. It is a creative force that pushes a living being towards new forms. However, in human being "vitality, in the full sense of the word, is human because man has intentionality."[82] Unlike other living beings, human vitality is not limited to certain environments. The dynamic in human beings "is open in all directions," because they are able to create new worlds, both in the technical and spiritual realms. As Tillich depicts, "Man is not only mind, statically related to the universals, but he is spirit, dynamically creating a world of his own beyond the world that he finds. And man is not only vital individuality, dynamically realizing himself as a natural process, but he is spirit, creating in unity with the eternal forms and norms of being."[83] However, human vitality is conditioned by human intentionality. By intentionality, Tillich means "being related to meaningful structures, living in universals, grasping and shaping reality."[84] Further, Tillich contends that "man's dynamics, his creative vitality, is not undirected, chaotic, self-contained activity. It is directed, formed; it transcends itself toward meaningful contents. There is no vitality as such and no intentionality as such. They are interdependent, like other polar elements."[85] Tillich continuously argues that "the dynamic character of being implies the tendency of everything to transcend itself and to create new forms."[86]

However, self-transcendence is based upon self-conservation. The human being is able to self-transcend, but "is limited only by the structure which makes man what he is a complete self which has a world."[87] That is to say, only if the essential selfhood is conserved, can humans transcend any given situation. Therefore, while maintaining their essential selfhood (form), at the same time humans transcend this form in the direction of a new form.

This self-transcendent aspect of human beings is critical to Tillich's understanding of human nature. As Guyton Hammond indicates, Tillich's idea of self-transcendence has two sides, "an expression of the power of being and a separation from its source." [88] Tillich acknowledges that "the self-transcendence of life, which reveals itself to man as the greatness of life, leads under the conditions of existence to the tragic character of life, to the ambiguity of the great and the tragic."[89] Tillich also states elsewhere that because of human existential freedom, human transcendence can also bring about chaos. "Man, transcending under the dynamic drive of his destiny, can fall into a formless, dynamic, overstepping his destiny, and with it every new form, and ending in a chaos which negates form and dynamics."[90] This chaos is what usually follows from the advent of freedom. Because of human pride, "the new is sought—and chaos is found, this is our predicament."[91]

Freedom and Destiny

The third ontological polarity, freedom and destiny, is significant in Tillich's theology, for in it "the description of the basic ontological structure and its elements reaches both its fulfillment"[92] and through the actualization of freedom in correlation with destiny makes existence possible. "Freedom in polarity with destiny is a structural element which makes existence possible because it transcends the essential necessity of being without destroying it."[93] Further, Tillich contends that the concept of freedom is important because "revelation cannot be understood without it."[94] In Tillich's view, although all beings participate in the polarity of freedom and destiny, it is only humans who embody this complete polarity. "Man is man because he has freedom, but he has freedom only in polar interdependence with destiny."[95] By referring to the self-world structure, Tillich argues that "man, who has a complete self and a world, is the only being who is free in the sense of deliberation, decision, and responsibility. Therefore, freedom and destiny can be applied to subhuman nature only by way of analogy; this parallels the situation with respect to the basic ontological structure and the other ontological polarities."[96] Distinct from humans and subhuman species, God is devoid of destiny because God is freedom and only humans who have freedom have a destiny.[97]

We express our freedom through "deliberation, decision, and responsibility." This expression of freedom is enacted in the world against the tendencies of determinism and indeterminism.[98] For Tillich, human freedom is the human capacity to determine human acts "neither by something outside him nor by any part of him but by the centered totality of his being."[99] And destiny is the world in which humans must interact; it is the situation out of which "man finds himself, facing the world to which, at the same time, he belongs."[100] As Tillich contends, human destiny is the basis of human freedom.

> When I make a decision, it is the concrete totality of everything that constitutes my being which decides, not an epistemological subject. This refers to body structure, psychic striving, spiritual character. It includes the communities to which I belong, the past unremembered and remembered, the environment which has shaped me, the world which has made an impact on me. It refers to all my former decisions. Destiny is not a strange power which determines what shall happen to me. It is myself as given, formed by nature, history, and myself. My destiny is the basis of my freedom; my freedom participates in shaping my destiny.[101]

Tillich in another article explicates what he means by freedom. "Freedom, I believe, should be described as the reaction of a centered self to a stimulus in such a way that the center, and not a part or partial process within the whole, determines the reaction."[102] Here the question of the center is raised again.

Continually, Tillich expands the concept that "the center is the point in which all motives, drives, impressions, insights, and emotions, coverage without any one of them determining the center. We experience the center in every deliberation, in every decision, in every act of self-awareness, of self-rejection, of self-acceptance. The center is, metaphorically speaking, a point and cannot be divided as long as there is an integrated self."[103] Like the above discussion of individualization and participation, the self-awareness of the human being has an inalterable center from which it evaluates reality. As long as the configuration of subject and object remains intact and operating, the human nature is implicitly a structure of self-awareness.

Although humans are free to act and transcend themselves, there remains a centered self with a world opposite itself to which it nevertheless belongs.[104] Due to this centeredness, human beings can transcend themselves; at the same time, due to this centeredness, human beings are also constrained by it. This is what Tillich describes as the paradox of self-transcendence. "It is self-transcendence because life is not transcended by something that is not life. Life, by its very nature is life, is both in and above itself, and this situation is manifest in the function of self-transcendence."[105] Once we exercise our free will in order to escape from determinism, we realize that our decision is predicated on the finiteness of our making the specific choice. This finiteness of our freedom is what Tillich calls destiny. "Man's freedom is limited by his destiny which has placed him at a definite place in a definite time under definite conditions. He cannot exercise his freedom at large; he can exercise it only within a extremely small margin on the basis of his concrete situation and individual character. Out of the determination of his destiny the acts of his freedom arise and, in turn, contribute their part to his destiny."[106]

However, once humans actualize themselves through freedom, they surpass the limits of their finitude. They aspire to infinity but are tragically rebuked by their destiny. This is how Tillich delineates human estrangement.[107] Essentially humans embody a myriad of possibilities, and yet as they come to human consciousness they have to make a decision. The initial decision is to actualize their existence, and then humans must continue to choose among many options. This problematic aspect will be discussed in the following chapter.

The Meaning of Existence

What Tillich means by being is not an abstract object but rather designates what is real. In reality, neither object nor subject is alone by itself. Subjects as well as objects are real. In other words, knowers as well as known are real. Unlike Hegel, Tillich does not agree that consciousness is real. Rather, he treats consciousness and thought as real aspects of being because being precedes and founds consciousness. Therefore, being manifests itself in and through all dimensions of our reality. Moreover, being appears in our awareness of our own being from the inside. In this respect, we realize that the category of being lies not in our external experience of objects, but in our inner awareness of ourselves as existing beings.[108] Since being manifests itself in our inner awareness of our own being, it actualizes the meaning of our existence. But at the same time, it presents us with the problematic of our existence. In order to discuss these problems further, we move to Tillich's analysis of being and finitude, which will help us to grasp Tillich's whole system of thought.

In Tillich's theology, the consciousness or awareness of our finitude implies two things. We are conscious of the meaning of our finitude through the relation of our finite being to nonbeing, on the one hand, and through the relation of our finite being to infinity, on the other. Therefore, only in the context of our relation to nonbeing and to infinity can we understand our finitude.[109]

Being and Nonbeing

According to Tillich, nonbeing is the threat to finite being. "Being, limited by nonbeing, is finitude. Nonbeing appears as the 'not yet' of being and as the 'no more' of being."[110] Every finite being is mixed with nonbeing that "it is being in process of coming from and going toward nonbeing."[111] In this sense, nonbeing is a part of being. To illustrate a dialectical relationship between being and nonbeing, Arthur Cochrane points out the correlation of the three key terms in Tillich's ontology: being, nonbeing, being-itself. There are three pairs of correlation in Tillich's system, such that there is a dialectical relationship between being and nonbeing in human beings, a dialectical relationship between Being-itself and nonbeing in God, and a dialectic relationship between humans as finite beings and God as Being-itself. "All three are interdependent and interpenetrable. Being reveals nonbeing and nonbeing reveals being. Together they reveal being-itself and at the same time being-itself (God) reveals finite being."[112]

Furthermore, Tillich avers that "nonbeing is literally nothing except in relation to being. Being precedes nonbeing in ontological validity, as the word 'nonbeing' itself indicates." [113] What Tillich means by nonbeing here is dialectical nonbeing (*me on*).[114] In this dialectical aspect, humans participate in nonbeing; nonbeing displays a definite ontological status. As Tillich states, "there can be no world unless there is a dialectical participation of nonbeing in being."[115]

In this dialectical relationship between being and nonbeing, the finite being has power to resist nonbeing because the human beings are more than finite beings. "In order to experience his finitude, man must look at himself from the point of view of a potential infinity."[116] "Reality is the power of resistance against dissolution into nothingness. Consequently, being can be described (not defined) as the power of resistance against nonbeing, or simply as the power of being, whereby power means the chance of carrying through one's own self-realization." [117] Our individual self-identity is real only as it manifests itself as inviolate. What "real" means is "what has the power to resist nonbeing and what cannot be resolved into something else. According to this criterion the self-related being is the most real being . . . It resists absolutely the dissolution into something else. It cannot be divided, it cannot be made a mere part of something else . . . (Thus) all genuine 'realism' is based on the Ego-Thou relation."[118] Here Tillich describes the situation that every individual struggles to maintain its power of being in the face of nonbeing. Nonbeing, as Tillich discusses it, is not an entity or event; instead, it is present in every act of being. In utilizing their finite freedom, humans constantly encounter, gain, and are rebuffed by the limits of their selves. "It is a continuous venture, a pushing forward and encountering other beings, constellations, and laws, a being thrown back and starting again."[119] The relationship between this ontological analysis and human existence will be described in the essential and existential nature of the human being.

Human Essential and Existential Nature

In order to explicate Tillich's view on the actualization of human consciousness and human self-transcendence, we now turn to Tillich's analysis of essential and existential nature. Tillich depicts the "state" of essential nature by positing the potential aspect of essential nature. "In psychological terms one can interpret this state as that of "dreaming innocence." Both words point to something that precedes actual existence. It has potentiality, not actuality. It has no place, it is *au topos* (utopia). It has no time; it precedes temporality, and it is suprahistorical . . . For the actual is present in the potential in terms of anticipation. For these reasons the metaphor "dreaming" is adequate in describing the state of essential being."[120] What Tillich means here is the central qualities of essential nature. The essential nature does not exist in actual space or time. It does not actually exist; rather it exists in a potential sense. Therefore, Tillich uses the imagery of "dreaming innocence" to designate it. As Donald F. Dreisbach comments, "the essential state, 'Dreaming Innocence,' is not perfection, but is the state of undecided potentialities."[121]

In his *Systematic Theology*, Tillich gives a long definition for the concept of essence. He writes:

> Essence can mean the nature of a thing without any valuation of it, it can mean the universals which characterize a thing, it can mean the ideas in which existing things participate, it can mean the norm by which a thing must be judged, it can mean the original goodness of everything created, and it can mean the patterns of all things in the divine mind. The basic ambiguity, however, lies in the oscillation of the meaning between an empirical and valuating sense. Essence as the nature of a thing, or as the quality in which a thing participates, has one character. Essence as that from which being has "fallen," the true and undistorted nature of things, has another character. In the second case essence is the basis of value judgments, while in the first case essence is a logical ideal to be reached by abstraction or intuition without the interference of valuations.[122]

Here Tillich acknowledges two types of essence. When essence is understood as the nature of a thing or as the quality or a universal in which things participate, then essence is used in its empirical or logical sense. When essence is understood as that from which being has "fallen," the true and undistorted nature of things, then essence is used in its valuational sense. Generally speaking, Tillich's concept of essence refers to the nature and the potentialities of all members of a species, or of an individual. Essence, in some sense, is potentiality. It makes a thing what it is (*ousia*). Both essence and *ousia* are identified with potentiality.[123]

Furthermore, in his discussion of existence, Tillich states that "existence can mean the possibility of finding a thing within the whole of being. It can mean the actuality of what is potential in the realm of essences, it can mean the 'fallen world,' and it can mean a type of thinking which is aware of its existential conditions or which rejects essence entirely. Again, an unavoidable ambiguity justifies the use of this one word in these different senses. Whatever exists, that is, 'stands out' of mere potentiality, is more than it is in the state of mere potentiality and less than it could be in the power of its essential nature."[124] Clearly, Tillich denotes essence as the realm of potentiality and existence as the actualization of or standing out from this potentiality.[125] However, even in the state of existence, essence is not completely lost. "The essential nature of man is present in all states of his development, although in existential distortion."[126] In comparison with Plato's position, Tillich states that "existence is the loss of true essentiality. It is not a complete loss, for man still stands in his potential or essential being. He remembers it, and, through his remembrance, he participates in the true and the good. He stands in and out of the essential realm."[127]

The distinction between essence and existence is the distinction between potential and actual being. In standing out of potentiality or essential being, the actuality of existential being is the distortion of essence. That is to say, human beings are responsible for this distortion through the exercise of their finite freedom. The actuality of existential being is cut off or separated from the power and ground of being. In existence we, as finite beings, are aware both of our belonging to and separation from the infinite. Since the essential being is not completely lost in existence, our essential natures are always hidden yet shine through the existential distortion.[128]

Moreover, Tillich refers to two types of nonbeing in order to explain the ontological status of essence. "*Ouk on* is the 'nothing' which has no relation at all to being; *me on* is the 'nothing' which has a dialectical relation to being. The Platonic school identified *me on* with that which does not yet have being but which can become being if it is united with essences or ideas."[129] Continuously, Tillich says, "as potential being, it is in the state of relative nonbeing, it is not-yet-being. But it is not nothing. Potentiality is the state of real possibility, that is, it is more than a logical possibility. Potentiality is the power of being which, metaphorically speaking, has not yet realized its power. This power of being is still latent; it has not yet become manifest."[130] Essence here means "not-yet-being," not absolute nonbeing (*ouk on*). It does not exist; rather it potentially exists. It participates in God; and its reality is in the divine mind. It is not separated from God's being[131]

In the Christian view, as Tillich contends, existence is the fulfillment of creation and the actualized expression of God's creativity. But at the same time the split between created goodness and distorted existence must be stressed. "The distinction between essence and existence, which religiously speaking is the distinction between the created and the actual world, is the backbone of the whole body of theological thought."[132] Essential being includes nonbeing, but is not disrupted or split. Existential being, however, is split, disrupted, and threatened by nonbeing.[133]

According to Tillich, every human being is born with this "essential" potentiality. However, once self-consciousness is developed, humans no longer remain in this "dreaming innocence;" instead, they are actual existence. In this passage from "dreaming innocence" of essential being to existential being, Tillich states that "in the difficult steps of transition from potentiality to actuality, an awakening takes place. Experience, responsibility, and guilt are acquired, and the state of dreaming innocence is lost."[134] There are two criteria for the transition from human essential nature to existential nature. First, actuality can be designated as awakening in this transition from potentiality to actuality; and second, this awakening is comprised of an assumption of experience, responsibility, and guilt. This is also what Tillich calls estrangement. Estrangement is existence. It is a fall, which is "the passage from essence to existence."[135] In other words, in our existence, we are "estranged from the ground of our being, from other beings and from ourselves."[136]

In sum, human essential nature is a potential nature. It is an unactualized level of being. Once there is the act of existing, of taking an actual being, there is the actualization of the potentialities. But in this process of actualization potentialities are deleted. Hence, existence is a distortion, a falling away from essential possibilities. So to be a human being is to be in continual tension between essence and existence, between what is and what could be.[137]

With the understanding of Tillich's structure of ontology, we realize that humans have both essential and existential nature, and this causes human the problem of human existence. In the following chapter our discussion will be focused upon the problematic nature of human being, or the problem of human existence.

Notes

1. Langdon Gilkey claims that the concept of being is Tillich's basic thought. See Langdon Gilkey, *Gilkey on Tillich* (New York: The Crossroad Publishing Company, 1990), 23-24.

2. Paul Tillich, *Systematic Theology*, vol. 1 (Chicago: University of Chicago Press, 1951), 14. Gilkey elucidates that ontology for Tillich means "for anything to be insofar as it is." See Gilkey, *Gilkey on Tillich*, 23-24.

3. Tillich, *Systematic Theology*, vol. 1., 163.

4. Ibid., 14.

5. Ibid.

6. Paul Tillich, *Biblical Religion and the Search for Ultimate Reality* (Chicago: University of Chicago Press, 1955), 6.

7. Ibid., 6.

8. "Our very being is a continuous asking for the meaning of our being, a continuous attempt to decipher the enigma of our world and heart." Paul Tillich, *Shaking of the Foundations* (New York: Charles Scribner's Sons, 1948), 111-2. "The ontological question is: What is Being itself? What is that which is not a special being or groups of being, not something concrete or something abstract, but rather something which is always thought implicitly, and sometimes explicitly, if something is said to?" Tillich, *Systematic Theology*, vol. I, 163. " But ontology asks the simple and infinitely difficult question: What does it mean to be? What are the structures, common to everything that is, to everything that participates in being." Paul Tillich, *Love, Power, and Justice* (New York: Oxford University Press, 1954), 19. "Philosophy asks the ultimate question that can be asked, namely the question as to what being, simply being, means." Paul Tillich, *The Protestant Era*, trans. James Luther Adams (Chicago: The University of Chicago Press, 1948), 85. "The search for ultimate reality beyond everything that seems to be real is the search for being-itself, for the power of being in everything that is. It is the ontological question, the root question of every philosophy." Tillich, *Biblical Religion and the Search for Ultimate Reality*, 13.

9. Paul Tillich, "What is Basic in Human Nature," *Pastoral Psychology*, xiv: 14.

10. Tillich, *Systematic Theology*, vol. 1, 14. Tillich's concept of being can have two meanings. One is the being of things and the other is the being of God. See Gilkey, *Gilkey on Tillich*, 24; Charles E. Winquist, "Heterology and Ontology

in the Thought of Paul Tillich," in *God and Being: The Problem of Ontology in the Philosophical Theology of Paul Tillich*, ed. Gert Hummel (Berlin, NY: Walter de Gruyter, 1989), 52.

11. Langdon Gilkey, *Gilkey on Tillich*, 27.

12. Ibid.

13. Ibid., 28.

14. "Person is individuality on the human level, with self-relatedness and world-relatedness and therefore with rationality, freedom, and responsibility. It is established in the encounter of an ego-self with another self, often called the 'I-Thou' relationship, and it exists only in community with other person." Tillich, *Biblical Religion and the Search for Ultimate Reality*, 23.

15. Paul Tillich, *Systematic Theology*, vol. 2 (Chicago: University of Chicago Press, 1951), 169.

16. Ibid.

17. Ibid., 168. "One can rightly say that man is the being who is able to ask questions." Tillich, *Biblical Religion and the Search for Ultimate Reality*, 1. "Every being participates in the structure of being, but man alone is immediately aware of this structure." Tillich, *Systematic Theology*, vol. 1, 168.

18. See Adrian Thatcher, *The Ontology of Paul Tillich* (Oxford: Oxford University Press, 1978), 15.

19. Paul Tillich, "Being and Love," in *Moral Principle of Action*, ed. By Ruth N. Anshen (New York: Harper and Brothers, 1952), 300.

20. Tillich, *Systematic Theology*, vol. 1, 163.

21. George F. Thomas, *Religious Philosophies of the West* (New York: Charles Scribner's Sons, 1965), 398.

22. Tillich, *Biblical Religion and the Search for Ultimate Reality*, 11.

23. Ibid.

24. Ibid., 20.

25. Tillich, *Systematic Theology*, vol. 1, 170.

26. Thatcher, *The Ontology of Paul Tillich*, 15.

27. Thatcher argues that the existential, not the logical, is what Tillich wants to emphasize. See Thatcher, *The Ontology of Paul Tillich*, 22.

28. Tillich, *Biblical Religion and the Search for Ultimate Reality*, 11.

29. Ibid., 12.

30. Tillich, *The Shaking of the Foundations*, 112.

31. See. Donald F. Dreisbach, *Symbols and Salvation: Paul Tillich's Doctrine of Religious Symbols and his Interpretation of the Symbols of the Christian Tradition* (Lanham: University Press of America, 1993), 52-53.

32. Tillich, *Systematic Theology*, vol. 1, 164.

33. Ibid., 168.

34. Ibid., 169.

35. Ibid.

36. Ibid., 170.

37. Ibid.

38. Ibid.

39. Ibid., 169-170.

40. Ibid., 171.

41. Ibid.

42. Gilkey, *Gilkey on Tillich*, 86-7, quoted in Tillich, *Systematic Theology*, vol. 1, 171.

43. Ibid., 87.

44. Tillich, *Systematic Theology*, vol. 1, 171.

45. Donald R. Ferrell, *Logos and Existence*, 38.

46. Tillich, *Systematic Theology*, vol. 1, 75.

47. Ibid., 73.

48. Ibid., 172.

49. Ibid., 164-5.

50. Ibid., 169.

51. Ibid., 170.

52. Ibid., 174-5. Tillich also indicates that the concept of individualization is derived from the major concept of difference in the western classical philosophy, i.e. Plato's "spread over all things" and Aristotle's telos. See Tillich, *Systematic Theology*, vol. 1, 174.

53. Paul Tillich, *The Courage to Be* (New Haven & London: Yale University Press, 1952), 88.

54. Tillich, *Systematic Theology*, vol. 1, 176.

55. Tillich, *Systematic Theology*, vol. 3 (Chicago: University of Chicago Press, 1963), 20.

56. Ibid., 21.

57. Ibid., 32.

58. Ibid., 34.

59. Ibid.

60. Ibid., 33.

61. Ibid., 35.

62. Ibid., 36.

63. Ibid.

64. Ibid.

65. Ibid.

66. Ibid., 37.

67. Tillich, *Love, Peace and Justice*, 78. Also Tillich applies this concept to the moral act of how humans realize the ought-to-be in their encounter with the others. The answer for this question is "oughtness." It is basically experienced in the ego-thou relation. See Tillich, *Systematic Theology*, vol. 3, 40.

68. Tillich, *Systematic Theology*, vol. 3, 40.

69. Tillich, *Systematic Theology*, vol. 1, 173.

70. Tillich, *Systematic Theology*, vol. 3, 261.

71. Tillich, *Systematic Theology*, vol. 1, 176-7.

72. Ibid., 178.

73. Ibid.

74. Ibid., 179.

75. Thatcher, *The Ontology of Paul Tillich*, 65.

76. Tillich, *Systematic Theology*, vol. 1, 179.

77. Ibid.

78. Thatcher, *The Ontology of Paul Tillich*, 65.

79. Ibid.

80. Donald R. Ferrell, *Logos and Existence*, 44.

81. Tillich, *Systematic Theology*, vol. 1, 180.

82. Ibid.

83. Paul Tillich, "the Conception of Man in Existential Philosophy," *Journal of Religion*, vol. xix, no. 3, (July)1939: 206.

84. Tillich, *Systematic Theology*, vol. 1, 180.

85. Ibid., 180-1.

86. Ibid., 180.

87. Ibid., 181.

88. Guyton B. Hammond, *Man in Estrangement: A Comparison of the thought of Paul Tillich and Erich Fromm* (Nashville, Tennessee: Vanderbilt University Press, 1965), 107.

89. Tillich, *Systematic Theology*, vol. 3, 92.

90. Tillich, "What is Basic in Human Nature," 18.

91. Ibid.

92. Tillich, *Systematic Theology*, vol. 1, 182.

93. Ibid.

94. Ibid.

95. Ibid.

96. Ibid., 185.

97. Ibid.

98. Donald R. Ferrell argues that the problem of using the language of determinism and indeterminism is a pseudo-problem for Tillich. For he, unlike most of the analytic philosophers, does not rule out the attempt to deal with the perennial problems of philosophy because of the limit of language. See Ferrell, *Logos and Existence*, 82, n. 35.

99. Tillich, *Systematic Theology*, vol. 1, 184.

100. Ibid., 182-3.

101. Ibid., 184-5.

102. Tillich, "What is Basic in Human Nature," 16.

103. Ibid., 17.

104. Ibid.

105. Tillich, *Systematic Theology*, vol. 3, 31.

106. Tillich, "What is Basic in Human Nature," 17. Unlike humanism, Tillich's concept of freedom is not a doctrine of autonomous freedom. Not only is human freedom possible through human destiny, but also through the

ontological priority of being-itself, which is the condition for any finite entity to exist at all. See Ferrell, *Logos and Existence*, 63, n. 38. Also David E. Roberts points out that Tillich's view of the human freedom operates outside or transcendent of the self. As Roberts says, "in grasping his life as a whole as moving towards death, he transcends temporal immediacy. He sees his world in the setting of potential infinity, his participation in the setting of potential university, his destiny in the setting of potential all-inclusiveness. The power of transcending makes man aware of his own finitude, and at the same time marks him as belonging to Being itself." David E. Roberts, "Tillich's Doctrine of Man," in *The Theology of Paul Tillich*, eds. Charles W. Kegley and Robert W. Bretall (New York: the Macmillan Company, 1964), 120.

107. Tillich, "What is Basic in Human Nature," 17.

108. Gilkey, *Gilkey on Tillich*, 28-29.

109. Ibid., 91.

110. Tillich, *Systematic Theology*, vol. 1, 189.

111. Ibid.

112. Arthur Cochrane, *The Existentialists and God* (Dubuque, Iowa: The University of Dubuque Press, 1954), 78

113. Tillich, *Systematic Theology*, vol. 1, 189.

114. Tillich uses Plato's idea of *ouk on* (absolute nothing) and *me on* (relative nothing) to elucidate the concept of nonbeing. And here Tillich indicates the relative nothing of our finitude. See Tillich, *Systematic Theology*, vol. 1, 187-188.

115. Ibid., 187.

116. Ibid., 190.

117. Paul Tillich, "Being and Love," in *Moral Principles of Action*, ed. Ruth N. Anshen, (NewYork: Harper and Brothers, 1952) 664.

118. Ibid., 663.

119. Ibid., 664.

120. Tillich, *Systematic Theology*, vol. 2, 33.

121. Dreisbach, *Symbols and Salvation,* 77.

122. Tillich, *Systematic Theology*, vol. 1, 202-3.

123. Thatcher, *The Ontology of Paul Tillich*, 103. Also Thatcher indicates that Plato's *eidos*, idea or form, influences Tillich's concept of essence; and Hegel's essence obviously has some affinities with Tillich's. See Thatcher, *The Ontology of Paul Tillich*, 100.

124. Tillich, *Systematic Theology*, vol. 1, 203.

125. Dreisbach, *Symbols and Salvation*, 78.

126. Tillich, *Systematic Theology*, vol. 2, 33.

127. Ibid., 22.

128. See John P. Newport, *Paul Tillich* (Peabody, MA: Hendrickson Publishers, 1984), 68. In this argument, Arthur Cochrane questions how we can affirm that the creature is good if nonbeing belongs within being, if we participate in being and nonbeing, and if anxiety is an ontological quality of our nature. See Cochrane, *The Existentialists and God*, 81. And also Reinhold Niebuhr raises the similar question in "Biblical Thought and Ontological Speculation" in *The Theology of Paul Tillich*, eds. Charles W. Kegley and Robert W. Bretall (New York: the Macmillan Company, 1964), 216-227. Tillich replies that first, although the actualization of creation and the beginning of the fall are logically different, they are ontologically the same; and second, the fall is the work of finite freedom universally and no one can avoid it. See Tillich, "Reply" in *The Theology of Paul Tillich*, eds. Charles W. Kegley and Robert W. Bretall, 342-343.

129. Tillich, *Systematic Theology*, vol. 1, 188.

130. Tillich, *Systematic Theology*, vol. 2, 20.

131. Ibid.

132. Tillich, *Systematic Theology*, vol. 1, 204.

133. See Alexander McKelway, *The Systematic Theology of Paul Tillich* (New York: A Delta Book, 1966), 112-3.

134. Tillich, *Systematic Theology*, vol. 2, 34.

135. Gilkey, *Gilkey on Tillich*, 123.

136. Tillich, *Systematic Theology*, vol. 2, 44. See also Gilkey, *Gilkey on Tillich*, 122-126.

137. See Donald Dreisbach, "Essence, Existence, and the Fall: Paul Tillich's Analysis of Existence," *Harvard Theological Review*, vol. 73, (July-Dec.)1980: 521-538.

CHAPTER TWO
The Problem of Human Existence

In Paul Tillich's thought, human existence is problematic. In human experience, "it is not an exaggeration to say that today man experiences his present situation in terms of disruption, conflict, self-destruction, meaninglessness, and despair in all realms of life."[1] The reason for this can be traced to Tillich's ontological structure of human being. In his definition of a self, Tillich contends that "being a self means being separated in some way from everything else, having everything else opposite one's self, being able to look at it and act upon it. At the same time, however, this self is aware that it belongs to that at which it looks. The self is 'in' it."[2] This is the character of what the human beings are. They possess a consciousness of self-reflection. Thus, the dialectical relationship between self and other, being and nonbeing, or the configuration of subject-object becomes the problematic structure of human existence.

As discussed in the previous chapter, in the ontological structure of all beings, finiteness is a constituent character. However, the uniqueness of the human beings is that they realize their finiteness cognitively. As Tillich contends, "man is not only finite, as is every creature, he is also aware of his finitude. And this awareness is anxiety."[3] This human awareness arises out of the relations of human finitude to what lies beyond the finite. It is only by the awareness of infinitude that we can realize our finitude. In a sermon, Tillich says, "Only because we look at something infinite can we realize we are finite. Only because we are able to see the eternal can we see the limited time that is given us. Only because we can elevate ourselves above the animals can we see that we are like animals. Our melancholy about our transitoriness is rooted in our power to look beyond it."[4] Here, Tillich indicates that the awareness of human finitude is the human relation to infinity. "Infinity points to our relation, an experienced relation, beyond ourselves to our ground. . . . Infinity refers to the infinite self-transcendence of spirit."[5] It is "an expression of man's belonging to that which is beyond nonbeing, namely, to being-itself."[6]

On the other hand, the awareness of human finitude is also seen through the relation of human finite being to nonbeing. Without nonbeing, there cannot be the separation from a human's own being that leads to self-awareness. "There can be no world unless there is a dialectical participation of nonbeing in being."[7] In order to realize their humanity, humans participate positively in nonbeing as well as being.[8] Nonbeing is not merely negative; it is a positive and creative part of human being. It "appears as the 'not yet' of being and as the 'no more' of being."[9] In the activity of human living and creating, nonbeing is a part of human finite being that brings the new into reality. This aspect of nonbeing is 'dialectical nonbeing,' *me on*, "which has a dialectical relation to being."[10] Thus, "the dialectical problem of nonbeing is inescapable. It is the problem of finitude. Finitude unites being with dialectical nonbeing."[11]

Although nonbeing is a necessary ingredient in dynamic existence and can overcome that existence, it negates not only life itself but also what the human self strives to establish, namely, structures of meaning, value, and power.[12] As Gilkey indicates, this nonbeing, for Tillich, is the opposite of being, the undialectical negation of being. "The 'nothing' out of which God creates and so which has no relation (expect opposition) at all to being."[13] This is absolute nonbeing, *ouk on*. "The relation between being and *ouk on* defines finitude over against God; therefore, this aspect of nonbeing is by definition separated from God."[14]

To exist is to be finite. As finite beings, humans experience their infinity on the one side and nonbeing on the other. In relation to infinity, humans experience their infinite dimension of finitude. This is the essential humanity of the human. Due to this human infinite dimension and their interrelatedness to their divine ground, humans are aware of themselves in a world as "finite freedom" or finite spirit. On the other hand, in relation to nonbeing, human finite beings are threatened by it because "the end is anticipated."[15] This is also the sense of being not.[16] As Tillich, claims, "everything which participates in the power of being is 'mixed' with nonbeing. It is being in process of coming from and going toward nonbeing. It is finite."[17] Due to human finitude, anxiety arises. It is "rooted in the structure of being."[18]

Anxiety

What Tillich means by anxiety is finitude in awareness. "Anxiety is the self-awareness of the finite self as finite."[19] This awareness is the root of the problematic nature of human existence. "The first assertion about the nature of anxiety is this: anxiety is the state in which a being is aware of its possible nonbeing. The same statement in a shorter form would read: anxiety is the existential awareness of nonbeing. 'Existential' in this sentence means that it is not the abstract knowledge of nonbeing which produces anxiety but the awareness that nonbeing is part of one's own being."[20]

Further, Tillich distinguishes this anxiety from fear and pathological anxiety. In regard to the former, Tillich asserts that fear is different from anxiety because fear "has a definite object (as most authors agree), which can be faced, analyzed, attacked, endured."[21] "Fear is being afraid of something, a pain, the rejection by a person or a group, the loss of something or somebody, the moment of dying."[22] On the other hand, "anxiety has no object, or rather, in the paradoxical phrase, its object is the negation of every object. Therefore participation, struggle, and love with respect to it are impossible."[23] Although fear and anxiety can be distinguished, they cannot be separated. They are interrelated. "The sting of fear is anxiety, and anxiety strives toward fear."[24] However, as Tillich contends, anxiety cannot be extirpated and changed into fear because "it belongs to existence itself."[25]

In addition, Tillich discusses three types of anxiety that nonbeing brings about in human beings. These three types of anxiety are the three directions in which nonbeing threatens being.[26] In explicating his understanding of anxiety, Tillich contends that anxiety threatens human ontic self-affirmation both relatively and absolutely and appears in three forms.[27] These three forms of anxiety are existential, and "are immanent in each other but normally under the dominance of one of them."[28]

The first type of anxiety is that of fate and death. As Tillich writes, "the anxiety of fate and death is most basic, most universal, and inescapable. All attempts to argue it away are futile."[29] Fate and death are the relative and absolute threat to the ontic level of human beings respectively. In his understanding of fate, Tillich repeatedly stresses the finiteness and transitoriness of existential being. According to Tillich, "fate is the rule of contingency, and the anxiety about fate is based in the finite being's awareness of being contingent in every respect, of having no ultimate necessity. Fate is usually identified with necessity in the sense of an inescapable causal determination. Yet it is not causal necessity that makes fate a matter of anxiety but the lack of ultimate necessity, the irrationality, the impenetrable darkness of fate."[30] If we want to know how this polarity confronts the human beings, we have to look at the manner in which this type of anxiety manifests itself in the categories of existence. For Tillich, "categories are the forms in which the mind grasps and shapes reality," or "forms which determine content."[31] There are four categories that Tillich delineates as inclusive of all forms, namely, time, space, cause, and substance.

The central category of finitude is time. It comprises the transitoriness that characterizes all existence, but more exactly or more "actually" for human beings. Time is a symbol of human destiny. Humans are not only anxious about the moment of dying, but rather an ever-present shadow of "having to die" that is "potentially present in every moment."[32] This anxiety is so deeply rooted that "it permeates the whole of man's being; it shapes soul and body and determines spiritual life."[33] "The fear of death determines the element of anxiety in every fear. Anxiety, if not modified by the fear of an object, anxiety in its nakedness, is always the anxiety of ultimate nonbeing."[34]

The second category is that of space. The human temporal present implies space, because time creates the present through its union with space.[35] To exist means to be present in space. "Every being strives to provide and to preserve space for itself. . . . Thus in all realms of life striving for space is an ontological necessity."[36] However, the spatiality of finite being is subject to nonbeing. That means the spatial context of being is gained tentatively. Neither can we possess our space absolutely nor can we rely on our space to sustain us indefinitely. Our situation is that we have no ultimate claim on space, and our destiny is that we will lose every space in which we posit ourselves. "Finitude means having no definite place; it means losing every place finally and, with it, to losing being itself."[37] This anxiety of not-having-a-place is the expression of the ultimate insecurity of finitude.[38]

The third category is causality. It is ambiguous because "to look for causes means to look for the power of being in a thing;" and yet a thing that is caused does not come into being by its own power of being. "Things and events have no *aseity*."[39] Only God has *aseity*. As finite things, humans are caused and thrown into existence. "Causality expresses by implication the inability of anything to rest on itself. Everything is driven beyond itself to its cause, and the cause is driven beyond itself to its cause, and so on indefinitely. Causality powerfully expresses the abyss of nonbeing in everything."[40] The realization of this "abyss" impinges on human beings directly as we reflect on the causality of our own being. "The anxiety in which he is aware of this situation is anxiety about the lack of necessity of his being. He might not be! Then why is he? And why should he continue to be? There is no reasonable answer. This is exactly the anxiety implied in the awareness of causality as a category of finitude."[41]

The fourth category is substance. It is "the union of being and nonbeing in everything finite. . . . [It] points to something underlying the flux of appearances, something which is relatively static and self-contained."[42] It requires the notion of accidents. "The accidents receive their ontological power from the substance to which they belong."[43] Without the accidents, substance is nothing such that in both substance and accidents there is the unity of being and nonbeing. In addition, the category of substance "is effective in any encounter of mind and reality; it is present whenever one speaks of something."[44]

Anxiety is manifested in relation to substance because of the impact of change. Every change may result in nonbeing. "This anxiety about change is anxiety about the threat of nonbeing implied in change."[45] Most pertinently, human beings are anxious that their self-identities are being destroyed. This may occur in an individual self or group identity collapsing; and ultimately, it will be in the anticipation of the final loss of substance. "The human experience of having to die anticipates the complete loss of identity with one's self. Questions about an immortal substance of the soul express the profound anxiety connected with this anticipation."[46] However, whatever such religious notions are put forth regarding the nature of the soul, "the question of unchangeable substance cannot be silenced."[47]

In these categories of existence, we realize that anxiety arises out of our existential structure. This is our fate. Due to death, fate has its power. It is evident in the ontological categories.[48] "Fate would not produce inescapable anxiety without death behind it. And death stands behind fate and its contingencies not only in the moment when one is thrown out of existence but in every moment within existence."[49]

The second type of anxiety is the relative anxiety of emptiness and the absolute anxiety of meaninglessness. As death lies in the background of the vicissitudes of fate, the absolute threat of nonbeing, meaninglessness, also stands behind the relative threat of emptiness. This polarity of anxiety threatens our spiritual self-affirmation; and this threat is manifested in the anxiety of emptiness. As Tillich contends, "The anxiety of emptiness is aroused by the threat of nonbeing to the special contents of the spiritual life."[50] Human beings trying to seek themselves are the motif of this search for meaning. In the beginning of the ontological question, human beings could not seek any meaning unless there is a sense in them that their present mode of existence is somehow lacking in meaning. This lacking of meaning is recognized either through their personal reflection or through their contact with and influence from other selves. In responding to it, humans may come to realize that it is precisely the loss of a spiritual center, which took away the meaning from the special contents of the spiritual life.[51] With this realization, the element of doubt emerges in order to construct a new spiritual center.

With the threat of emptiness, we begin to doubt. As in the anxiety of fate, we doubt the contingencies of our beings. Avoiding being swallowed by nonbeing, our spiritual lives try "to maintain [ourselves] as long as possible by clinging to affirmations which are not yet undercut, be they traditions, autonomous convictions, or emotional preferences."[52] Under such circumstances, we doubt the contingencies of our beings and try to affirm something preliminary as ultimate. This is the way to save our spiritual life. We escape from our freedom "in order to escape the anxiety of meaninglessness." Therefore, "meaning is saved, but the self is sacrificed."[53] However, the affirmation that we rely on may also have failed. Here, Tillich provides the examples of fascism, communism, and Nazism as examples of this surrender of self to authority.[54]

As Tillich concedes, "The experience of meaninglessness, emptiness, and despair is not neurotic but realistic. . . . They are universally real, but they are not structurally necessary. They can be conquered by the presence of a healing power."[55] Therefore, there is the more primary concern, which is "a meaning which gives meaning to all meanings."[56] Tillich refers here to our ultimate concern. When we come to believe that we have lost our spiritual center, we feel the absolute anxiety of meaninglessness. "The anxiety of meaninglessness is anxiety about the loss of an ultimate concern."[57] However, when we confront this lack of meaning, we try to create or adopt an ultimate concern and this attempt must ultimately fail. For to regain a spiritual center is not only dependent upon our acceptance of the concern subjectively, but also that concern must grasp us objectively.[58]

If doubt is raised and our present spiritual affirmation is lacking, and we cannot create a spiritual center, then the question arises, "What are we to do?" This feeling of insufficiency gives rise to the third type of anxiety, namely, the anxiety arising from guilt and the threat of ultimate condemnation.[59]

The third type of anxiety is the relative anxiety of guilt and the absolute anxiety of condemnation. As human beings, we are responsible for our being. This is a characteristic of being a human. As Tillich explains, "Man's being ontic as well as spiritual, is not only given to him but also demanded from him. He is responsible for it; literally, he is required to answer, if he is asked, what he has made of himself. He who asks him is his judge, namely he himself, who, at the same time, stands against him."[60] This is our internal injunction; and it produces the relative anxiety of guilt and the absolute anxiety of self-rejection or condemnation. We are essentially finite freedom. We have freedom in contrast to other creatures. They have analogies to freedom but not freedom itself. However, since we are finite, excluded from the infinity to which we belong, we can only say that nature is finite necessity, God is infinite freedom, and we are finite freedom.[61]

Finite freedom means that we are free to transgress. And yet this transgression is unavoidable because of the moral imperfection of our existence. As Tillich depicts it, "Even in what he considers his best deed nonbeing is present and prevents it from being perfect. A profound ambiguity between good and evil permeates everything he does, because it permeates his personal being as such. Nonbeing is mixed with being in his moral self-affirmation as it is in awareness of this ambiguity is the feeling of guilt."[62] When we transgresses, the ensuing guilt brings with it anxiety. "The anxiety of guilt shows the same complex characteristics as the anxiety about ontic and spiritual nonbeing."[63]

To extirpate this feeling of guilt, two techniques may be employed. First, we may deny the negative feeling and reject the moral tenets that underlie these feelings. As Tillich interprets it, "No one is willing to acknowledge, in concrete terms, his finitude, his weakness and his errors, his ignorance and his insecurity, his loneliness and his anxiety. And if he is ready to acknowledge them he makes another instrument of hubris out of his readiness. A demonic structure drives man to confuse natural self-affirmation with destructive self-elevation."[64] The reason humans manifest this hubris is that they do not acknowledge their finitude.[65]

The second technique is to "take nonbeing into his moral self-affirmation." Rather than denying the guilt, one is to adopt a strict moral rigor and to replace guilt with a rational self-satisfaction derived from this moral action. However, in both sets of techniques, the anxiety of guilt lies in the background and breaks again and again into the open, producing the extreme situation of moral despair.[66] The result of both of these techniques to escape from guilt is hubris. As Tillich contends, "To be a self and to have a world constitute the challenge to man as the perfection of creation. But the perfection is, at the same time, his temptation. Man is tempted to make himself existentially the center of himself and his world."[67] Since the threat of fate and death has always awakened and increased the consciousness of guilt, it does exist in this response to guilt. Although suicide can liberate one from the anxiety of fate and death, as the Stoics knew, it cannot liberate one from the anxiety of guilt and condemnation.[68] Therefore, Tillich contends that "all three types of anxiety are implied in the existence of man as man, his finitude, and his estrangement."[69] And finally they lead humans to despair.

Having depicted the types of anxiety, Tillich discusses the major difference between existential anxiety and pathological anxiety. One of the major differences is that existential anxiety cannot be extirpated, but must be accepted through courage.[70] This existential anxiety cannot be removed because it is our ontological character. If one fails to accept this basic anxiety, "to take the anxiety upon itself,"[71] then pathological anxiety happens. This consequence of failure "leads to self-affirmation on a limited, fixed, and unrealistic basis and to a compulsory defense of this basis."[72] In relation to the anxiety of fate and death, pathological anxiety generates "an unrealistic security; in relation to the anxiety of guilt and condemnation, an unrealistic perfection; in relation to the anxiety of doubt and meaninglessness, an unrealistic certitude."[73] And the treatments for each anxiety are different. Medical healing is for pathological anxiety, and religion or spiritual counseling is for basic anxiety.

Despair

According to Tillich, all three types of anxiety "are fulfilled in the situation of despair to which all of them contribute."[74] "Despair is an ultimate or 'boundary-line' situation. One cannot go beyond it. Its nature is indicated in the etymology of the word despair: without hope."[75] It expresses the feeling of a situation from which Sartre says there is "no exit," or to Kierkegaard means "death" that is beyond possible healing.[76] As Gilkey depicts it, in the feeling of despair, "one finds one's self caught in an unbearable and terrifying situation, a menacing slide into nothingness."[77] In such a situation, although one feels that nonbeing is victorious, its victory is limited because there is still the implication that humans retain a capacity to feel. That means being is still present.[78]

However, there is no solace in this realization for the despairing humans; instead this is the root cause of the pain of despair. Even though humans feel being is still present, they also feel the irresistible power of nonbeing. Such a circumstance is what Tillich calls "the despair within the despair."[79] "The pain of despair is that a being is aware of itself as unable to affirm itself because of the power of nonbeing. The pain of despair is that a being is aware of itself as unable to affirm itself because of the power of nonbeing."[80]

In facing this pain, Tillich claims that human life can be interpreted as a continuous attempt to avoid despair.[81] However, despair means "no escape."[82] As Tillich preaches, "Despair is 'the sickness unto death'. But the terrible thing about the sickness of despair is that we cannot be released, not even though open or hidden suicide. For we all know that we are bound eternally and inescapably to the Ground of our being."[83] Repeatedly, Tillich claims that "the pain of despair is the agony of being responsible for the loss of the meaning of one's existence and of being unable to recover it. One is shut up in one's self and in the conflict with one's self. One cannot escape, because one cannot escape from one's self."[84]

Although the pain of despair is inevitable and inescapable, humans still attempt to alleviate this pain. Tillich indicates two possible ways to avoid the "question of nonbeing"—logical and ontological—and yet he also shows their shortcomings. Logically, "one can ask whether nonbeing is anything more than the content of logical judgment—a judgment in which a possible or real assertion is denied. One can assert that nonbeing is a negative judgment devoid of ontological significance."[85] The shortcoming of the logical denial is that the very ability to posit a denial presumes a type of being which can transcend the immediately given situation by means of expectations which may be disappointed. For instance, if an anticipated event does not happen, it implies that the judgment concerning that event is mistaken, and the expected event and conditions are nonexistent. "Thus, disappointed, expectation creates the distinction between being and nonbeing."[86] From this instance, we know that humans must be separated from their being in order to enable them to have an expectation. In order to actualize such a separation, humans must participate not only in being but also in nonbeing. "Therefore, the very structure of which makes negative judgments possible proves the ontological character of nonbeing. Unless man participates in nonbeing, no negative judgments are possible."[87]

In regard to the ontological attempt at healing, there is the strategy of trying to deprive it of its dialectical character. This dialectical approach places nonbeing within a dialectical relationship with being. This is what Tillich depicts *me on*, which is the "nothing" and has a dialectical relation to being. However, "the mystery of nonbeing was not removed, for in spite of its 'nothingness' nonbeing was credited with having the power of resisting a complete union with the ideas."[88]

Although Tillich contends that people are successful in avoiding despair most of the time, the rare occasions on which despair is fully manifested do "determine the interpretation of existence as a whole."[89] As Gilkey comments, "Despair is the realization of our destruction by the nonbeing that suffuses our own reality and that of our world, combined with the sharp awareness that our destruction has been a self-destruction, a union of tragic destiny and bound freedom from which there is neither respite nor escape."[90] Due to this structure of anxiety and despair, humans can begin to see that this morass of anxiety and despair is their problem of existence. And due to meaninglessness and despair, humans come to doubt. They doubt themselves and the reality and efficacy of the Ultimate. Then, the only thing remaining is the vestige of being which despairs. It is from this despairing element of being that the ontological question arises. And this is the question about the aim of our existence.

Notes

1. Tillich, *Systematic Theology*, vol. 1, 49

2. Ibid., 170.

3. Tillich, *Systematic Theology*, vol. 2, 34.

4. Tillich, *The Shaking of the Foundations*, 67.

5. Gilkey, *Gilkey on Tillich*, 92.

6. Tillich, *Systematic Theology*, vol. 1, 91.

7. Ibid., 187.

8. Gilkey, *Gilkey on Tillich*, 90.

9. Tillich, *Systematic Theology*, vol. 1, 189.

10. Ibid., 188. In his *The Ontology of Paul Tillich*, Adrian Thatcher argues that Tillich's concept of non-being extends beyond Plato's use of it because Tillich was influenced by the philosophy of Boehme, Schelling, and Hegel. See Thatcher, *Ontology of Paul Tillich*, 49-51.

11. Tillich, *Systematic Theology*, vol. 1, 189.

12. Dreisbach, *Symbols and Salvation*, 100

13. Gilkey, *Gilkey on Tillich*, 92. quoted in Tillich, *Systematic Theology*, vol. 1, 188,

14. Ibid..

15. Tillich, *Systematic Theology*, vol. 1, 190.

16. "The shock of nonbeing is the shock of not being in the sense of a radical negation, in the sense of 'being not.'" Tillich, *Systematic Theology*, vol. 1, 186, n. 5.

17. Tillich, *Systematic Theology*, vol. 1, 189.

18. Ibid., 194.

19. Ibid., 191.

20. Tillich, *The Courage to Be* (New Haven, CT: Yale University Press, 1952), 35. "Anxiety is independent of any special object which might produce it; it is dependent only on the treat of nonbeing which is identical with finitude." Tillich, *Systematic Theology,* vol. *1*, 191.

21. Tillich, *The Courage to Be*, 36.

22. Ibid., 37.

23. Ibid., 36.

24. Ibid., 37.

25. Ibid., 39.

26. Ibid., 41.

27. Ibid.

28. Ibid., 42.

29. Ibid.

30. Ibid., 44-45.

31. Tillich, *Systematic Theology,* vol. 1, 192.

32. Ibid., 193.

33. Ibid., 193-4

34. Tillich, *The Courage to Be*, 38.

35. Tillich, *Systematic Theology*, vol. 1, 194.

36. Ibid., 194.

37. Ibid., 195.

38. Ibid.

39. Ibid.

40. Ibid.

41. Ibid., 196.

42. Ibid., 197.

43. Ibid.

44. Ibid.

45. Ibid.

46. Ibid., 198.

47. Ibid.

48. Ann Belford Ulanov argues that the answer to this anxiety is not courage, but rather something that proceeds from that courage, namely, love. See Ann Belford Ulanov, "The Anxiety of Being," in *The Thought of Paul Tillich*, eds., James Luther Adams, Wilhelm Pauck, and Roger Lincoln Shinn (San Francisco: Harper and Row, Publishers, 1985), 128. We will discuss this concept later.

49. Tillich, *The Courage to Be*, 45.

50. Ibid.,47.

51. Ibid., 48.

52. Ibid., 48-9.

53. Ibid., 49.

54. Ibid., 99.

55. Tillich, "What is Basic in Human Nature," 20.

56. Tillich, *The Courage to Be*, 47.

57. Ibid.

58. The concept of ultimate concern and the insufficiency of any attempt at self-salvation will be discussed in the next chapter.

59. "The answer to such anxiety is again, not the power of courage, though it may issue from courage; it is a responsive opening, a motion of love, a love tough enough not to pull into itself, a love that allows us to be ourselves." Ulanov, "The Anxiety of Being," 131.

60. Tillich, *The Courage to Be*, 51.

61. Tillich, *Systematic Theology*, vol. 2, 31.

62. Tillich, *The Courage to Be*, 52.

63. Ibid.

64. Tillich, *Systematic Theology*, vol. 2, 51.

65. Ibid.,50.

66. Tillich, *The Courage to Be*, 53.

67. Tillich, *Systematic Theology*, vol.2, 49.

68. Tillich, *The Courage to Be*, 55. Again, "this radical anxiety of being can be met only by love. Only love is strong as death." Ulanov, "The Anxiety of Being," 133.

69. Tillich, *The Courage to Be*, 54.

70. Ibid., 77.

71. Ibid.

72. Ibid.

73. Ibid.

74. Ibid., 54.

75. Ibid.

76. Tillich, *Systematic Theology*, vol. 2, 75.

77. Gilkey, *Gilkey on Tillich*, 133.

78. Tillich, *The Courage to Be*, 55.

79. Ibid.

80. ibid.

81. Ibid., 56.

82. Tillich, *The Shaking of the Foundations*, 160.

83. Ibid.

84. Tillich, *Systematic Theology*, vol. 2, 75.

85. Tillich, *Systematic Theology*, vol. 1, 187.

86. Ibid.

87. Ibid.

88. Ibid., 188.

89. Tillich, *The Courage to Be*, 57.

90. Gilkey, *Gilkey on Tillich*, 134.

CHAPTER THREE
The Aim of Existence

In their existence, humans experience the pain of existence.[1] But only for those who have experienced such pain, i.e., the shock of transitoriness, can the anxiety in which they are aware of their finitude, the threat of nonbeing, understand what the notion of God means.[2] For Tillich God is the answer to the problem of existence and so is the aim of existence. As Tillich claims, "God is the answer to the question implied in man's finitude; he is the name for that which concerns man ultimately."[3] What Tillich means is that any concern that is truly ultimate is concern towards God. But does this mean that anything can be our God?" "Is God relative to individual interpretation?"

In his *Ultimate Concern: Tillich in Dialogue*, Tillich replies to a student's question about ultimate concern in two parts: the first is a rephrasing of ultimate concern as "taking something with ultimate seriousness, unconditional seriousness." [4] Although Tillich feels "concern" is a better word, "take seriously," he believes, may be easier to comprehend than "concern."[5] In answering the question regarding people who say that they have no ultimate concern, Tillich suggests that there must be something that people take with unconditional seriousness, something people would be ready to suffer for or even die for.[6] Tillich says that even the most ardent cynic, atheist, or nationalist arrives at something they take with unconditional seriousness, even if it is their own cynicism, atheism, or nationalistic fervor.[7]

It seems that the term, ultimate concern, has been clarified, and yet it does not explain the charge of relativism. Therefore, Tillich continues, saying that a genuine "ultimate concern" is not only an object for us to grasp, but rather its true strength lies in us "being grasped" by it.[8] We cannot say that we make this or that a matter of our ultimate concern. Instead, we are being grasped by it when we begin to reflect on it.[9]

According to Tillich, faith is the state of being that is manifest in the individual who has been grasped by ultimate concern. In the third volume of the *Systematic Theology*, Tillich contends that "faith, formally or generally defined, is the state of being grasped by that toward which self-transcendence aspires, the ultimate in being and meaning. In a short formulation, one can say that faith is the state of being grasped by an ultimate concern."[10] In his another works, Tillich gives an elaboration on this formulation. "Faith is the concern about our existence in its ultimate 'whence' and 'whither.' It is a concern of the whole person; it is the most personal concern and that which determines all others. It is not something that can be forced upon us; it is not something which we can produce the will be believe, but that by which we are grasped."[11]

In addition, the manifestation of this ultimate concern is "revelation." As Tillich claims, "Revelation is the self-manifestation of what concerns us ultimately. The subjective state is an ecstatic experience. The content is the mystery of being, taking hold of us. The expression is the set of symbols. The consequence is a transformation of those who receive a social group, and indirectly, individuals."[12] For Tillich, revelation is "a special and extraordinary manifestation which removes the veil from something which is hidden in a special and extraordinary way."[13] What Tillich means by hidden is "mystery." He delineates two sides to the mystery, positive and negative. On the negative side, "the genuine mystery appears when reason is driven beyond itself to its 'ground and abyss,' to that which 'precedes' reason, to the fact that 'being is and nonbeing is not' (Parmenides), to the original fact (*UrTatsache*) that there is something and not nothing."[14] This is the ecstatic manifestation of revelation that "the shock which grasps the mind when it encounters the threat of nonbeing."[15] And this is an indispensable element in revelation. On the positive side, mystery, which includes the negative side, "appears as ground and not only as abyss. It appears as the power of being, conquering nonbeing. It appears as our ultimate concern."[16] Therefore, revelation, for Tillich, "is the manifestation of what concerns us ultimately. The mystery which is revealed is of ultimate concern to us because it is the ground of our being."[17]

In his *Love, Peace and Justice*, Tillich contends that "God is the basic and universal symbol for what concerns us ultimately. As being itself, he is ultimate reality, the really real, the ground and abyss of everything that is real."[18] Now, the question is what Tillich means by God as being-itself.[19] For Tillich, the fundamental doctrine of God is that God is not a being alongside others. God is not even the highest being. "If God is a being, he is subject to the categories of finitude, especially to space and substance."[20] God is extrinsic to finite being. The best understanding of God is God as being-itself. God is neither alongside things nor above them. As Tillich avers, "Being-itself cannot have a beginning and an end. Otherwise it would have arisen out of nonbeing. . . . Being is the beginning without a beginning, the end without an end. It is its own beginning, the end, the initial power of everything that is."[21]

To say God is being-itself is to say God is *prior to* the split between essential and existential being. God as being-itself "is beyond the contrast of essential and existential being."[22] God cannot be the universal essence because God is not the unity and totality of finitude potentialities.[23] God cannot even be identified with existence. For God is not a being. If God exists as a being, God's existence does not fulfil God's essential potentialities.[24] Therefore, "God is being-itself, not a being." Rather, God is the ground of things.

Furthermore, Tillich explains the power of God in existence. The power of being, for Tillich, is "another way of expressing the same thing in a circumscribing phrase."[25] God as the power of being is the power of resisting and conquering nonbeing. "Therefore, instead of saying that God is first of all being-itself, it is possible to say that he is the power of being in everything and above everything, the infinite power of being."[26]

As the power of being, Tillich claims, "God transcends every being and also the totality of beings the world."[27] This power is so inexhaustible and limitless that being-itself infinitely transcends every finite being. The power of being emphasizes the infinite power, inexhaustibility, and creativity of being-itself. "The power of being is the divine omnipotence. It is unfathomed creativity of God, for it is by this power that beings are created and sustained in being."[28] What Tillich means here is that the power of being is in everything and, at the same time, above everything. In other words, God is being present in all existence, while at the same time, transcending all existence.

Regarding the concept of the power of being, Tillich contends that God is not a static absolute. Rather, "the power of being" symbolizes God as the living God and has the meaning of dynamics, moving, and impelling symbolically. In this regard, God is not only being-itself but also the living God. However, God as the living God is a symbol taken from human finite being. In this respect, the living God may be understood in terms of the structure of being as it appears in human life,[29] because "God lives in so far as he is the ground of life."[30] That is to say, as Tillich puts it, "God must be approached cognitively through the structural elements of being-itself. These elements make him a living God, a God who can be man's ultimate concern. They enable us to use symbols which we are certain point to the ground of reality."[31]

In the structure of being, there are three pairs of the ontological elements, individualization and participation, dynamics and forms, and freedom and destiny. In the polarity of individualization and participation, God can be called "the absolute individual" as well as "the absolute participant." In fact, there is no separation between individualization and participation in God. "This can only mean that both individualization and participation are rooted in the ground of the divine life and that God is equally near to each of them while transcending them both."[32] Therefore, God cannot be a person as God cannot be a being; and God's participation does not mean that something alongside of God with which God has to do.[33] "God participates in everything that is. . . . But the divine participation creates that in which it participates."[34]

With regard to the polarity of dynamics and form, it is a mistake to declare that God is the pure form in which everything potential is actual. To say God is the pure form is to neglect the dynamic element in God. As Tillich points out, "The divine creativity, God's participation in history, his outgoing character, are based on this dynamic element."[35] Without the dynamic element, God would be a "fixed result," *actus purus*, pure actuality without potentiality. "The God who is *actus purus* is not the living God."[36] In the polarity of dynamics and form, potentiality and actuality is always in perfect balance within the divine life. Symbolically, the element of form in the dynamics-form polarity is applied to the divine life. God as life expresses the actualization of God's potentialities. But still, there is no distinction between potentiality and actuality in God. Therefore, those elements can be merely applied to God symbolically.

In the third polarity, divine life is free and yet has a destiny. God is free because God is not a being and has *aseity*, God is *a se*, self-derived. "There is no ground prior to him which could condition his freedom; neither chaos nor nonbeing has power to limit or resist him."[37] Therefore, God is free. But how can God be said to have destiny? How can it be possible? "It is possible, provided the connotation of a destiny—determining power above God is avoided and provided one adds that God is his own destiny and that in God freedom and destiny are one."[38] Further, "if we say that God is his own destiny, we point both to the infinite mystery of being and to the participation of God in becoming and in history."[39]

Since God has no separation of individualization and participation, of potentiality and actualization, and of destiny and freedom, God as the living God is to be understood symbolically and beyond any distinction whatsoever. "For God is not timeless nor changeless but the 'moving-permanent,' the 'changeless-changing' ground of change."[40] Therefore, in order to protect the transcendence of God, humans have access to God in a relationship symbolically. As Tillich claims, "As the God, with whom I have a person-to-person encounter. He is the subject of all the symbolic statements in which I express my ultimate concern. Everything we say about being-itself, the ground and abyss of being, must be symbolic."[41]

In addition, although humans objectify God, God is not an object among other objects. Instead, God transcends the subject-object relationship. Therefore, humans cannot speak of God because language itself is limited by the subject-object cleavage.[42] The only possibility for overcomeing the ambiguities and the subject-object scheme is the Spirit-created symbol.[43] Unlike a sign, a symbol is not created by the individual. It points beyond itself to the Ultimate from which it is generated. As Tillich contends, "Religious symbols are double-edged. They are directed toward the infinite which they symbolize and toward the finite through which they symbolize it."[44] Thus, religious symbols, which point to the divine, can be judged only on the accuracy with which they express that to which they point. That is to say, "a religious symbol possesses some truth if it adequately expresses the correlation of revelation in which some person stands. A religious symbol is true if it adequately expresses the correlation of some person with final revelation."[45]

With these understandings, how can humans approach God? How can one with a finite self approach God, who "cannot be called a self, because the concept of 'self' implies separation from and contrast to everything which is not self."[46] Moreover, can one encounter God, who cannot be drawn into the context of the ego-world and the subject-object correlation because of the holiness of God?[47] What recourse do humans have? In regard to these questions, Tillich's answer is love.

Notes

1. As James Luther Adams clearly indicates, humans must raise a question about their existence and seek an answer to that question in a state of ontic cleavage. See James Luther Adams, *Paul Tillich's Philosophy of Culture, Science, and Religion* (New York: Harper and Row, Publishers, 1965) 24-25.

2. Tillich, *Systematic Theology*, vol. 1 61-2.

3. Tillich, *Systematic Theology*, vol. 1, 211.

4. Paul Tillich, *Ultimate Concern: Tillich in Dialogue*, ed. D. Mackenzie Brown (New York: Harper and Row, 1965), 7.

5. William L. Rowe indicates that what Tillich means by "concern" is not only concern the special sense of 'commitment to,' but also in the more ordinary sense of something one is "anxious about." See William L. Rowe, *Religious Symbols and God: A Philosophical Study of Tillich's Theology* (Chicago: The University of Chicago Press, 1968) 20-21.

6. Tillich, *Ultimate Concern: Tillich in Dialogue*, 8.

7. Ibid.

8. Ibid., 11.

9. Ibid., 8.

10. Tillich, *Systematic Theology*, vol.3, 130.

11. Tillich, *Biblical Religion and the Search for Ultimate Reality*, 51-2.

12. Paul Tillich, "Christian and Non-Christian Revelation," Lecture given at Lycoming College on 10/28/61, Tillich Archives, Andover-Harvard Theological Library, Cambridge, 4. Gilkey explains that Tillich's idea of revelation is the dimension of depth, the depth of reason, the unconditional mystery of reality, truth, and value. It is the promise of reunion that heals us in body, spirit, and community. See Gilkey, *Gilkey on Tillich*, 48-9.

13. Tillich, *Systematic Theology*, vol. 1, 108.

14. Ibid.

15. Ibid., 110.

16. Ibid.

17. Ibid.

18. Tillich, *Love, Peace, and Justice*, 109.

19. Adrian Thatcher contends that Tillich's concept of God as Being-itself can be literal due to its ontological implication, but it is also symbolical due to the infinite mystery of God. See Thatcher, *The Ontology of Paul Tillich*, 37-40. See also Robert C. Coburn, "God, Revelation, and Religious Truth: Some Themes and Problems in the Theology of Paul Tillich," *Faith and Philosophy*, Vol. 13, No. 1(January 1996): 3-33.

20. Tillich, *Systematic Theology*, vol 1, 235.

21. Ibid., 189.

22. Ibid.

23. Ibid.

24. Ibid.

25. Ibid., 236.

26. Ibid.

27. Ibid., 237.

28. Lewis S.Ford, "Tillich's Tergiversations towards the power of being" *Scottish Journal of Theology*, 28 (1975): 325.

29. Alexander J. McKelway, *The Systematic Theology of Paul Tillich: A Review and Analysis* (Richmond, Virginia: John Knox Press, 1964), 125.

30. Tillich, *Systematic Theology*, vol. 1, 242.

31. Ibid., 238.

32. Ibid., 245.

33. McKelway, *The Systematic Theology of Paul Tillich: A review and Analysis,* 126.

34. Tillich, *Systematic Theology*, vol. 1, 245.

35. Ibid.,246.

36. Ibid.

37. Ibid., 248.

38. Ibid., 248-9.

39. Ibid., 249.

40. Gilkey, *Gilkey on Tillich*, 108.

41. Tillich, *Love, Justice, and Peace*, p.109; "Man's ultimate concern must be expressed symbolically, because symbolic language alone is able to express the ultimate." Paul Tillich, *The Dynamics of Faith* (New York: Harper Torchbook, 1958),41.

42. Tillich, *Systematic Theology*, vol. 3, 253.

43. Ibid., 254.

44. Tillich, *Systematic Theology*, vol. 1, 240. Donald F. Dreisbach indicates that there are some critics who have remarked that Tillich paid no attention to the distinction between the symbolic and the ontological. See Dreisbach, *Symbols and Salvation*, 131.

45. Tillich, *Systematic Theology*, vol. 1, 240.

46. Ibid., 244.

47. Ibid., 272.

CHAPTER FOUR
The Concept of Love

In his essay "Being and Love," Tillich defines ontology as "the rational explanation of the structure of Being itself. . . . Ontology deals with the structure of Being itself."[1] Tillich articulates the meaning of "the ontology of love." "If we speak of the ontology of Love we indicate that Love belongs to the structure of Being itself, that every special being with its special nature participates in the nature. Love since it participates in Being itself. The participation of a being in the nature of Love can happen even as the negation of love, as indifference, or as hate."[2] Tillich tries to depict love in relation to Being itself. What Tillich means by "every special being with its special nature" refers not only to human beings but also by analogy to other loving beings. This implies that love is a universal phenomenon.

With this connection between Being itself and love, Tillich shows that love has ontological dignity. "Love, power, and justice are metaphysically speaking as old as being itself. They precede everything that is, and they cannot be derived from anything that is. They have ontological dignity."[3] Everyone can trace the integral ontic role of love from the very beginning of Being itself. Moreover, the elements of power and justice, as Tillich clearly indicates, have fundamental relationships to love. They are "ever repeated subjects of ontology." Therefore, in this chapter we will discuss the various expressions of love, the relation of love to power and justice, and love as a dynamic resolution to the problematic nature of human existence.

The Forms of Love

As Alexander C. Irwin clearly notes, love is the most crucial category of Tillich's theology.[4] Tillich has described love as "the moving power of life,"[5] life's "inner dynamics,"[6] the foundation of all social and political power structures, the "ultimate moral principle" and "the source of all moral norms,"[7] "the infinite which is given to the finite," and the power that "rescues life from death."[8] In order to formulate his ontology of love, Tillich indicates that love is understood in many ways and usually depicted as an emotional or ethical state.[9]

However, Tillich contends that those formulations are insufficient. They each have a partial truth. "Love is not an emotion, but strong emotional elements are implied in it, as are the other functions of the human mind."[10] Also, "the ethical nature of love is dependent on its ontological nature, and . . . the ontological nature of love gets its qualifications by its ethical character."[11] Tillich defines love as "the drive towards the reunion of the separated; this is ontologically and therefore universally true."[12] That is to say, in Tillich's concept of essence and existence, once we come to exist, we are estranged from our essential nature. This is the depth dimension of our existence and the problematic structure of existence. The resolution to this problem is to reunite with Being-itself from which we are separated. This reunion can be depicted as a resolution of love.

If love is the drive towards the reunion, this reunion must lie beyond or transcend the limits of finitude. "Love is the state of being taken into the transcendent unity of unambiguous life."[13] As Tillich indicates, "the moment of love is a moment of self-transcendence. This implies the ecstatic character of Being in the sense of our transcending into the other self while remaining within our own self. This ecstatic self-transcendence is as original as the self-relatedness."[14] In this love relation, we experience that the distinction between subject and object, namely lover and loved, is overcome. And there is the transcendent movement of love towards Being itself. Tillich states "if love in all its forms is the drive towards the reunion of the separated, the different qualities of the one nature of love become understandable."[15] These forms of love are immanent manifestations of the transcendent union of Being-itself. Tillich presents them through four traditional categories, which are inherited from classical philosophy and theology, namely *libido/epithymia, philia, eros*, and *agape*.

In his *Systematic Theology*, Tillich delineates the meaning of these different forms of love. "Love as *libido* is the movement of the needy toward that which fulfils the need. Love as *philia* is the movement of the equal toward union with the equal. Love as *eros* is the movement of that which is lower in power and meaning to that which is higher."[16] Obviously, as Tillich notes, the element of desire is present in all these three kinds of love. However, "this does not contradict the created goodness of being, since separation and the longing for reunion belong to the essential nature of creaturely life."[17] But to a certain extent, these three kinds of love are "dependent on contingent characteristics which change and are partial."[18] They are also "dependent on repulsion and attraction, on passion and sympathy."[19] The fourth type of love is *agape*. "It affirms the other unconditionally, that is, apart from higher or lower, pleasant or unpleasant qualities. . . . *Agape* is universal; no one with whom a concrete relation is technically possible (the neighbor) is excluded; nor is anyone preferred."[20] It is a form of love that transcends the other three kinds of love, and yet is not totally separated from the other kinds of love. "*Agape* is a quality of love, that quality which expresses the self-transcendence of the religious element in love. If love is the ultimate norm of all moral demands, its *agape* quality points to the transcendent source of the content of the moral imperative. For *agape* transcends the finite possibilities of man."[21] For Tillich, *agape* is the type of love that characterizes Divine Love and is also connected with the other kinds of love.

In order to understand these four kinds of love in Tillich's thought thoroughly, we need some further explications. The first one, *libido*, is usually associated with Freud, and frequently understood as the sex drive. From the Latin meaning of *libido* as "desire" or "dust," this association is not totally erroneous. Tillich also defines *libido* as "culminating in sex."[22] However, Tillich's use of *libido* is a slightly different than Freud's because Freud put too much stress on the negative aspect of *libido*. As Tillich comments, "Insofar as Freud describes *libido* as the desire of the individual to get rid of tensions, he has described the perverted form of *libido*. . . . Freud describes man's *libido* in its perverted, self-estranged stage. But his description . . . misses the meaning of *libido* as the normal drive towards vital self-fulfilment."[23]

Instead of emphasizing *libido* as the desire for pleasure, Tillich stresses the positive aspect of desire in moving towards a sense of unity to overcome the estrangement of its existence, namely, the relationship of desire to love. "First of all it must be said that *libido* to use the Latin word is misunderstood if it is defined as the desire for pleasure. . . . But it is not the pleasure as such which is desired, but the union with that which fulfils the desire. . . . Only a perverted life follows the pain-pleasure principle. Unperverted life strives for that of which it is in want, it strives for union with that which is separated from it, though it belongs to it."[24] Tillich acknowledges that pleasure has a purpose in us.[25] Undoubtedly, humans seek pleasure and avoid pain. But there is the deepest level of the pain-pleasure cycle that we want to escape. As we realize that we are alienated from world, God, and ourselves, we realize we are being trapped in our existence. This is reflected in Freud's "death instinct." And Tillich describes the "death instinct" as "the desire to escape the pain of the never satisfied *libido*" and "it is the never satisfied *libido* in man, whether repressed or unrestrained, which produces in him the desire to get rid of himself as man."[26] However, with this realization, we are still presented with the capacity to understand that we belong to what we are separated from. In it there lies the possibility and hope of reunion.

The second type of love is *philia*. It designates fraternal or brotherly love or the love between friends in Greek. For Tillich, this kind of love "presupposes some amount of familiarity with the object of love."[27] "It is the self-transcendence toward the equal of a different Self."[28] This kind of self-transcendence creates a community in which one participates with the other, thereby forming a unity. In doing so, both parties may gain self-affirmation. As Tillich says, "Friendship depends on the participation of both sides as equals in an embracing unity."[29]

Eros is commonly associated with physical love and sexual desire. In contrast to this common understanding, Tillich focuses upon its content. In his lecture entitled, "Love as *Eros* and the Integration of Personality," Tillich says that

> The problem of *eros* is the liberation of the divine in us from the bondage to the material element. Therefore its movement is upwards from the world of senses to the world of forms. The highest form is the good and beautiful itself. Those who have been saved from the shadows and have seen reality: "their souls are continually pressing on to dwell in the world above." (Plato. Symp.517c) The *Eros* in this sense is the longing of the finite towards its infinite ground. The

> basis of this longing is the subconscious remembrance of the world above, once seen, (Reunion) making the soul feel estranged in this world. The function of the things is to remember the soul, to make the unconscious remembrance conscious.[30]

Undoubtedly, *eros* is part of physical love and desire, but it also indicates a transcendent dimension in which *eros* moves towards overcoming the material beyond the form of the world. Tillich acknowledges that "there is epithymia in every *eros*. But *eros* transcends epithymia."[31] "*Eros* drives beyond the individual things and persons. It uses the concrete as a starting point. But then it transcends it and dissolves it into the universal. The fulfillment of *eros* is the mystical union with the one, in which all concreteness has disappeared."[32] Tillich uses the Platonic idea of forms to argue that "*eros* drives finally beyond any special form to the principle of form, the true and beautiful itself."[33] It "carries the soul in its search for ultimate reality;"[34] and "drives the soul through all levels of reality to ultimate reality, to truth itself, which is the good itself."[35] As Tillich contends, "Without the *eros* towards truth, theology would not exist, and without the *eros* towards the beautiful, no ritual expressions would exist. Even more serious is the rejection of the *eros* quality of love with respect to God."[36]

In other words, as one moves towards the immanent forms, one strives for reunion with the transcendent forms. This kind of movement is for self-affirmation. In this movement, we strive for reunion with Being-itself. However, Tillich alerts us that *eros* may be identified with the immanent form of love, *libido*, and become a relative form of love. Genuine *eros*, as Tillich says, "participates in the ultimate. And in this participation the self is affirmed and denied at the same time."[37]

With this understanding, the function of *eros* for Tillich, as Irwin correctly argues, is "a concept that can embrace feelings and experiences traditionally thought of in widely separated areas of human life. *Eros* offers a category that reconciles the 'higher' and 'lower' aspects of love and desire."[38] Since Tillich states that "love as *eros* is the movement of that which is lower in power and meaning to that which is higher,"[39] *eros* has its united dimension.[40] In his *Love, Power and Justice*, Tillich argues that "*eros* is united with *epithymia* if *epithymia* is the desire for vital self-fulfilment and not for the pleasure resulting from the union."[41] And also "*philia* is dependent on *eros*. Concepts like participation and communion point to the *eros* quality in every *philia* relation."[42]

Moreover, *eros* has the quality of love with respect to God. Without *eros*, love towards God becomes obedience and it is not love at all. That is to say, we must have the desire to love God. Otherwise, love will become a meaningless word.[43] Our love for God is of the nature of *eros*. However, on the other hand, although *eros* is "a force woven through the whole fabric of human life,"[44] it, including *philia* and *epithymia* or *libido*, can become "profanized in a merely sexual direction"[45] without unifying with the fourth type of love, namely *agape*.

From the above discussion, all three kinds of love, *libido*, *philia*, and *eros*, have the element of desire. Although "this does not contradict the created goodness of being,"[46] they are "dependent on contingent characteristics which change and are partial;"[47] and "dependent on repulsion and attraction, on passion and sympathy."[48] That is to say, they are not without limitation and not potentially unambiguous. However, *agape*, the fourth type of love, is "independent of these states. It affirms the other unconditionally, that is, apart from higher or lower, pleasant or unpleasant qualities."[49]

In his "Being and Love," Tillich defines *agape* as ecstatic love. It transcends the given self of the loving and the loved toward the unity of fulfillment. "It is self-sacrificing not for the sake of the other Self as such, but for the sake of the ultimate destiny of the other Self. The union of *agape* is the union with the other Self in the realm of the ultimate meaning."[50] Moreover, "*agape* is an ecstatic manifestation of the Spiritual Presence. It is possible only in unity with faith and is the state of being drawn into the transcendent unity of unambiguous life."[51] Unlike the other types of love, *agape* is an independent expression of love and "is able to unite with them, to judge them, and to transform them. Love as *agape* is a creation of the Spiritual Presence which conquers the ambiguities of all other kinds of love."[52] With this direct creation, "*agape* unites the lover and the beloved because of the image of fulfillment which God has of both. Therefore, *agape* is universal."[53] In other words, "*agape* accepts the other in spite of resistance. It suffers and forgives. It seeks the personal fulfillment of the other."[54] This idea of *agape* is identical with the quality of love in the New Testament. And it is basically "God's love toward us."[55]

As Tillich contends, although *agape* transcends the other three types of love, it does not mean that they are viewed as inherently evil. For *agape* can be characterized in terms of the *libidinal*, *philial*, and *erotic* energies. Since *agape* is usually connected with the other types of love, although it is not always and is not even a necessary connection, "it is natural that Christian symbolism has used these types in order to make the divine love concrete."[56] Thus, these three types of love—*libido*, *philia* and *eros*—are vital elements in union with *agape*. For this reason, as Irwin argues, "the ontological unity of the different types of love must be recognized as the basic condition of love's expression in human life."[57]

Furthermore, Tillich argues that *eros* and *agape* cannot be separated. Otherwise, "*agape* toward God is impossible."[58] As Irwin clearly denotes, "the project of reconciling *eros* and *agape* is an imperative of Tillich's doctrine of love, one to which he returns with regularity."[59] Although *agape* is basically God's love, it is also relevant to human love toward God and to relationships between human beings. Due to *agape* in our human level needs to express ourselves in the concrete, it unites with the other types of love, namely, *libido*, *philia*, and *eros*. As Tillich says, "*agape* seeks that which is concrete, individual, unique, here and now. *Agape* seeks the person, the other one who cannot be exchanged for anything or anyone else. . . . *Agape* accepts the concrete in spite of the power of the universal which tries to swallow the concrete."[60]

In addition, "*agape* is first of all the love God has toward the creature and through the creature toward himself."[61] We love because God's love instills and awakens love in us. This kind of love forces us to "seeks the other because of the ultimate unity of being with being within the divine ground."[62] Our love toward God is neither *agape* nor *phila* nor *eros* nor *libido* alone. Instead, it is all of them united. It is "the life finding itself and its substantial love-character and the affirmation of this character."[63] In this respect, *agape* acts as the ultimate criterion of the other types of love as well. *Agape* as ultimate reality manifest itself and transforms life and love. It is love cutting into love and enters into all types of love and elevates them.[64] As Tillich illustrates, "in the holy community the *agape* quality of love cuts into the *libido*, *eros*, and *philia* qualities of love and elevates them beyond the ambiguities of their self-centredness."[65] In other words, *agape* as the ultimate criterion that transforms life and love. It does not deny the existing world or the other types of love. Rather, it enters, transforms and brings them to completion.[66] In a lecture, Tillich articulates the view that "the vital basis of every act of love is *libido*, the metaphysical ground of every act of love is *eros*, the human expression of every act of love is *philia*, and the ultimate criterion and corrective of every act of love is *agape*."[67]

Moreover, *agape* has a spirit of forgiveness in a relationship with others. It expresses itself as the character of charity which "sees in the other his potential fulfillment and makes the union not dependent on the judging wrath or the lack of *philia*. In this sense, *agape* has always the forgiving element in itself."[68] This is what *agape* is. However, we will misunderstand the whole concept of *agape* if we merely see the element of forgiveness. For Tillich would argue that if we have this kind of misunderstanding, it is because we consider *agape* as a kind of emotion. We overlook the fact that *agape* is also judgmental. For this reason, Tillich contends that there is an aspect of judgment and power in love.

Love, Power, and Justice

It seems odd to put love and power in the same category and try to discuss their relationship. This is especially strange, if love is understood from its emotional side and power from its image of the use of coercion of one partner against another. These two concepts are often contrasted. "Love is identified with a resignation of power and power with a denial of love. Powerless love and loveless power are contrasted."[69] However, Tillich argues that this kind of understanding is completely in error and confused. On the contrary, "love is not weakness, not resignation of power but the perfect power of Being."[70] "The perfect power of Being, for Tillich, is God as Being-itself and "is the bearer of the powerful love."[71] That is to say, the ontological foundation of love and power is God as Being-itself. In God, "love and power are identical."

"Love is real only as the power of being. It is not the negation but the affirmation of power." [72] In addition, "power is real only in its actualization, in the encounter with the other bearers of power and in the ever-changing balance which is the result of these encounters. Life is the dynamic actualization of being."[73] In our human capacity, we manifest this power to self-affirm ourselves against the threat of non-being. As Tillich avers, "power is the possibility of self-affirmation in spite of internal and external negation. It is the possibility of overcoming non-being. Human power is the possibility of man to overcome non-being indefinitely."[74]

Furthermore, if love is the reunion of the separated, power conquers that separation. In this regard, "the more conquered separation there is the more power there is. . . . The more reuniting love there is, the more conquered non-being there is, the more power of being there is."[75] Therefore, love and power cannot be separated in their manifestation. One cannot be manifested without the other. In order to exercise its charity and forgiveness, love needs judging and punishing to provide for a place where this can be done. In order to destroy what is against love, love must be united with power.[76] If love and power are united and if compulsion is inescapable in every actualization of power, then justice is the next category to keep them in balance.

Tillich argues that love demands the reunion of the separated and is the pre-condition for justice, or the principle of justice.[77] "Love as the power of reunion of the independent elements of reality judges every process of self-realization and demands venturing self-affirmation as much as venturing self-negation. This judgement of Love is Justice immanent in Being and therefore identical with the power of Being."[78] Justice here is "the form of uniting love."[79] In this sense, Tillich claims this justice is creative justice in its ultimate meaning.[80] Moreover, justice is the form in which the power of being actualizes itself.[81] If love demands reunion, justice preserves that which is to be reunited and is the form in which and through which love performs its work.[82] Therefore, Tillich clearly argues that "love, justice, and power are inseparable in Being-itself."[83] They are ontologically blended together. In order to understand one, we have to refer to the others.

Nevertheless, at the human existential level, love, power, and justice are separable. For "every self-realization is partially unjust, because it is a partial self-realization. Its power of being conflicts with other powers of being."[84] In this respect, every self-affirmation is necessarily a self-denial of some other agent seeking self-affirmation. At the personal level as well as at the societal level, justice can be abused and misused when deprived of justice. In such cases, justice indeed demands love seeking self-affirmation in the light of the power of love in Being-itself against injustice. Only through reunion with Being-itself can self-affirmation be totally fulfilled. As Tillich states, this quality of love is what Luther called "power breaking unjust power is Love's strange work, while Love's proper work is the mutual self-surrender to Love itself."[85]

Through this understanding, love aims at the self-affirmation of human beings through reunion with God as Being-itself. Essentially, humans can transcend themselves in order to reunite with God. However, once we actualize our freedom in our finite existence, we can only partially bridge the gap between the infinite and ourselves. This self-transcendence can be called the action of love. This is the movement of self-affirmation. But this movement alone is not sufficient to break through our existential situation. What we need is the other side of the reunion, namely, God as Being-itself. Through the power of God and the acceptance of God, this reunion will then be achieved. This is also a movement of love. In Tillich's theology, love can be understood as a dynamic resolution of human estrangement.

The Dynamic Resolution

In his *Systematic Theology*, Tillich contends that "God is love. And, since God is being-itself, one must say that being-itself is love."[86] What does this mean? Tillich answers that due to the ecstasy of Love, we experience the Ground of Being. God as Love means that "the Ground of Being from which every being takes its power of being has the character of self-separating and self-returning life. Self-separating is the abbreviation for complete individualization. Self-returning is the abbreviation for the return of life to itself in the power of reuniting love."[87] Love, for Tillich, "is the meaning of separation as well as of the return."[88] Moreover, God and love are not separable and they are one. "God's being is the being of love and God's infinite power of Being is the infinite power of love."[89] In his sermons, Tillich preaches that "God is love, and the divine love is triumphantly manifest in Christ the Crucified."[90] And "love alone does not disappear; it endures forever. For God himself is love, according to John who carries through the thought of Paul."[91]

Time and again, Tillich argues that the statement of "God is love" does not mean that "God is first something else and then has Love."[92] Rather, God is love and love is God's very nature. Therefore, God as love is dependent on the act in which God manifests Godself to us as love.[93] By drawing the distinction between conceiving God as love and God as having love, Tillich uses Hegel's idea of a serious otherness.[94] In order to say that God is love, there must be an independent being in relation to God who is loved. That is to say, there must be a lover and a loved in the loving relationship.[95] Furthermore, as God, the Ground of Being, is the principle of Love, that grounding love is actual only in relation to the beings. "For the beings are separated from their Ground by their freedom."[96]

Although humans and God are separated, this does not deny that they are essentially united. It does not mean that humans and God are the same entity. It means that humans are essentially in union with God. However, in their existential situation, humans are estranged from what they essentially are. Therefore, as Tillich claims, "The difference actualizes the identity and transforms identity into love. The love structure of Being is secondly the structure of reunion."[97] Again, Tillich contends that "love is the drive towards the unity of the separated. Reunion presupposes separation of that which belongs essentially together. . . . It is impossible to unite that which is essentially separated."[98]

To reiterate the previous chapters, Tillich distinguishes between the essential and the existential nature of human beings. Human essential nature is unbroken union with God; and is the foundation of existential brokenness. Separation, or existential brokenness, is for love to manifest. But the fulfillment of love depends on the promise of unity with God as love.

Due to their existential estrangement, humans are separated from what they belong to, and they move towards reunion with that from which they are separated. This movement towards this reunion is a movement of love. And with God as love, this movement can be fulfilled. "Love is that state of being taken by the Spiritual Presence into the transcendent unity of unambiguous life."[99] Therefore, love, for Tillich, has its dynamic dimension. As he says, "Life is being in actuality and love is the moving power of life. In these two sentences the ontological nature of love is expressed. They say that being is not actual without love which drives everything that is towards everything else that is."[100] Furthermore, Tillich indicates that only if one participates in God's love, can one know the knowledge of God.[101] Our knowledge of God then depends on our relationship with God. Here Tillich tries to delineate the structure of human essential nature, which has been separated from in actuality. And now humans long to return to their essential nature. This returning movement is through the dynamic movement of love. For love is the drive toward the unity of the separated, and through the human experience of love, the meaning of life becomes manifest.[102]

One thing we have to note is that what Tillich calls "return" is not a return to the essential state of existence, but rather to the essential state of unity.[103] That is to say, this return has a meaning of progression. In other words, separation is the state of estrangement. The estranged is striving for reunion. Therefore, love can be understood as the reunion of the estranged. "Estrangement presupposes original oneness. Love manifests its greatest power there where it overcomes the greatest separation."[104] With love, not only will the separation of the self and Being-itself be reunited, but the separation of self from self will be resolved as well. For Tillich, the greatest separation in the human existence is the split between selves. Most importantly, the source of this "earthly *agape*" is from God's unconditional love. And this love is given to us by the grace of God

Grace

As one is reunited with God as Being-itself, one participates in God. This participation has both objective and subjective sides. One receives subjectively the objective movement of God's love. No one can coerce or create this objective movement. One can only receive this movement. This is what Tillich means by grace. "Grace means that the Spiritual Presence cannot be produced but is given. The ambiguity of self-determination is overcome by grace, and there is no other way of overcoming it and of escaping the despair of the conflict between the command of self-determination and the impossibility of determining oneself in the direction of what one essentially is."[105] In this regard, grace is a free gift inaugurated by God. It is God's love for us. Despite separation and estrangement, grace is the reunion of life with life and the reconciliation of the self with itself. "Grace transforms fate into a meaningful destiny; it changes guilt into confidence and courage."[106]

The subjective side of grace is the human reception of grace. This reception is totally dependent on the accepted being. However, the question arises: "How can I accept that I am accepted? . . . The only possible answer is: God himself as Spiritual Presence."[107] "Spiritual

Presence" for Tillich has been treated analogously to the term "Accepting Acceptance," that is, it is a partly symbolic, partly ontological term. It denotes one's awareness of participation in God and one's response to this awareness.[108] Moreover, the objective side then is the result of the acceptance. As the movement of divine love or *agape*, grace comprises the resolution to the estrangement in human existence. "The divine love is the final answer to the question implied in human existence, including finitude, the threat of disruption, and estrangement."[109] Now the question is, how can humans encounter the movement of divine love objectively? The answer is, the only way humans are able to encounter God's love is through the symbol of Jesus as the Christ.

As Tillich contends, "Christianity is what it is through the affirmation that Jesus of Nazareth, who has been called 'the Christ,' is actually the Christ, namely, he who brings the new state of things, the New Being."[110] Jesus as the Christ is the medium of the final revelation. Through his sacrifice of himself on the cross, he retains "his complete transparency to the ground of being."[111] Jesus as the Christ is the symbol of the ground of being, manifests the power of God presenting in a person, a person subject to all the conditions of existence. Through Jesus as the Christ, we can see the divine participation in existential estrangement.[112]

Furthermore, Jesus as the Christ's victory over existential estrangement brings the New Being to all humanity.[113] New Being is the new reality in which the self-estrangement of our existence is overcome. It is a reality of reconciliation and reunion, of creativity, meaning, and hope.[114] "New Being is essential being under the conditions of existence conquering the gap between essence and existence."[115] New being is new because it is the undistorted manifestation of essential being within and under the existential conditions. It is new because it is not the merely potential character of essential being; and it is new because it overcomes the estranged character of existential being. In other words, New Being is actual, conquering the estrangement of actual existence.[116] Thus, New Being is the healing of human estrangement, and yet is not a mere return to the essential nature. Instead, it is a reconciliation within actual existing nature with its essence and its ground.[117]

New Being, for Tillich, "can be characterized as the Being of Love. Love is the drive toward reintegration of what has been alienated."[118] Now the question is raised, how can we experience the New Being? Tillich provides the answer that, if we "asked with existential seriousness, the answer is implied in the question, for existential seriousness is evidence of the impact of the Spiritual Presence upon an individual."[119] If we are ultimately concerned about our state of estrangement and about the possibility of reunion with the ground, we are already in the grip of the Spiritual Presence.[120] At this moment, our question is already answered. The New Being as the Being of Love is the "ultimate criterion of every healing and saving process."[121] Through Jesus as the Christ, the continuing salvation of God is manifested.

With the concept of the New Being, Tillich offers his concept of atonement. Basically, there are six principles of atonement. First, God alone creates the atoning processes. The Christ as the bearer of the New Being mediates the reconciling act of God to us. Second, there are no conflicts in God between God's love and God's justice. Third, there is no implication that human sin or human existential estrangement is being denied in God's atoning act. Fourth, God's atoning act does not mean that God removes human estrangement and its consequences. Instead, God participates in human estrangement and transforms those who participate in God's participation. Fifth, the Cross of the Christ is the manifestation of God's participation in existential estrangement and the criterion of all other manifestations of God's participation in the suffering world. Last, when one participates in the New Being, which is the being of Jesus as the Christ, one also participates in the manifestation of the atoning act of God.[122] These principles of atonement are God's saving act in Christ, but it cannot be effective alone. It needs humans to participate in God's participation, to accept it, and to be transformed by it.[123] These principles are also the basis for Tillich's threefold description of the state of salvation.

According to Tillich, the threefold character of salvation is regeneration or participation, justification or acceptance, and sanctification or transformation. In regeneration, humans are in "the state of having been drawn into the new reality manifest as Jesus as the Christ."[124] Humans participate in this reality and are reborn through participation. Justification, as the second character of salvation, is placed after regeneration. "Justification brings the 'in spite of' into the process of salvation."[125] Objectively, justification is an eternal act of God, totally without any human effort. God alone accepts those who are indeed estranged from God and takes them into the unity of the New Being, the Christ. On the subjective side, justification depends on the acceptance.

What this means is that humans must accept that God accepts them. They must accept acceptance.[126] Actually, regeneration and justification are one and describe the reunion of what is estranged. Regeneration is the reunion and justification is the paradoxical character of this reunion.[127] The final character of salvation is sanctification or transformation, which is distinguished from the previous two "as a process is distinguished from the event which it is initiated. . . . Sanctification is the process in which the power of the New Being transforms personality and community, inside and outside the church."[128]

In order to understand this threefold character of salvation completely, we have to understand its relation to Tillich's idea of faith. The only way humans can know that they are accepted is through faith. Once humans understand the reality of the New Being, they take their steps through faith toward the New Being and its promise of salvation. After being established in faith, then humans will be assured that they are accepted in spite of their existential estrangement.

To reiterate Tillich's idea of faith, it is "the state of being grasped by the ultimate concern."[129] This is the formal or general definition of faith. According to this definition, Tillich argues that everyone has faith because everyone is concerned ultimately about something. Thus, this formal definition of faith is basic and universal.[130] Moreover, there is the material definition of faith. "Faith is the state of being grasped by the Spiritual Presence and opened to the transcendent unity of unambiguous life. . . . One could say that faith is the state of being grasped by the New Being as it is manifest in Jesus of the Christ."[131] In this material definition, Tillich argues that there are three elements of faith. The first one is the element of being opened up by the Spiritual Presence. It is faith in its receptive character, which is regeneration. The second one is the element of accepting it in spite of the infinite gap between the divine Spirit and the human spirit. It is faith in its paradoxical character, and hence it is justification. And the third moment is the element of expecting final participation in the transcendent unity of unambiguous life. It is faith in its anticipatory character, which is sanctification.[132] The first two of these elements are like accepting acceptance and the final one is a process toward the future.

Furthermore, Tillich elucidates the relationship between faith and courage. Although "Spiritual Presence" or "New Being" is unambiguous, it is fragmentary in its manifestation in time and space. That is to say, the

New Being is only fragmentary in human existential experience. Therefore, "faith is certain in so far as it is an experience of the holy. But faith is uncertain in so far as the infinite to which it is related is received by a finite being. This element of uncertainty in faith cannot be removed, it must be accepted. And the element in faith which accepts this is courage."[133] Due to the element of uncertainty in faith, courage is "the daring self-affirmation of one's own being in spite of the powers of 'nonbeing' which are the heritage of everything finite."[134] Courage is the element of faith and is related to the risk of faith. But we cannot replace faith by courage, and yet we cannot describe faith without courage.[135]

Finally, we turn back to love as representative of Tillich's *raison d'etre*. "Whereas faith is the state of being grasped by the Spiritual Presence, love is the state of being taken by the Spiritual Presence into the transcendent unity of unambiguous life."[136] Like faith, love also has the receptive, paradoxical, and anticipatory character of the New Being. First, it accepts the object of love without restrictions. Second, it holds this acceptance in spite of the estranged, profanized, and demonized state of its objects. And third, it re-establishes the holiness, greatness, and dignity of its object; and takes its object into the transcendent unity of unambiguous life.[137] In this regard, "the concern of faith is identical with the desire of love: reunion with that to which one belongs and from which one is estranged."[138] Therefore, faith and love are two sides of a coin. "Faith without love is a continuation of estrangement and an ambiguous act of religious self-transcendence. Love without faith is an ambiguous reunion of the separated without the criterion and the power of the transcendent union."[139] Both faith and love move in the same way. "Being grasped by God in faith and adhering to God in love is one and the same state of creaturely life. It is participation in the transcendent unity of unambiguous life."[140]

Notes

1. Tillich, "Being and Love," 661.

2. Ibid..

3. Tillich, *Love, Power, and Justice*, 21.

4. Alexander C. Irwin, *Eros Toward the World: Paul Tillich and the Theology of the Erotic* (Minneapolis, MN: Augsburg Fortress, 1991), 8.

5. Tillich, *Love, Power, Justice*, 25.

6. Tillich, *Systematic Theology*, vol.3, 137.

7. Tillich, *Morality and Beyond* (New York: Harper Torchbook, 1963), 38, 42.

8. Irwin, *Eros Toward the World: Paul Tillich and the Theology of the Erotic,* 8.

9. Tillich, *Love, Power, and Justice*, 3-4.

10. Tillich, *Systematic Theology*, vol.3, 135.

11. Tillich, *Love, Power, and Justice*, 5.

12. Tillich, *Systematic Theology*, vol. 3, 134.

13. Judith Plaskow, *Sex, Sin and Grace: Woman's Experience and the Theologies of Reinhold Niebuhr and Paul Tillich* (Washington, D.C.: University Press of America, 1980), 129.

14. Tillich, "Being and Love," 666.

15. Tillich, *Love, Power, Justice*, 28.

16. Tillich, *Systematic Theology*, vol. 1, 280.

17. Ibid.

18. Ibid.

19. Ibid.

20. Ibid.

21. Tillich, *Morality and Beyond*, 40; also "Agape as the self-transcending element of love is not separated from the other elements that usually are described as *epithymia*—the *libido* quality of love, *philia* – the friendship quality of love, and *eros* – the mystical quality of love." *Morality and Beyond*, 40.

22. Tillich, "Being and Love," 666.

23. Tillich, *Love, Power, Justice*, 29-30.

24. Ibid., 28-29.

25. "The joy of eating and drinking, its intoxicating character is a part of the ecstasy of libido." Tillich, "Being and Love," 666.

26. Tillich, *Systematic Theology*, vol. 2, 54.

27. Tillich, *Love, Power, and Justice*, 32.

28. Tillich, "Being and Love," 668.

29. Ibid.

30. Tillich, "Love as Eros and the Integration of Personality." In "Unity of Love and Its Healing Power," (A Series of eight lectures), unpublished, Tillich Archives, Harvard Divinity School, 39-40.

31. Tillich, *Love, Power, and Justice*, 30.

32. Tillich, *Biblical Religion and the Search for Ultimate Reality*, 51.

33. Tillich, "Being and Love," 667.

34. Tillich, *Biblical Religion and the Search for Ultimate Reality*, 50.

35. Ibid., 72.

36. Tillich, *Love, Power, and Justice*, 31.

37. Tillich, "Being and Love," 667.

38. Irwin, *Eros Toward the World: Paul Tillich and the Theology of the Erotic,* 13.

39. Tillich, *Systematic Theology*, vol. 1, 280.

40. See Irwin, *Eros Toward the World: Paul Tillich and the Theology of the Erotic,*

43-98. Irwin tries to prove that *eros* is one of the major categories in Tillich's thought.

41. Tillich, *Love, Power, and Justice*, 30.

42. Ibid., 31-32.

43. Ibid., p.31.

44. Irwin, *Eros Toward the World: Paul Tillich and the Theology of the Erotic,* 17.

45. Tillich, *Systematic Theology*, vol. 3, 137.

46. Tillich, *Systematic Theology*, vol. 1, 280.

47. Ibid.

48. Ibid.

49. Ibid.

50. Tillich, "Being and Love," 668.

51. Tillich, *Systematic Theology*, vol. 3, 137.

52. Ibid.

53. Tillich, *Systematic Theology*, vol. 1, 280.

54. Ibid.

55. Tillich, "Being and Love," 668.

56. Tillich, *Systematic Theology*, vol. 1, 281. Tillich notes that the *libido* element of love is a form of poetic-religious symbolism for the devotional language, the *philia* element of love symbolizes the relation between God and us, and the erotic element of love symbolizes the drive toward ultimate fulfillment. Tillich, *Systematic Theology*, vol.1, 281.

57. Irwin, *Eros Toward the World: Paul Tillich and the Theology of the Erotic,* 9-10.

58. Tillich, *Systematic Theology*, vol. 1, 281.

59. Irwin, *Eros Toward the World: Paul Tillich and the Theology of the Erotic,* 10.

60. Tillich, *Biblical Religion and the Search for Ultimate Reality*, 50.

61. Tillich, *Systematic Theology*, vol. 3, 138.

62. Tillich, *Systematic Theology*, vol. 1, 280-1.

63. Tillich, "Being and Love," 668.

64. Tillich, *Love, Power, and Justice*, 33, 116.

65. Ibid., 116.

66. Irwin, *Eros Toward the World: Paul Tillich and the Theology of the Erotic,* 15.

67. Tillich, "The Unity of Love and Its Healing Power," 58.

68. Tillich, "Being and Love," 668.

69. Tillich, *Love, Power, Justice*, 11.

70. Tillich, "Being and Love," 664.

71. Ibid.

72. Ibid.

73. Tillich, *Love, Power, and Justice*, 41.

74. Ibid., 40.

75. Ibid., 48.

76. Tillich, *Love, Power, Justice*, 49.

77. Ibid., 57.

78. Ibid., 665.

79. Tillich, "Being and Love," 665.

80. Tillich, *Love, Power, Justice*, 71.

81. Ibid., 56.

82. Ibid., 71.

83. Tillich, "Being and Love," 665.

84. Ibid.

85. Ibid.

86. Tillich, *Systematic Theology*, vol. 1, 279.

87. Tillich, "Being and Love," 671.

88. Ibid.

89. Tillich, *The New Being* (New York: Charles Scribner's Sons, 1955), 26.

90. Ibid., 26-7.

91. Tillich, *The Shaking of the Foundations*, 109.

92. Tillich, "Being and Love," 662.

93. Ibid.

94. Ibid. Tillich uses Hegel's dialectic in most of his theology. See Adrian Thatcher, *Ontology of Paul Tillich*, 89-94; Kenan Osbornes, *New Being* (The Hague, Netherlands: Martinus Nijhoff, 1969), 20-1.

95. Tillich, "Being and Love," 663.

96. Ibid.

97. Ibid.

98. Tillich, *Love, Power, and Justice*, 25.

99. Tillich, *Systematic Theology*, vol. 3, 134.

100. Tillich, *Love, Power, and Justice*, 25.

101. Tillich, "Being and Love," 662.

102. Tillich, *Love, Power, and Justice*, 25.

103. Guyton B. Hammond suggests that Tillich's idea of reunion preserves human individualization as well as overcomes their separation from the Ground of Being. See Guyton B. Hammond, *Man in Estrangement*, 167-8.

104. Tillich, *Love, Power, and Justice*, 25.

105. Tillich, *Systematic Theology*, vol. 3, 211.

106. Tillich, *The Shaking of the Foundation*, 156. Also see Plaskow, *Sex, Sin and Grace: Women's Experience and the Theologies of Reinhold Niebuhr and Paul Tillich*, 120-121.

107. Tillich, *Systematic Theology*, vol. 3, 222.

108. Donald F. Dreisbach argues that Tillich has two different possibilities for understanding Spiritual Presence. One is a symbol of one's awareness of participation of God, and the other is a power that causes unambiguous life. However, I think these are the two sides of a coin. Tillich does mean both. See Dreisbach, *Symbols and Salvation*, 174.

109. Tillich *Systematic Theology*, vol. 1, 286.

110. Tillich *Systematic Theology*, vol. 2, 97.

111. Tillich *Systematic Theology*, vol. 1, 136.

112. Dreisbach, *Symbols and Salvation*, 145.

113. Plaskow, *Sex, Sin and Grace*, 126. Langdon Gilkey contends that the New Being is the central category or symbol for Tillich's theology. See Gilkey, *Gilkey on Tillich*, 138.

114. Tillich, *Systematic Theology*, vol. 1,49.

115. Tillich, *Systematic Theology*, vol. 2, 118-9.

116. Ibid., 119.

117. Dreisbach, *Symbols and Salvation*,.146; also see Kenan B. Osborne, *New Being*, 182-184.

118. Tillich, "The Importance of New Being for Christian Theology," in *Man and Transformation*, ed. by Joseph Campbell (Princeton, NJ: Princeton University Press, 1964), 174.

119. Tillich, *Systematic Theology*, vol. 3, 223

120. Ibid.

121. Tillich, *Systematic Theology*, vol. 2, 168.

122. Ibid., 175-6.

123. Ibid., 176.

124. Ibid., 177.

125. Ibid., 178.

126. Ibid., 179.

127. Ibid., 179.

128. Ibid., 179-180.

129. Tillich, *Systematic Theology*, vol. 3, 130.

130. Ibid.

131. Ibid., 131.

132. Ibid., 133-4.

133. Tillich, *The Dynamics of Faith*, 16.

134. Ibid.17. "Courage is the self-affirmation of being in spite of the fact of nonbeing. It is the act of the individual self in taking the anxiety of nonbeing upon itself." Tillich, *Courage to Be*, 155.

135. Tillich, *The Dynamics of Faith*, 103. Guyton B. Hammond argues that courage is a power of being, which is derive from the ground of being. See Guyton B. Hammond, *Man in Estrangement*, 140.

136. Tillich, *Systematic Theology*, vol. 3, 134.

137. Ibid., 138.

138. Tillich, *The Dynamics of Faith*, 112.

139. Tillich, *Systematic Theology*, vol. 3, 129.

140. Ibid., 138.

PART TWO
The Thought of Chu Hsi

The second part of the dissertation now discusses the thought of Chu Hsi. In the initial chapter, a brief induction to the inheritance of Chu Hsi's thought will be provided. The development of Confucianism before Chu Hsi will be briefly described. Chu Hsi's synthesis of the thought of his Northern Sung masters provides innovative ideas for a renewed Confucianism will also be explored.

In the sixth chapter, Chu Hsi's ontological structure of principle (*li*) and vital energy (*ch'i*) will be analyzed. The relationship between the Great Ultimate (*T'ai-chi*) and principle (*li*), between Tao and principle, between principle and vital energy will be elucidated. Based on his concepts of principle and vital energy, Chu Hsi's theory of human nature will be discussed in the seventh chapter. Chu Hsi's concept of human nature as well as heart-mind will be expounded. And the relationship between human nature, heart-mind, and feelings will also be examined.

In the eighth chapter, Chu Hsi's concept of *jen* will be analyzed. By discussing the development of the concept of *jen* in the Confucian tradition, we will show that Chu Hsi's innovative Confucian concept of *jen* is the resolution of human estrangement. In so doing, we will examine his two important statements, namely, *jen* as the character of the heart-mind and *jen* as the principle of love. Also the relationship between *jen* and self-realization (*ch'eng*) will be explored.

CHAPTER FIVE
The Inheritance of Chu Hsi's Thought

The term Confucianism is used generally to denote the Chinese term "*ju chia*." Although the term Confucianism is considered ambiguous by some scholars, it is still a common usage for denoting the school of thought that is traditionally refered to as *ju chia* and to phenomena associated with that school. It refers to the teaching of Confucius and the entire development of the Confucian tradition.[1] Before Chu Hsi, there were three major periods of the development of Confucianism.[2] The first period is called the classical period (551-221 BCE). In this period, there were three masters of Confucianism, Confucius (551-479 BCE), Mencius (371-289 BCE), and Hsün Tzu (fl. 298-238). Although Confucius only claimed to be a transmitter of the teachings of the early sages, he is treated as the founder of this tradition by later generations. In this period, the main concern for Confucius to Hsün Tzu is what humans must do in order to achieve humanity (*jen*). The answer for Confucius was to restore the rites. Basically, the classical period of Confucianism was focused upon the ethical dimension of society.

The second period was the rise of the Han dynasty (206 BCE- 220 CE). Confucianism in this period became the state-sponsored imperial Confucian orthodoxy and the civil ideology for the Han imperial state. Not only did the Han Confucians develop political theories, but they also preserved the classical Confucian tradition by writing commentaries and historical compilations of earlier texts. In this period, Tung Chung-shu (c. 179-104 BCE), one of the Han Confucians, combined the theory of other schools of thought, particularly the Yin-Yang School, with classical Confucianism in order to develop a pan-Chinese cosmology which assumed that the universe is not static but rather dynamic and an organic whole.

After the fall of the Han dynasty was the period of the Neo-Taoism of the Wei-Chin (220-420) and the rise and success of Buddhism in the T'ang dynasty (618-907). In the Wei-Chin period, there was a revival of the study of classical Taoism, particularly Lao Tzu and Chuang Tzu. The Neo-Taoists were interested in the metaphysics of being and nonbeing as well as a universal ground of logic. Thus, they developed a concept of principle (*li*), which became a central concept of later Neo-Confucianism.[3] In the T'ang dynasty, there were different schools of Buddhism established in China such as T'ien-t'ai, Hua-yen, Ch'an, and Pure Land. And through China, the Buddhist heritage has spread to East Asia and then to the North Atlantic world.[4] However, although Buddhism was successfully flourishing in the T'ang dynasty, it did not mean that Confucianism disappeared from Chinese soil.

By the end of the T'ang dynasty, Han Yü (768-824) and Li Ao (fl. 798), two of the most famous T'ang Confucians, defended and preserved the Confucian Tao against the Buddhist challenge. Although Han Yü can be treated as a leader of the revival of Confucianism and a founder of Neo-Confucianism, some historians of Chinese philosophy treat his influence as merely literary.[5] However, Han Yü and Li Ao intended to retain the traditional Confucian goals of a moral being and a moral society by criticizing the Taoist idea of inaction and Buddhist ideas of silence and annihilation.[6]

Following the late T'ang Confucianism came to its fourth period. This is the Northern and Southern Sung (960-1279) revival of Confucianism. A group of intellectuals desired to revive the Confucian tradition. Two important leaders were Fan Chung-yen (989-1052), a prominent official, and Hu Yüan (993-1059), a famous educator. They emphasized the importance of the Confucian Classics and socio-political responsibility. Although these intellectuals were Confucians, they were not strong speculative thinkers. Their contribution was in the context of literary development and social reform rather than the formation of a new world-view in contrast with that of Buddhism. Their main concern was to engage in social and political affairs and to enjoy spiritual self-cultivation. Thus, eclecticism arose from this dominant school. After Fan and Hu, the tendency was continued by Wang An-shih (1021-1086), and the Su brothers, Su Shih (1036-1101) and Su Ch'e (1039-1112). This group occupied a middle position in the transition from Buddhism to Neo-Confucianism.[7]

Another group, which arose out of this eclecticism, were named Neo-Confucians in the West.[8] This group responded to two important needs. The first is the promotion of morality in the rising literate class; and the second is the rationalization of the gradually consolidating socio-political structure by incorporating the conception of law in its metaphysics.[9] Although the term Neo-Confucianism is ambiguous, it is still useful for referring to schools of thought in the Northern and Southern Sung. According to Wm. Theodore de Bary, Neo-Confucianism is the most vital system of thought that links "modern China" and the rest of East Asian intellectual history. It was the primary force in shaping a new common culture in East Asia. In contrast to the speculative and meditative learnings of Buddhism and Taoism in the T'ang dynasty, a more realistic group of Confucian scholars emerged in the Sung dynasty. These scholars developed an inclusive humanist vision that integrated personal self-cultivation with social ethics and moral metaphysics into a holistic philosophy of life. They understood classical Confucian thought as the establishment of the lineage of the "Learning of the Tao." This group of Confucians can be traced through a line of scholars from Chou Tun-i (1017-1073), via Chang Tsai (1020-1077), Ch'eng Hao (1032-1085), and Ch'eng I (1033-1107), to the great synthesizer, Chu Hsi (1130-1200).[10]

In his *Confucian Discourse and Chu Hsi's Ascendancy*, Hoyt Cleveland Tillman argues that Chu Hsi's system of thought was shaped by his relationships and interchanges with his major contemporaries.[11] And yet Chu Hsi is still the most influential thinker in Chinese history since Confucius and Mencius, the two most important of classical Confucian thinkers.[12] His thought has been dominant in China for over eight hundred years and has also influenced many phases of Asian life throughout East Asia. He has been described as the "*chi ta-ch'eng,*" or "the one gathering into a great completion," the greatest synthesizer of Neo-Confucianism.[13] One of his major contributions to later generations was to group the *Analects*, *Mencius*, the *Great Learning*, and the

Doctrine of Means together as the "Four Books." Ever since Chu Hsi completed his commentaries on these texts in 1190, the "Four Books" became the focus of Confucian thought and later the basic texts in civil service examinations and school education. Since 1313 his commentaries on the "Four Books" provided the orthodox interpretation of the texts and the basis for the imperial examinations till 1905.[14] In this regard, Chu Hsi can be said to be the foremost Confucian of the Neo-Confucian movement in China as well as East Asia.

Although Chu Hsi's thought was shaped by his relationships and interchanges with his major contemporaries, we can still affirm that Chu Hsi indeed synthesized the thought of Northern Sung masters in order to reconstruct his own system of thought, also known as the school of principle. Chu Hsi borrows the concept of the Great Ultimate from Chou Tun-i and even identifies it with principle. Although his thought has some Taoist elements, Chou Tun-i's idea of the Great Ultimate provided a concept of one universal principle for the ceaselessly generative cosmos. Also this universal principle is manifested in every particular thing or event as its principle.

In Chang Tsai's thought, vital energy (*ch'i*) is the most important element of reality. Chu Hsi borrows this notion of vital energy for his ontological structure. Vital energy (*ch'i*) is the dynamic, unceasing energy of the production of the myriad things. For Chu Hsi, it refers to physical form, individuality, and the transformation of things. In terms of human beings, the heart-mind is the highest and most refined form of vital energy. Principle and vital energy are two pivotal elements in Chu Hsi's ontological structure. In his *Reflections on Things at Hand*, Chu Hsi excluded Shao Yung as one of the major masters of the Northern Sung. The problem with Shao Yung is that his thought was too numerological in character and his philosophy of symbols and numbers was derived from Taoist thought.[15]

Most conclusively, Chu Hsi followed the thought of the two Ch'engs. The Ch'eng brothers, Ch'eng Hao and Ch'eng I, treated principle as the foundation of their philosophy. To understand principle is the way to understand knowledge as well as morality. According to them, principle was manifested in everything and governed everywhere. It is the universal order as well as the universal form of creation, and can be identified with the nature of human beings and things.[16] Chu Hsi followed their idea of principle in a very insightful way. He related principle to vital force and identified principle with the Great Ultimate. These philosophic moves prior to the Ch'eng brothers had never been tried before.

In the following chapters, I will discuss the thought of Chu Hsi. We will then see how Chu Hsi synthesized the thought of the Northern Sung masters and provided the innovative teachings of Confucianism. As the greatest synthesizer of Neo-Confucianism, Chu Hsi's thought indeed took Confucianism to a new level.

Notes

1. See Julia Ching, *Confucianism and Christianity*, 7; Kwong-loi Shun, *Mencius and Early Chinese Thought* (Stanford, California: Stanford University Press, 1997), 3-4. Eno discusses the early development of *ju* in the appendix B of his *The Confucian Creation of Heaven* (Albany: State University of New York, 1990), 190-197.

2. See Berthrong, *All Under Heaven*, 77-83.

3. Chan, *A Source Book of Chinese Philosophy*, 315.

4. Berthrong, *All Under Heaven*, 79.

5. See Peter K Bol, *"This Culture of Ours":Intellectual Transition in T'ang and Sung China* (Stanford, California: Stanford University Press, 1992), 23.

6. Chan, *A Source Book of Chinese Philosophy*, 451.

7. Chung Tsai-chun, *The Development of the Concepts of Heaven and of Man in the Philosophy of Chu Hsi* (Taiwan, Republic of China: Institute of Chinese Literature and Philosophy, Academia Sinica, 1993), 37-8.

8. Hoyt Cleveland Tillman argues that Neo-Confucianism and *Tao-Hsüeh* are not the same because Neo-Confucianism traditionally has excluded some Confucians, who were certainly influential in their period of time but did not even mention in Chu Hsi's *Tao-t'ung*. See Hoyt Cleveland Tillman, "A New Direction in Confucian Scholarship: Approaches to Examining The Differences Between Neo-Confucianism and *Tao-Hsüeh*," *Philosophy East & West*, vol. 42, no. 3, (July) 1992: 455-474.

9. Chung Tsai-chun, *The Development of the Concepts of Heaven and of Man in the Philosophy of Chu Hsi*, 39.

10. See Wm. Theodore de Bary, *East Asian Civilizations: A Dialogue in Five Stages* (Cambridge, MA: Harvard University Press, 1988), 43-66; Tu Wei-Ming, "Confucianism" in *Our Religions*, ed. Arvind Sharma (San Francisco: Harper Collins Publishers, 1993), 168.

11. See Hoyt Cleveland Tillman, *Confucian Discourse and Chu Hsi's Ascendancy* (Honolulu: University of Hawaii Press,1992).

12. Wing-tsit Chan, *Chu Hsi: New Studies* (Honolulu: University of Hawaii Press,

1989), vii.

13. Wing-tsit Chan, *Chu Hsi Life and Thought* (Hong Kong: Chinese University of Hong Kong Press, 1987), 38.
14. Ibid., 130.
15. Wing-tsit Chan, *Chu Hsi Life and Thought*, 109.
16. Ibid., 110.

CHAPTER SIX
Ontological Structure: Principle and Vital Energy

Li (principle) is a crucial concept not only in Chu Hsi's thought but also in Chinese thought in the last 800 years. Neo-Confucianism can be called *Li-hsüeh* (School of Principle) in Chinese.[1] If the concept of *li* has already been philosophically accepted in China for so many years, what is the difference between Chu Hsi and Confucians before him? In his articles, Wing-tsit Chan argues that one of the new ideas in Chu Hsi's philosophical system is the concept of *li*.[2] According to Chan, Chu Hsi synthesized all the important elements in the philosophy of the two Ch'engs[3] in a new insightful way. "He distinguished principle that is naturally so (*tzu-jan*), principle that is originally so (*pen-jan*), principle that is necessarily so (*pi-jan*), principle that should be so (*tang-jan*)."[4] Most importantly, Chu identifies the Great Ultimate (*t'ai-chi*) with *li*.[5] In *Yü-lei* (Classified Conversations of Chu Hsi), Chu says, "The Great Ultimate is nothing other than principle."[6] Since there is only one Great Ultimate (*t'ai-chi*), then there is only one *li*. Although *li* is one, its manifestations are many. For the myriad things have been endowed with *li*. In the case of humans, every human being has a particular *li*.[7]

T'ai-chi and *Li*

In regard to the relation between *li* and *t'ai-chi*, Chung-ying Cheng suggests that there are at least six types of *li* in Chu Hsi's thought. They are (i) the ontological *li* of the Great Ultimate, (ii) the objective *li* of things--order, structure, and law of things, (iii) the rational *li* of mind--the ordering and analytical-synthetic activities of mind, (iv) the latent *li* of mind--the ideas and concepts in mind, (v) the technological *li* of mind and things--design of artifacts, and (vi) nomological *li* of mind-conduct-pattern of moral conduct and correct social behavior.[8] Cheng explains that at first all *li* are ultimately rooted in the ontological *li*, which is the ground for all the other types of *li*. In this respect, Chu Hsi conceives that *li* is the objective principle inherent in things and yet is ultimately one.[9] What Chu Hsi means by *li* is that *t'ai-chi* is the ultimate unity in which things share. In other words, *T'ai-chi* is *li* in its ultimate state. It embodies *yin* and *yang*, which is the operation of myriad things.[10] As Chu Hsi says, "The *T'ai-chi* is not a thing, it is in *yin-yang* (passive and active cosmic forces) where *yin-yang* is; it is in *wu-hsing* (the Five Powers, Metal, Wood, Water, Fire, and Earth) where *wu-hsing* is; it is in all things where all things are. It is only a *li*. But in so far as it reaches the ultimate, it is the *T'ai-chi*."[11] Thus, this concept "*li* is *t'ai-chi*" implies that "every person has a *T'ai-chi* and everything has a *T'ai-chi*."[12] What this means is that "every person and everything has a *li* that makes it what it is and that represents the same ultimate *li*."[13]

What then is the Great Ultimate? According to Wing-tsit Chan, the concept of the Great Ultimate (*T'ai-chi*) is one major aspect of Chu Hsi's completion of the thought of Neo-Confucianism. Before Chu His's time, the Great Ultimate was not an important concept. Among the Five Masters of the Northern Sung, only Chou Tun-i (1017-1073) wrote a treatise on *the Diagram of the Great Ultimate*. The others, Ch'eng brothers, Chang Tsai (1032-1085), and Shao Yung (1011-1077), had never or rarely mentioned *t'ai-chi*. However, Chu Hsi utilizes Chou's treatise to develop his concept of *t'ai-chi* and it becomes one of the major concepts of his philosophical system.[14]

According to Teng Aimin, *t'ai-chi* in Chu Hsi's thought is first of all the highest being or ground of the universe. It is not something which exists in time and space. Rather, "it is what it is in itself and conceived through itself. It possesses mystical energy and effect, and is capable of generating all beings."[15] *T'ai chi* is the synthesis of being and nonbeing, on the one hand, and neither being nor nonbeing, on the other. As Teng Aimin cites, "the operations of Heaven have neither sound nor smell, that is to say, nonbeing exists in being. The Ultimate of Nonbeing is also the Great Ultimate, that is to say, being exists in nonbeing."[16] What Chu Hsi means by "neither sound nor smell" is that "the Great Ultimate has neither spatial restriction nor physical form or body. There is no spot where it may be placed."[17] In this respect, *t'ai-chi* can be understood as both being and nonbeing. On the other hand, Chu Hsi uses Chou Tun-i's statement, "the Great Ultimate is also the Ultimate of nonbeing (*wu-chi*)," to elucidate the concept of the Great Ultimate. Fundamentally, the Great Ultimate is the Ultimate of Nonbeing (*wu-chi*) because *t'ai-chi* has "no shape or appearance, spatial restriction, or physical form."[18] As Chu Hsi says, "What is called '*Wu-chi erh T'ai-chi*' (the Great Ultimate is also the Ultimate of nonbeing) does not mean that on top of the Great Ultimate there is separately an Ultimate of Nonbeing. It merely says that the Great Ultimate is not a thing, as in the saying, The operations of Heaven have neither sound nor smell."[19] Chu Hsi's idea of the Ultimate of nonbeing is merely to indicate "the formless, abstract, intangible condition of the concept of *t'ai-chi*."[20] Therefore, *t'ai-chi* cannot be something. Moreover, "*t'ai chi* is the greatest extent to the highest degree."[21] That means *t'ai-chi* has a transcendental characteristic. Thus, it is beyond anything, neither being nor nonbeing.[22]

Not only is *t'ai-chi* transcendental, but it is also immanent. As Chu Hsi argues, "The Great Ultimate is merely the principle of heaven and earth and the myriad things. With respect to heaven and earth, there is the Great Ultimate in them. With respect to the myriad things, there is the Great Ultimate in each and every one of them. Before heaven and earth existed, there was assuredly this principle. It is the principle that "through movement generates the yang." It is also this principle that "through tranquillity generates the *yin*."[23] Here Chu Hsi tries to indicate that *t'ai-chi* is the highest norm or principle and manifests in every individual creature. Logically speaking, *t'ai-chi* is the highest principle and everything has principle, therefore it implies that everything has *t'ai-chi* in it. As the result *t'ai-chi* is the principle of the myriad things and at the same time everything involves *t'ai-chi* in itself.[24] As Chu Hsi contends, "Fundamentally there is only one Great Ultimate. Yet each of the myriad things has been endowed with it and each in itself possesses the Great Ultimate in its entirely. This is similar to the fact that there is one moon in the sky but when its light is scattered upon rivers and lakes, it can be seen everywhere. It cannot be said that moon has been split."[25]

This is also the concept of *li-i fen–shu* (Principle is one but its manifestations are many). With the analogy of the moon and its beams, Chu Hsi avers that there is only one general principle governing the universe. As moonlight is scattered upon the myriad things, such as rivers and lakes, it produces myriad reflections. And all myriad reflections come originally from one moon. In other words, every person and everything has *t'ai-chi* as *li* that makes it what it is and that represents the same *T'ai-chi.*[26] As *li* can be diversified into different types and orders of things, the ontological *li* of the Great Ultimate can manifest different types and orders of *li*, such as the objective *li*, the rational *li*, the latent *li* of mind, the technological *li*, and the nomological *li*. And these five types of *li* are unified in the ontological *li* of the Great Ultimate.[27] Therefore, *t'ai-chi* can be understood as the perfected goal of each person in the universe and also the perfection of the whole universe.[28]

Finally, *t'ai-chi* is "the norm of the *yin-yang* forces. It is the essence of this activity."[29] It possesses *tung* (activity) and *ching* (tranquillity). In Chou Tun-i's Treatise, "the Great Ultimate through movement generates *yang*. . . . Through tranquillity the Great Ultimate generates *yin*."[30] For Chou, *t'ai-chi* involves activity and tranquillity and is identical with *ch'i* (vital energy). However, for Chu Hsi, *t'ai-chi* cannot be activity and tranquillity nor can it be identified with them. Rather, it is just the principle of activity and tranquillity. Chu Hsi argues that *t'ai-chi* is merely principle and principle can not be reduced to activity and tranquillity.[31] "Due to the principle of activity, *yang* can be generated through activity; and due to the principle of tranquillity, *yin* can be generated through tranquillity."[32] In other words, the activity of *t'ai-chi* is *yang* and the tranquillity of *t'ai-chi* is *yin*. "The activity and tranquillity of *t'ai-chi* consists in the unity of their opposition."[33] As Teng Aimin clearly indicates, the distinction between activity and tranquillity and *t'ai-chi* is the distinction between things existing after physical form and things existing before physical form.[34] *T'ai-chi* cannot embody any activity because it is principle. It is "a term for explaining how things act and not the action itself."[35] "The Great [Supreme] Ultimate is only the supreme good and perfected principle of the Tao. Each person has a Great [Supreme] Ultimate and each thing has its Great [Supreme] Ultimate."[36]

Tao and *Li*

In his *Pei-hsi tzu-i (Neo-Confucian Terms Explained)*, Ch'en Ch'un elaborates on Chu Hsi's term *li* in terms of the idea of Tao. "Generally speaking, the Way and principle are the same thing. But since they are distinguished by two different words, there must be a difference between them."[37] In his *Further Reflections on Things at Hand*, Chu Hsi distinguishes Tao from *li*. "Tao is a roadway. Principle is its ordered pattern."[38] And "what the word Tao encompasses is very great. Principle is the myriad streaks and veins coursing within Tao."[39] What "Tao is a roadway" means is that "it is that which all men travel on. Each principle has a linear system and circumscribed limits."[40] As Ch'en Ch'un contends, "Compared with 'principle,' the 'Way' is broader while 'principle' is more concrete. 'Principle' has the idea of being definitely unchanging. Hence, the way is that which can be followed forever, and principle is that which is forever unchanging."[41] Both Tao and *li* are not the concrete events or things. Rather, they are the formal norm of the events and things. They are the norm by which every events and things ought to be so.[42] Or using Tillich's terms, they are the essence of being, namely, what being ought to be. Ontologically speaking, Tao is the formal norm of being; while cosmologically speaking, *li* is the formal norm of our universe. This is the basic difference between Tao and *li*. As Ch'en Ch'un indicates, Tao is more abstract whereas *li* is more concrete. *Li* then points to the ordered patterns of the events and things and reflects the greatest Tao in it.[43]

Li and *Ch'i*

Although *li* is the major philosophical category of Chu Hsi's thought, we still cannot understand this concept thoroughly without relating it to *ch'i* (vital energy). According to Wing-tsit Chan, one of the Chu Hsi's completions of Neo-Confucianism is the clarification of the relation between principle and vital energy. Before Chu Hsi, the relation between *li* and *ch'i* was vague. Chang Tsai had the concept of *ch'i* but he did not relate it to *li*. Although the Cheng brothers had made *li* as their foundation of their thought, they did not demonstrate how *li* and *ch'i* relate to each other.[44] In his philosophy, Chu Hsi advocates that there are two fundamental ontological elements, namely *li* and *ch'i*. Although *li* is incorporeal and *ch'i* is corporeal, *ch'i* still belongs to the metaphysical ground of things. Both of them, *li* and *ch'i*, are the necessary elements in the original substance of things. Stanislaus Lokuang argues that Chu Hsi defines the Great Ultimate as the supreme principle. Not only is *T'ai-chi* as *li* the highest principle of the universe the origin of the universe, but also it is the most relevant principle of everything.[45] In traditional Confucianism, since the universe is the flux of life and everything possesses life, life then was simply the existence of things. The *yin-yang* force formed the existence of the myriad things. Continuously and unceasingly this force produces the myriad things. This *yin-yang* force has its own principle of operations, namely, the principle of perpetual renewal of life. Originally this principle of perpetual renewal of life in each thing is the same principle. But actually things are different from each other. Why? It is because there is *ch'i* (vital energy) in each physical body. Each individual thing possesses different *ch'i*.[46]

However, it is impossible to understand Chu Hsi's concept of *ch'i* without *li* or vice versa. Chu Hsi emphasizes over and over again that *li* and *ch'i* cannot be separate or independent. We can analyze Chu Hsi's relation of *li* and *ch'i* into three points. First, there is only one *li* but different *ch'i*. As Chu Hsi claims, "Throughout the universe there are both principle and material force. Principle refers to the Way, which exists before physical form [and is without it] and is the root from which all things are produced. Material force refers to material objects, which exists after physical form [and is with it]; it is the instrument by which things are produced. Therefore in the production of man and things, they must be endowed with principle before they have their nature, and they must be endowed with material force before they have physical form."[47] In this respect, principle is used to explain what the reality and universality of things ought to be, and yet it is not a thing itself. Rather, "it is incorporeal, one, eternal and unchanging, uniform, constituting the essence of things, indestructible, the reason for creation, and always good."[48] Principle is also prior to everything and is the root from which all things are produced. All things that exist partake of it; everything, whether it is living or non-living, natural or artificial, has *li*. On the other hand, *ch'i* is used to explain physical form, individuality, and the transformation of things. "It is physical, many, transitory and changeable, unequal in things, constituting their physical substance, destructible, the vehicle and material for creation, and involving both good and evil."[49] It exists before physical form; it is the instrument by which things are produced.

Since Chu Hsi identifies *li* with *t'ai-chi*, and says that "each and every person has in him the *t'ai-chi* and each and everything has in it the *t'ai-chi*,"[50] this indicates that there is the ultimate identity of things and the ultimate unity which things share. Due to the fact that every person and everything has a *li* that makes it what it is, the myriad things share the same ultimate *li*. If this is the case, why are things different? Chu Hsi's answer is that "considering the fact that all things come from one source, we see that their principle is the same but their vital energy [material force] different."[51] Originally, *li* is one, but its manifestation is many because there is *ch'i*. In other words, there is a unified *li* in the universe, but due to differences of *ch'i* things are formed differently. Therefore, the differences of things do not come from *li* but from *ch'i*.[52]

Moreover, Chu Hsi suggests that due to the difference in the degree of purity of *ch'i*, there will be a difference in the degree of the manifestation of *li*. As Chu Hsi says, "the difference in material force is due to the inequality of its purity or impurity, whereas the difference in principle is due to its completeness or partiality."[53] For this reason, there are animals and human beings. *Li* in animals is only manifested partially and in human beings is manifested completely. Originally, the myriad things have the same *li* but different *ch'i*. However, when we see the different shapes and forms of the myriad things, we see their *ch'i* is similar but their *li* utterly different. It is because *li* has been manifested completely in one thing and partially in the others.[54] Compared with animals, human beings have more pure *ch'i*, and yet they still have differences in the degree of purity. Chu Hsi makes an analogy in this point clearly. He says, "The principle is like a precious jewel. When a saint or wise man possesses it, it is like being placed in clear water. Its brilliance naturally can be seen. When stupid or unworthy persons possess it, it is like being placed in turbid water. Clearing turbid water and removing mud and sand so that its brilliance can be seen."[55] On the one hand, there is no distinction between animals because they all have the same *li*. However, on the other hand, animals and humans are indeed different because of *ch'i*. It causes animals to receive *li* partially and humans to receive it thoroughly. Due to this *ch'i*, things are different, some are higher and others are lower.[56] Concerning to human beings, *li* is their nature. There is only one nature as there is only one *li*. Again due to *ch'i* each physical body that humans possess is different. In addition, the difference of *ch'i* can cause human nature good and evil. "The nature of all men is good, and yet there are those who are good from their birth and those who are evil from their birth. This is because of the difference in vital energy [material force] with which they are endowed."[57]

Second, *li* and *ch'i* are not separated or mixed. In the first chapter of *Yü-lei*, Chu Hsi argues that "in the universe there has never been any material force without principle or principle without material force."[58] That means both *li* and *ch'i* are intermingled and cannot be separated. "Principle has never been separated from material force."[59] Although *li* is embedded intimately and necessarily in every individual thing, it is not a thing. It needs *ch'i*, which is the immanent, experiential and tangible constituent, in order to complete or formalize the phenomenal world. Therefore, *li* exists right in *ch'i*.[60] Chu Hsi clearly contends that "*li* is not a separate entity. It exists right in *ch'i*. Without *ch'i*, *li* would have nothing to adhere to."[61] "As there is *li*, there is *ch'i*; whereas there is *ch'i*, there is *li* in it."[62] Someone asked Chu Hsi about the evidence that *li* is in *ch'i*. Chu Hsi answered that "there is order in the complicated interfusion of the *yin* and the *yang* and of the Five Agents. Principle is there. If material force does not consolidate and integrate, principle would have nothing to attach itself to."[63]

However, on the other hand, *li* and *ch'i* are indeed two different entities. The former is incorporeal and the latter is corporeal. As Chu Hsi contends, "What are called principle and material force are certainly two different entities. But considered from the standpoint of things, the two entities are merged one with the other and cannot be separated with each in a different place. However, this does not destroy the fact that two entities are each an entity in itself."[64] Although there has never been *ch'i* without *li* or *li* without *ch'i* in the universe, they are indeed two different entities. The different characteristics of *li* and *ch'i* set them apart from each other, but their necessary mutual involvement binds them together. In other words, in relation to *ch'i*, *li* is neither immanent nor transcendent; instead, it is both.[65] *Li* attaches to *ch'i* in order to be realized in the world; and *ch'i* needs *li* as its own law in order to actualize and impose its character on things in the process of creation.[66]

Finally, *li* and *ch'i* have no priority over each other. In terms of the characteristics of *li* and *ch'i*, can we say that *li* is first and then *ch'i* comes after? In *Yü-lei*, Chu Hsi answers that "Fundamentally principle and material force cannot be spoken of as prior or posterior. But if we must trace their origin, we are obliged to say that principle is prior. However, principle is not a separate entity. It exists right in material force. Without material force, principle would have nothing to adhere to."[67] Over and ever, Chu Hsi argues that we cannot know if *li* is first and then *ch'i* comes after; or *ch'i* is first and then *li*. They are not separated from each other. *Ch'i* operates according to *li*. As there is *ch'i*, there is also *li*. *Ch'i* can integrate and create, but not *li*.[68] When someone asked Chu Hsi whether *li* must precede *ch'i*. Chu Hsi answered that basically *li* and *ch'i* cannot be spoken of as prior or posterior. However, logically "*li* exists before there is the universe. But after all, *li* will remain even if the mountains and rivers and the earth itself all cave in."[69] What Chu Hsi means is that *li* has no beginning or end. Actually, *li* exists before any physical form and is the principle of being, the essence of things. "When considered from the standpoint of principle, before things existed their principles of being had already existed. Only their principles existed, however, but not yet really the things themselves."[70] But logically speaking, *li* exists before *ch'i* due to its operation being in accordance with *li*. Nevertheless, there is no *li* without *ch'i* or vice versa. There is not something outside of *ch'i* that imparts a *li* of being into it.[71] This is the reason why Chu Hsi said that *li* has never been separate from *ch'i*. Actually, neither of them can be considered to be prior to the other. *Li* is not a separate entity. It exists right in *ch'i*.

Furthermore, *li* is *hsing-erh-shang* (incorporeal) and *ch'i* is *hsing-erh-hsia* (corporeal). In other words, *li* has no form or cannot have form, whereas *ch'i* forms the physicality of things. *Li* is static but *ch'i* is dynamic. *Li* is the source from which things emerge, while *ch'i* is the force by which things are produced. Therefore, in the process of creation, things must be endowed with *li* before they have their nature, and they must be endowed with *ch'i* before they have their physical form.[72] "As there is principle, there is therefore material force to operate everywhere and nourish and develop all things."[73] Thus, Chu Hsi contends that *li* and *ch'i* cannot be seen as sequential, and yet when we are reasoning, *li* is first and then *ch'i* follows it.[74] But in the reality, there is no priority between them.

In addition, there is another question concerning whether *li* produces *ch'i*. In the *Yü-lei*, Chu Hsi mentions that "because there is this principle, there is produced afterward this material force."[75] And elsewhere in the *Yü-lei*, Chu Hsi says that "although *ch'i* is produced by *li*, once *ch'i* is produced, *li* no longer controls it."[76] What Chu Hsi means by *li* produces *ch'i* is that *li* does not by itself create *ch'i*. In fact, *li* does not create anything. It is merely a static principle from which the myriad things emerge. But if we must trace them to their origin, *li* is prior to *ch'i*; and *ch'i* operates in accordance with *li*. In this respect, we can say that *li* produces *ch'i*. However, once *ch'i* is produced, *li* has no control of it. "As material force gathers, principle is also there. Material force can integrate and create, but principle has no intention and does not deliberate or create."[77] Further, Chu Hsi contends that heaven creates and transforms the myriad things. *Ch'i* thereby forms physical shape, and *li* is also endowed.[78] Therefore, both *li* and *ch'i* are created by heaven. In other words, *ch'i* is not produced by *li*, but by heaven.

Two-Wheel Patterns

In order to get a deeper understanding of Chu Hsi's concept of *li* and *ch'i,* an illustration of Chu Hsi's two-wheel patterns, such as *t'ai-chi* and *yin-yang* forces, *Tao* and concrete things, and substance and function, will provide an avenue for us.

T'ai-chi and *Yin-Yang* Force

Whenever Chu Hsi mentions *yin-yang* forces, he relates them to *t'ai-chi*. Chu Hsi identifies *t'ai-chi* with *li* and *yin-yang* with *ch'i*. *T'ai-chi* is nothing other than *li*.[79] And *yin-yang* is merely *ch'i*.[80] Like *li* and *ch'i*, *t'ai-chi* and *yin-yang* are not separated or mixed. "The Great Ultimate contains all principles of the Five Agents and *yin* and *yang*."[81] *T'ai-chi* antedates any physical things and standes outside *yin* and *yang*. It exists before all things of the universe and is beyond the realm of matter. However, on the other hand, *t'ai-chi* remains in all things, which are produced by *yin-yang* forces. In other words, *t'ai-chi* as *li* already exists within the state of the two forms, namely, *yin-yang*. Since the movement of the *yin-yang* forces produces the myriad things, whereas *t'ai-chi* is merely an absolute one, there is no intermingling of *t'ai-chi* with the *yin-yang* forces.[82] In Chou Tun-i's philosophy, *t'ai-chi* involves the activity and tranquillity of *yin* and *yang* because *t'ai-chi* is *ch'i*. On the contrary, Chu Hsi treats *t'ai-chi* as *li*; therefore, *t'ai-chi* cannot involve activity and tranquillity.[83] Instead, it is the principle of activity and tranquillity. Through the principle of activity and tranquillity, *yang* and *yin* are generated respectively.

Second, like *li* and *ch'i*, *t'ai-chi* is embedded in *yin-yang*. As Chu His contends, "*t'ai-chi* is embedded in *yin-yang*, it does not separate from *yin-yang*."[84] When activity generates *yang*, *t'ai-chi* then is embedded in *yang*. When tranquillity generates *yin*, *t'ai-chi* then is embedded in *yin*. In other words, when there is activity, there is the *t'ai-chi* of activity. When there is tranquillity, there is the *t'ai-chi* of tranquillity. For *t'ai-chi* is the principle of activity and tranquillity.[85] Finally, not only are *t'ai-chi* and *yin-yang* not separated from each other, but they are interdependent upon each other as well. Chu Hsi clarifies that *t'ai-chi* is not something above *yin-yang*. But rather what we call *t'ai-chi* is embedded in *yin-yang*; and what we called *yin-yang* is also embedded in *t'ai-chi*.[86] What Chu Hsi means is that the interdependence of *t'ai-chi* and *yin-yang* is viewed from the side of *yin-yang*. Viewed from the side of *t'ai-chi*, however, there will be no *yin-yang* because *t'ai-chi* is prior to all things in the universe. Therefore, ontologically speaking, *t'ai-chi* is the origin and the source of the myriad things; and it "has neither spatial restriction nor physical form or body. There is no spot where it may be placed."[87] Before physical form, *t'ai-chi* is merely an undifferentiated principle. It contains *yin-yang* and the Five Agents.[88] In physical form, *t'ai-chi* as embod*ying* *yin* and *yang*. Thus, Chu Hsi claims that "each and every person has in him the Great Ultimate and each and every thing has in it the Great Ultimate."[89] But this does not mean that *yin* and *yang* are not produced by *t'ai-chi*, although Chu Hsi does not clearly explain how *t'ai-chi* can produce *yin* and *yang*.[90] As Chu Hsi contends, "viewing from the side of things, *t'ai-chi* is embedded in *yin-yang*; but originally speaking, *t'ai-chi* produces *yin-yang*."[91]

Tao and Concrete Things

The relation of Tao and concrete things resembles the relation of *li* and *ch'i* and of *t'ai-chi* and *yin-yang*. In Chu Hsi's philosophy, *T'ai-chi* and *li* is *hsing-erh-shang* (incorporeal) and *yin-yang* and *ch'i* is *hsing-erh-hsia* (corporeal). Similarly, Tao is *hsing-erh-shang* (incorporeal) and concrete things are *hsing-erh-hsia* (corporeal). Originally, the concept of *hsing-erh-shang* and *hsing-erh-hsia* are derived from the *Book of Changes*. However, the interpretations of this concept are different. Chang Tsai elucidates *hsing-erh-shang* as formless and called it the Way, while *hsing-erh-hsia* is form and is called a concrete thing. Moreover, he indicates that *ch'i* originally comes from Great Vacuity (*T'ai-hsu*), and therefore it should be formlessness and belong to *hsing-erh-shang*. However, if the Way and *ch'i* have no form and the concrete thing has form, then they cannot exist in the same physical body. Therefore, Chu Hsi follows the thought of Ch'eng I and Ch'eng Hao and instead of using the form and formless as the description of *hsing-erh-shang* and *hsing-erh-hsia* respectively, he contends that *hsing-erh-shang* is "prior to physical form" and *hsing-erh-hsia* is "posterior to physical form." In this respect, Chu Hsi explains *hsing-erh-shang* and *hsing-erh-hsia* in terms of "prior to" and "posterior to."[92] He claims that "when you use *shang* and *hsia* to describe the difference clearly, you are only drawing a clear distinction, not separating them from each other. A concrete thing is the Way. The Way is also a concrete thing. They are distinct but not separate."[93] The major difference between Chu Hsi and Chang Tsai is that *ch'i* in Chang's thought belongs to the formless, which is *hsing-erh-shang*, while for Chu Hsi *ch'i* is posterior to physical form, which is *hsing-erh-hsia*.[94]

Like *t'ai-chi* and *yin-yang*, Tao and the concrete things are not separated. As Chu Hsi clearly argues, "What is called *hsing-erh-shang* is Tao and what is called *hsing-erh-hsia* is concrete things. Tao is the principle of the Way. Every event and thing must have the principle of the Way. A concrete thing has form. Every event and thing must have a form. If there is Tao, there must be a concrete thing or vice versa. Every thing must have this principle."[95] Tao cannot be separated from the concrete thing or vice versa. Otherwise, what will a concrete thing be like if it is separated from the Tao? For instance, "a chair is a concrete thing on which everybody can sit. This is the principle of a chair. Humans are concrete things. Language and action are the principle of humans."[96] In this respect, Tao as principle and concrete things are inseparable. They are interdependent upon each other. As Ch'en Ch'un, one of the brilliant students of Chu Hsi, comments, "From the point of view of what transcends physical form, what is hidden and cannot be seen is called the Way. From the point of view of what possesses physical form, what is manifested and can be seen is called a concrete thing. But in reality, the Way is not separated from concrete things; it is merely their concrete principle. Human affairs that have physical shape or form are called concrete things. The principle that underlies human affairs is the Way."[97] This inseparable relationship between Tao and concrete things is much more similar to the relationship between *t'ai-chi* and *yin-yang* and between *li* and *ch'i*. From this view, the difference between Tao and concrete things in terms of *hsing-erh-shang* and *hsing-erh-hsia* is clear.

Moreover, not only are Tao and concrete things not separated, but also Tao dwells in concrete things. Chu Hsi claims that what is called *hsing-erh-shang* is Tao and what is called *hsing-erh-hsia* is a concrete thing. Speaking of a concrete thing which is *hsing-erh-hsia*, there is Tao inside it."[98] From the view point of concrete things, Tao is embedded in them. Through concrete things, Tao can be comprehended. In reality, Tao is not separated from concrete things. Otherwise, it will be something empty and cannot be comprehended. In this regard, Chu Hsi treats Tao and a concrete thing as one entity after the *hun-lun* (undifferentiated) state, the production of things. They cannot be separated. Yet Tao originally belongs to the incorporeal, whereas concrete things are corporeal. They cannot be intermingled. Therefore, the relation of Tao and concrete things is as similar as that of *li* and *ch'i*.

Substance and Function

The concept of substance and function has a long tradition. The earliest Chinese philosopher to use this concept is Wang Pi (226-249 C.E.). In his commentary on the *Lao-Tzu*, he comments that "as non-being is its [Tao's] function, all things will be embraced. Therefore in regard to things, if they are understood as non-being all things will be in order, whereas if they are understood as being, it is impossible to avoid the fact that they are products (phenomena)."[99] Even in the early Chinese Buddhist tradition, this concept had also been used. In his *Seng Chao's Treatises* chapter three, Seng Chao (384-414) claims that speaking of function, there is distinction, whereas speaking of substance, there is no difference. In addition to that, the real founder of the Hua-Yen

School, namely Fa-tsang (643-712 C.E.) also used the concept of substance and function in his *Treatise on the Golden Lion.*[100]

In Ch'eng I's (1033-1170) thought, "substance and function come from the same source, there is no gap between the manifest and the subtle."[101] However, Chu Hsi extends and refines Ch'eng's thought: "Substance explains why a thing is so, whereas function explains how a thing is so."[102] As Chu Hsi illustrates, "Substance is the reason for being, whereas function is its utility. Take, for example, the hearing of the ear or the seeing of the eye. It is naturally so and is substance, whereas to direct the eye to see things or to turn one's ear to listen is function."[103] Wing-tsit Chan gives an elucidation of Chu Hsi's concept of substance and function in six points.[104] First, substance and function are different. Before we say that substance and function come from the same source, we have to differentiate these two. If they have no differentiation, there is no need to say that they come from the same source. Therefore, Chu Hsi gives many examples of the difference between substance and function. "In case of the Change, Change is substance, and *ch'ien* (strength) and *k'un* (obedience) are function. . . . In case of the Way, the Way is substance, while moral principles are function."[105] In case of our body, ears and eyes are substance, while hearing and seeing are function.[106] And in case of a concrete thing, a fan with a frame and shape is substance, whereas waving it is function.[107]

Second, substance and function are not separated. Take the example of the hearing of the ear or the seeing of the eye again. Of course, hearing and seeing come from the ear and the eye. Can we separate hearing from the ear or seeing from the eye? The answer is no. We can hardly imagine hearing without the ear or seeing without the eye. Thus, hearing and seeing cannot be separated from the ear and the eye. "Since substance and function are not separated, there is certainly no substance without function."[108] In addition to that, Chu Hsi depicts substance and function as a continuum. Substance is prior to function because function is merely the operation of substance. However, in reality, they are not two different entities. Thus, they are not separated from each other.[109]

Third, substance and function come from the same source. What Chu Hsi means by "the same source" is merely the principle[110] Like *t'ai-chi*, the principle of activity and tranquillity is embodied in it. Tranquillity is the substance of *t'ai-chi* and activity is the function of *t'ai-chi*. Although activity and tranquillity are two different entities, they come from the same source, or the principle. Chu Hsi uses an example of a fan. "When it is waved, that is function, and when it is laid down, that is substance. When it is laid down, there is only one principle, and when it is waved, there is also only one principle."[111] Thus, not only are substance and function not separated from each other, but they embrace or encompass each other as well.[112]

Fourth, everything has its own substance and function. Although substance and function are different, substance is in function and vice versa. Substance is still substance and function is still function. They cannot be intermingled. However, in Chu Hsi's thought, "everything has its own substance and its own function."[113] In other words, everything can be both substance and function. As Chu Hsi illustrates, "Speaking from the point of view of what is above physical shape, what is empty and tranquil is of course substance, while what is revealed in things and affairs is function. Speaking from the point of view of what has physical shape, however, things and affairs are substance and the principle that is revealed is function."[114] Here we can see that substance and function are relative. However, since they come from the same source originally and they are not separated from each other, each concrete thing has its nature as both substance and function.[115]

Following the fourth point that everything has its own substance and function, substance and function then have no fixed position. However, we should not treat the concept of substance and function as relativistic. For substance and function indeed have their positions. Chu Hsi contends that substance and function have fixed positions. Fundamentally, substance has its fixed position. Once it manifests itself, then function emerges. Just as the body is substance, actions are function. Heaven itself is substance, but Heaven as the origin of the myriad things is function. Earth is substance, but Earth as the production of the myriad things is function.[116] Originally speaking, substance and function have fixed positions because substance is prior to function and function is merely the operation of substance. However, since everything can be substance and function, substance and function have no fixed position relatively. Chu Hsi gives an example that "when one faces north, then here is south and there is north. When one moves to the north, then in the north there are its north and south. Substance and function are not fixed. The substance and function in this place appertain here, while the substance and function in that place appertain there. This principle knows no limit and is applicable in any direction, penetrating hundreds of items and thousands of details."[117] Although substance and function originally have fixed positions and cannot be intermingled, when they are utilized for differentiating things, they have no fixed positions.

Finally, there is the case of what is the same in substance but different in function. Using an example of rites and music, Chu Hsi avers that although rites and music are different in function, they have the same substance. Basically, reverence is what rites aim at, whereas harmony is what music aims at. Both rites and music have a different function, and yet they depend upon the heart-mind, which is their substance, to manifest their proper forms. In this regard, reverence and harmony have no difference. Once reverence is attained, harmony will emerge; and also once harmony is attained, reverence will emerge.[118] As Chan comments, "not only reverence and harmony but all virtues issue from the heart-mind, for the one foundation diversifies into many manifestations."[119] Also, this is what Chu His calls "the principle is one but its manifestations are many."

Having discussed the relation of *t'ai-chi* and *yin-yang* force, of Tao and concrete things, and of substance and function, we can also seen the same relation of *li* and *ch'i* in them. Basically, *t'ai-chi* and *Tao* can be identified with *li*, and *yin-yang* and concrete things can be related to *ch'i*. In addition to that, generally speaking, *li* is substance and *ch'i* is function in their relationships. Moreover, Chu Hsi's concept of *li* and *ch'i* cannot be understood in terms of formal logic. Ontologically speaking, *li* is prior to *ch'i*, and yet in reality there is no priority between *li* and *ch'i*. That is to say, there is no *li* without *ch'i*, or *ch'i* without *li*. They are not sequential. They coexist at the same time. However, even though *li* and *ch'i* are not separated, they are not intermingled with each other. They are originally two different entities. The interplay of *li* and *ch'i* then produces the order of our world. That is to says, throughout the universe there are many things, but they all share one *li* (principle), which is identified with the Great Ultimate. It is the root from which the myriad things emerge. *Ch'i*, on the other hand, refers to material objects, which exist after physical form. It is the instrument by which the myriad things are produced. "Therefore in the productions of man and things, they must be endowed with principle before they have their nature, and they must be endowed with material force before they have physical form."[120] Based upon this ontological structure of *li* and *ch'i* Chu Hsi develops his concept of human nature, which will be elucidated in the next chapter.

Notes

1. Wing-tsit Chan argues that the entire Neo-Confucianism movement is called *Li-hsüeh*. See "The Evolution of the Neo-Confucian Concept *Li* as Principle," in *Neo-Confucianism, Etc.: Essays by Wing-tsit Chan*, ed. Charles K. H. Chen (Hanover, NH: Oriental Society, 1969), 45-87. Also both John H Berthrong and Ch'en Lai argue that *li* is the crucial concept of Chu Hsi's philosophical system. See John H. Berthrong, *All Under Heaven: Transforming Paradigms in Confucian-Christian Dialogue* (Albany, NY: State University of New York Press, 1991), 88-89; and Ch'en Lai, 朱熹哲學研究 [Research on Chu Hsi's Philosophy] (Peking: Chung-Kuo she-hui k'o hsüeh, 1987).

2. See Wing-tsit Chan, *Chu Hsi: Life and Thought* (Hong Kong: The Chinese University of Hong Kong Press, 1987), 103-138.

3. Ch'eng Hao (1032-1085) and Ch'eng I (1033-1107) are brothers and two of the Five Master in the Northern Sung (960-1126). See Wing-tsit Chan, *A Source Book in Chinese Philosophy* (Princeton, NJ: Princeton University Press), 518.

4. Chan, *Chu Hsi: Life and Thought*, 49.

5. See Chan, *Chu Hsi: Life and Though,* 49, no. 49.

6. Chu Hsi, *ChuTsu yü-lei* [Classified Conversations of Chu Hsi], vol. 1, ch.1, sec. 4 ,1270, ed. Li Ching-te (Peking: Chung- hua shu-chü, 1994) 2. (Hereafter cited as *Yü-lei*). Translated by Wing-tsit Chan in Wing-tsit Chan, *Chu Hsi: New Studies* (Honolulu: University of Hawaii Press), 147.

7. Chan, "The Evolution of the Neo-Confucian Concept *Li* as Principle," 77.

8. Chung-ying Cheng, "Methodology and Theory of Understanding," in *Chu Hsi and Neo-Confucianism*, ed. Wing-tsit Chan (Honolulu: University of Hawaii Press), 170.

9. Chung-ying Cheng, "Methodology and Theory of Understanding," 170.

10. Chan, *Chu Hsi: Life and Thought*, 115.

11. *Yü-lei*, vol. 6, ch. 94, 2371. Translated by Chung-ying Cheng in "Methodology and Theory of Understanding,"171-2.

12. *Yü-lei*, vol. 6, ch. 94, 2371.

13. Chung-ying Cheng, "Methodology and Theory of Understanding," 172.

14. See Chan, *Chu Hsi: Life and Thought,* 115-119. And also as Chan points out, Professor Yanamoi attests that *t'ai-chi* is not woven into Chu Hsi's philosophy. For most of the discussions in the *Yü-lei* and the *wen-chi* (Collection of Literary Works) on *t'ai-chi* are references to the *Book of Changes* (one of the Five Classics); and *t'ai-chi* is not used in the *Ssu-shu chi-chu* (Collected commentaries on the Four Books) and the *Ssu-shu huo-wen* (Questions and Answers on the Four Books). However, Chan argues that *t'ai-chi* is a concept in cosmology and ontology. It is the ground of the concept of *li* (principle). See Chan, *Chu Hsi: New Studies,* 146-148.

15. Teng Aimin, "Chu Hsi's Theory of the Great Ultimate," in *Chu Hsi and Neo-Confucianism*, ed. Wing-tsit Chan (Honolulu: University of Hawaii Press), 94.

16. Teng Aimin, "Chu Hsi's Theory of the Great Ultimate," 94.

17. *Yü-lei*, ch. 94, sec. 19, 2369. Translated by Wing-tsit Chan in *Chu Hsi: Life and Though,* 116.

18. Ch'en Ch'un, *Neo-Confucian Terms Explained*, trans. Wing-tsit Chan (New York: Columbia University Press, 1986), 116-7.

19. *Wen-chi*, 49:10a-b. Translated by Wing-tsit Chan in *Chu Hsi: New Studies,* 145.

20. Allen Wittenborn, "The Philosophy of Chu Hsi," in *Further Reflections on Things at Hand: A Reader, Chu Hsi*, trans. Allen Wittenborn (Lanham: University Press of America, Inc., 1991), 16.

21. Ch'en Ch'un, 117.

22. Teng Aimin, "Chu Hsi's Theory of the Great Ultimate," 95.

23. Wing-tsit Chan, *A Source Book in Chinese Philosophy*, 638.

24. Chan, *Chu Hsi: Life and Though,* 117.

25. Wing-tsit Chan, *A Source Book in Chinese Philosophy*, 638-9.

26. Chiu Hansheng avers that Chu Hsi's idea of *li-i fen-shu* is an important component of his philosophy of nature. This concept can elucidates the relation of the entity and its various ramifications, of the universe and all creation, and the one principle and the principle found in every being. See Chiu Hansheng, "*Zhu Xi's* Doctrine of Principle," in *Chu Hsi and Neo-Confucianism*, ed. Wing-tsit Chan (Honolulu: University of Hawaii Press), 120-122; and also Chung-ying Cheng, "Methodology and Theory of Understanding," 172.

27. Chung-ying Cheng, "Methodology and Theory of Understanding," 173.

28. John H. Berthrong, *All Under Heaven*, 98.

29. Berthrong, *All Under Heaven*, 98

30. Chan, *A Source Book in Chinese Philosophy*, 463.

31. *Yü-lei*, ch.94, sec.20, 2370. Translated by the author. Otherwise, it will indicate.

32. *Yü-lei*, ch.94, sec.37, 2373.

33. Teng Aimin, "Chu Hsi's Theory of the Great Ultimate," 96.

34. Ibid.

35. Berthrong, *All Under Heaven*, 99.

36. *Yü-lei*, ch. 94, sec.21, 2371. Translated by John H. Berthrong in *All Under Heaven*, 99.

37. Ch'en Ch'un, *Neo-Confucian Terms Explained*, 112.

38. Chu Hsi, *Further Reflections on Things at Hand*, trans. Allen Wittenborn (Lanham: University Press of America, 1991), 67.

39. Ibid., 67.

40. Ibid..

41. Ch'en Ch'un, *Neo-Confucian Terms Explained*, 112.

42. John H. Berthrong uses the notion of form, dynamics and unification to elucidate Chu Hsi's philosophical system. He treats Chu's concept of *li* as the formal element. See Berthrong, *All Under Heaven*, 85-87.

43. "Master Chu said: Tao is a comprehensive name. Principle is a specific item. In the mind it is called nature; in daily affairs it is called principle." Chu Hsi, *Further Reflections on Things at Hand*, ch.1, sec.59, 68.

44. See Chan, *Chu Hsi: Life and Though,* 110-113.

45. Stanislaus Lokuang, "Chu Hsi's Theory of Metaphysical Structure," in *Chu Hsi and Neo-Confucianism*, ed. Wing-tsit Chan (Honolulu: University of Hawaii Press), 66.

46. Ibid.

47. Chan, *A Source Book in Chinese Philosophy*, 636. Here Chan translates *ch'i* as material force instead of vital energy. Goto Toshimizu argues that although Chu Hsi's concept of *ch'i* is used in a materialistic sense, *ch'i* refers basically to "give birth to" the myriad creatures in traditional Confucianism and Taoism. Thus, it is vital rather then material. Also Julia Ching argues that *ch'i* should be translated as "vital force" instead of "material force." See Chung Tsai-chun, *The Development of the Concepts of Heaven and of Man in the Philosophy of Chu Hsi* (Taiwan, Republic of China: Institute of Chinese Literature and Philosophy, Academia Sinica, 1993), 174-177. John H. Berthrong contends that it is impossible to give an elegant, suitable and reliable English translation to *ch'i*. It is vital, energetic, and dynamic. See Berthrong, *All Under Heaven*, 217, n.7.

48. Chan, *Chu Hsi: Life and Though,* 111-2.

49. Ibid., 112.

50. Chan, *A Source Book in Chinese Philosophy*, 640. Chan comments that although some scholars try to make much of the similarities between Chu's *t'ai-chi* and Plato's the idea of the Good and Aristotle's idea of God, the western polarities still do not apply in Chinese philosophy. However, I do not think it cannot be done. The Western polarities do not necessary entail duality. One counter example is the thought of Paul Tillich. In addition, Chinese philosophical thought has used polarities as well. Chu Hsi is a good example.

51. Chan, *A Source Book in Chinese Philosophy*, 637.

52. See Lokuang, "Chu Hsi's Theory of Metaphysical Structure," 66.

53. Chan, *A Source Book in Chinese Philosophy*, 637.

54. Ibid.; also *Yü-lei*, ch.4, sec. 9, 57.

55. *Yü-lei*, ch.17, sec 23, 375.

56. Chan, *A Source Book in Chinese Philosophy*, 622; also *Yü-lei*, ch,4, sec. 17, 59.

57. Chan, *A Source Book in Chinese Philosophy*, 624.

58. *Yü-lei*, ch.1, sec. 6, 2. Translated by Wing-tsit Chan in Chan, *A Source Book in Chinese Philosophy*, 634.

59. Chan, *A Source Book in Chinese Philosophy*, 634.

60. See Wing-tsit Chan, *Chu Hsi: New Studies,* 140. And also see Chang Li-wen, 朱熹思想研究 [A Study of Chu Hsi's Thought] (Peking: Chug-kuo she-hui k'o-hsüeh ch'u-pan-she, 1981), 230.

61. *Yü-lei*, ch.1, sec, 11, 3. Translated by Wing-tsit Chan in *Chu Hsi: New Studies,* 140.

62. *Yü-lei*, ch.94, sec.37, 2374.

63. *Yü-lei*, ch.1, sec, 12, 3. Translated by Wing-tsit Chan in *A Source Book in Chinese Philosophy*, 635.

64. Chan, *A Source Book in Chinese Philosophy*, 637

65. Chan, *Chu Hsi: Life and Though,* 112.

66. See Chan, *Chu Hsi: Life and Though,* 110-113.

67. *Yü-lei*, ch.1, sec.11, 3. Translated by Wing-tsit Chan in *A Source Book in Chinese Philosophy*, 634.

68. See *Yü-lei*, ch.1, sec. 13, 3. Also Chan, *Chu Hsi: New Studies,* 140.

69. *Yü-lei*, ch.1, sec. 14, 4. Translated by Chiu Hansheng in "Zhu Xi's Doctrine of Principle," in *Chu Hsi and Neo-Confucianism*, ed. Wing-tsit Chan (Honolulu: University of Hawaii Press), 117.

70. Chan, *A Source Book in Chinese Philosophy*, 637.

71. See Chan, *Chu Hsi: Life and Though,* 110-113. Also Chang Li-wen, 朱熹思想研究 [A Study of Chu Hsi's Thought], 231.

72. See Chan, *A Source Book in Chinese Philosophy*, 636.

73. Chan, *A Source Book in Chinese Philosophy*, 635.

74. See Liu Shu-hsien, 朱熹哲學思想的發展與完成 [Development and Completion of Chu Hsi's Philosophical Thought] (Taipei: Hsüeh-sheng shu-chü, 1984), 276-277.

75. *Yü-lei*, ch.1, sec.5, 2. Translated by Wing-tsit Chan in *Chu Hsi: New Studies,* 139.

76. *Yü-lei*, ch.4, sec. 65, 71. Translated by Wing-tsit Chan in *Chu Hsi: New Studies,* 138.

77. *Yü-lei*, ch. 1, sec.13, 3. Translated by Wing-tsit Chan in *Chu Hsi: New Studies,* 140.

78. See Wing-tsit Chan, *Chu Hsi: New Studies,* 140

79. *Yü-lei*, ch. 1, sec.4, 2.

80. *Yü-lei*, ch. 65, sec. 1, 1602.

81. Chan, *A Source Book in Chinese Philosophy*, 641.

82. See Chang Liwen, "Chu Hsi's System of Thought of I," in *Chu Hsi and Neo-Confucianism*, ed. Wing-tsit Chan (Honolulu: University of Hawaii Press), 298-9.

83. See Chan, *A Source Book in Chinese Philosophy*, 636.

84. *Yü-lei* ch. 5, sec.43, 87.

85. See Chang Li-wen, 朱熹思想研究 [A Study of Chu Hsi's Thought], 237.

86. *Yü-lei*, ch. 95, sec. 80, 2437.

87. Chan, *A Source Book in Chinese Philosophy*, 639.

88. *Yü-lei*, ch. 75, sec. 84, 1929. As Wing-tsit Chan claims, Stanislaus Lokuang had an original observation that Ch'en Ch'un added the term *hun-lun* (undifferentiated) to explain *t'ai-chi* and this is different from Chu Hsi's thought. However, the term *hun-lun* is indeed found in *Yü-lei*. Therefore, I do think Ch'en Ch'un invented this term for explaining Chu Hsi's idea of *t'ai-chi*. It was already in Chu Hsi's thought. See Wing-tsit Chan, *Chu Hsi: New Studies,* 144.

89. Chan, *A Source Book in Chinese Philosophy*, 640.

90. See Chan, *A Source Book in Chinese Philosophy*, 639.

91. *Yü-lei*, ch. 75, sec.79, 1929.

92. See Lokuang, "Chu Hsi's Theory of Metaphysical Structure," 58-9.

93. *Yü-lei*, ch. 75, sec.101, 1935.

94. See Lokuang, "Chu Hsi's Theory of Metaphysical Structure," 59.

95. *Yü-lei*, ch. 75, sec.102, 1935.

96. *Yü-lei*, ch. 75, sec. 103, 1935.

97. Ch'en Ch'un, *Neo-Confucian Terms Explained*, 107.

98. *Yü-lei*, ch. 77, sec. 72, 1496.

99. Chan, *A Source Book in Chinese Philosophy*, 322.

100. See Wing-tsit Chan, 宋明理學之概念與歷史 [The Concept and History of the School of Principle in Sung and Ming] (Taiwan, Republic of China: Institute of Chinese Literature and Philosophy, Academia Sinica, 1996), 175-178.

101. Chan, *Chu Hsi: New Studies,* 222.

102. Chan, *Chu Hsi: New Studies,* 222.

103. *Yü-lei*, ch.6, sec.22, 101. Translated by Chan in *Chu Hsi: New Studies,* 222.

104. See Chan, *Chu Hsi: New Studies,* 222-231.

105. Chan, *Chu Hsi: New Studies,* 223.

106. *Yü-lei*, ch.6, sec.22, 101.

107. See *Yü-lei*, ch.6, sec.23, 102.

108. Chan, *Chu Hsi: New Studies,* 225.

109. Ibid., 226.

110. Ibid., 227.

111. *Yü-lei*, ch.94, sec.29, 2372. Translated by Wing-tsit Chan in *Chu Hsi: New Studies,* 227.

112. Chan, *Chu Hsi: New Studies,* 227.

113. Ibid., 228.

114. *Wen-chi*, 48:16b. Tanslated by Wing-tsit Chan in *Chu Hsi: New Studies,* 228.

115. See Chan, *Chu Hsi: New Studies,* 228.

116. *Yü-lei i*, ch. 6, sec. 21, 101.

117. Chan, *Chu Hsi: New Studies,* 230.

118. Ibid.

119. Ibid.

120. Chan, *A Source Book in Chinese Philosophy*, 636.

CHAPTER SEVEN
Chu Hsi's Concept of Human Nature

In classical Confucianism, one of the controversial issues was the question of the goodness or evilness of human nature. This had been one of the major differences between Mencius (371-289 BCE?) and Hsün Tzu (298-238 BCE). Generally speaking, the original nature of human beings, for Mencius, is good whereas the original nature of human beings, for Hsün Tzu, is evil.[1] However, the Han Confucian, Yang Hsing (53 BCE- A.D. 18) asserted that human nature is a mixture of good and evil. This issue has been continuously discussed for centuries. In the T'ang dynasty (618-907), Han Yü (768-824) argued that there are three grades of human nature, namely, good, intermediate, and bad. Li Ao (fl. 798), a disciple of Han Yü, agreed with Mencius' idea of the goodness of human nature whereas Tu Mu (b. 803) agreed with Hsün Tzu's idea of the evilness of human nature.[2]

In the Northern Sung (960-1126), Chou Tun-i claimed that human nature "may be good or it may be evil."[3] Like Mencius, Chang Tsai asserts that "nature in man is always good;"[4] and Ch'eng Hao argues that human basic nature is good because it issues from the Way.[5] Ch'eng I advocated the thesis that nature is principle. This is called the principle of nature. The principle of Heaven and Earth is the foundation of the myriad things. Before it is aroused, it is good.[6] This is a new conceptualization of the Mencian theory of human nature; and Chu Hsi follows and enhances this new concept in his theory of human nature.[7]

Nature

Chu Hsi extends his concept of *li* and *ch'i* into his crucial theory of human nature. For Chu Hsi, there are three elements in human beings, namely, nature, feelings, and mind-heart. These three elements are blended together. Following the philosophy of Ch'eng I, Chu Hsi identifies nature with *li*. As Ch'en Ch'un elucidates, "Nature is principle. Why is it called nature and not principle? The reason is that principle is a general term referring to the principles common to all things in the world, while nature is principle in oneself. It is called nature because principle is received from Heaven and is possessed by the self."[8] Here nature is *li*, which is possessed by us. That is to say, *li* dwells inside human nature. It is the essence of the human beings. Therefore, Chu Hsi claims that nature is principle only.[9]

Logically speaking, if nature is *li* and *li* is identified with *t'ai-chi* and Tao, then nature is also *t'ai-chi* and Tao. In the *Yü-lei*, someone asked Chu Hsi about the identity of *t'ai-chi* and *li* and Chu Hsi answered that they are identical due to *li*.[10] Chu Hsi argued that *t'ai-chi* is "simply the principle of the highest good. Each and every person has in him the Great Ultimate and each and every thing has in it the Great Ultimate."[11] Similarly, nature is also Tao. "The Way is identical with the nature of man and things and the nature is identical with the Way."[12] "Tao is nature and nature is Tao. They are only one thing."[13] Due to the logical structure of Chu Hsi's system, *li*, *t'ai-chi*, and Tao are identical and share the same characteristics, such that nature is *li*, and thus is identical with *t'ai-chi* and Tao.

In addition, as *li* resides in different places, nature then refers not to human beings only. Actually, for Chu Hsi, nature means not only human nature, but also the nature of things. "The nature consists of innumerable principles created by Heaven."[14] If it dwells in humans, it is human nature. If it dwells in things, it is the nature of things. Since Chu Hsi argues that every person and thing has in it the Great Ultimate, every person and thing then must have in it principle, and this also implies that every person and thing has nature. Chu Hsi argues that "the nature of man and the nature of things are in some respects the same and in other respects different."[15] Similarly, both the nature of human beings and the nature of things have the same origin, namely, *t'ai-chi*. However, in the process of creation, "the two material forces and the Five Agents, in their fusion and intermingling, and in their interaction and mutual influence, produce innumerable changes and inequalities. This is where they are different."[16] In this regard, both natures are the same due to having the same *li*, but, on the other hand, they are different due to the fact that they have different *ch'i*.

Furthermore, Chu Hsi explains that due to the fact that they have the same source, humans and things cannot be distinguished as higher and lower creatures. But due to *ch'i*, which humans receive as perfection and which things receive as partial and obstructed, the nature of human beings is higher than the nature of things.[17] *Li* in animals is only manifested partially and in human beings is manifested completely. That is to say, the difference between the nature of human beings and the nature of things is not in their consciousness and movement because they are the same in this respect. Rather, their difference lies in the fact that humans are endowed with humanity, righteousness, propriety, and wisdom. What makes the nature of human beings a higher or more perfect nature are these Four Virtues.[18] This is the major difference between humans and things. Using the analogy of sunlight, Chu Hsi argues that the nature of human beings receives more light than other natural things do.[19] Compared with animals, human beings have more pure *ch'i*, and yet they still have differences in the degree of purity.

In Chu Hsi's philosophy, nature is *li*. Since *li* and *ch'i* are not separated, nature, then, cannot be separate from *ch'i*. In this regard, Chu Hsi divides nature into *t'ien-ti chih hsing* (the nature of Heaven and Earth or the original nature) and *ch'i-chih chih hsing* (vital force and matter of nature or physical nature)[20] In Chang Tsai's thought, "with the existence of physical form, there exists physical nature (*ch'i-chih chih hsing*). If one skillfully returns to the original nature endowed by Heaven and Earth (*t'ien-ti chih hsing*), then it will be preserved. Therefore in physical nature there is that which the superior man denies to be his original nature."[21] What Chang Tsai means by *t'ien-ti chih hsing* is the original nature. This original nature exists even before humans and things have their physical form. Thus, their original nature is the same. After they have their physical forms, humans and things have different physical natures. The Ch'eng brothers followed Chang's argument that the original nature is basically *li*, whereas the physical nature is *ch'i*. In Ch'eng Hao's philosophy, "what is inborn is called nature. Nature is the same as material force and material force is the same as nature. They are both inborn."[22] In Ch'eng I's thought, human nature is the same as *li*. From sage-emperors Yao and Shun to the common people in the street, they have the same *li*. Capacity is an endowment from *ch'i*. *Ch'i* may be clear or turbid. Humans endowed with clear *ch'i* are wise, while those endowed with turbid *ch'i* are stupid.[23]

Following the philosophy of Chang Tsai and the Ch'engs brothers, Chu Hsi claims that the nature of Heaven and Earth is merely *li*.[24] It does not include *ch'i*. However, "when we speak of the physical nature, we refer to principle and material force combined. Before material force existed, basic nature was already in existence."[25] Since the nature of Heaven and Earth is *li*, it is originally good. It does not have any defect. As Chu Hsi claims, "nature is principle. And *li* does not have any evil. Therefore, what Mencius means by nature is the original nature of humans."[26] If that is the case, is there any obscurity or obstruction in the nature of Heaven and Earth? Chu Hsi answers "no." If there is any obscurity or obstruction, it is due to the impurity of the physical nature.[27] Moreover, although the nature of Heaven and Earth is *li*, without *ch'i*, it would not have anything in which to inhere. In other words, the nature of Heaven and Earth is not detachable from physical nature.

In formulating his concept of physical nature, Chu Hsi argued that physical nature has *li* and *ch'i* combined.[28] In physical nature, *li* and *ch'i* are closely related, but not identical. As Chu Hsi illustrates, "Nature is like water. If it flows in a clean channel, it is clear; if it flows in a dirty channel, it becomes turbid. When physical nature that is clear and balanced is received, it will be preserved in its completeness. This is true of man. When physical nature that is turbid and unbalanced is received, it will be obscured. This is true of animals."[29] Originally, nature is like pure water. But when it flows in a channel, its purity or turbidity is thoroughly dependent upon the channel. Similarly, there is only one principle in Heaven and Earth. Nature is *li*. Due to the endowment of *ch'i*, human nature is differentiated as good or bad.[30] Continuously, "the nature of all men is good, and yet there are those who are good from their birth and those who are evil from their birth. This is because of the difference in material force with which they are endowed."[31] That is to say, the goodness or badness of the physical nature is based upon the endowment of *ch'i*. The completeness or partiality of the endowment of *ch'i* determines the uprightness or baseness of the type of creature. Whereas the clarity or turbidity of the endowment of *ch'i* determines humans to be wise or foolish.

Although the nature of Heaven and Earth and physical nature are different, they are interdependent. Without physical nature, the nature of Heaven and Earth has no place to inhere. "The nature of Heaven and Earth runs through the physical nature;"[32] whereas physical nature emerges from the nature of Heaven and Earth.[33] Chu Hsi contends that if there is physical nature without the nature of Heaven and Earth, there will be no human beings, while if there is the nature of Heaven and Earth without physical nature, there will be also no human beings.[34] In this respect, there cannot be one without the other. On the other hand, although they are not separated, they are not intermingled. Logically speaking, one exists prior to the other. Heaven and Earth are not *ch'i* and matter or vice versa. They have their own unique characteristics.

Heart-Mind

The history of heart-mind in the Confucian tradition is very complex. Generally speaking, there were the distinctions between *li-hsüeh* (the School of Principle) and *hsin-hsüeh* (the School of Heart-Mind) in Sung-Ming Neo-Confucian thought. However, this kind of division of Sung-Ming Neo-Confucianism is hardly adequate. Chu Hsi, who is a leader of *li-hsüeh*, was more concerned about the concept of the mind-heart than anyone else.[35] In Chu Hsi's philosophy, heart-mind is a pivotal element of human beings and performs many functions. Following his concept of human nature, Chu Hsi also divides the mind-heart into *Tao hsin* (Tao heart-mind) and *jen hsin* (human heart-mind).[36] Both of them inhere in the heart-mind.[37]

In relation to *ch'i*, the heart-mind is the most refined and subtle kind of *ch'i*.[38] As the actualizing agent of all things, *ch'i* also imparts a concrete specificity to heart-mind, so that it has a creative or generative function. Therefore, the heart-mind is the source of bodily movements, and of the emotions and feelings. In this respect, the heart-mind is the human heart-mind, and contrasts the Tao heart-mind, which is really nothing other than humanity (*jen*).[39] In relation to *li*, the heart-mind embraces all *li*.[40] As Chu Hsi claims, "The heart-mind embraces all principles and all principles are complete in this single entity, the heart-mind. If one is not able to preserve the heart-mind, he will be unable to investigate principle to the utmost. If he is unable to investigate principle to the utmost, he will be unable to exert his heart-mind to the utmost."[41] Here Shu-Hsien Liu gives an elucidation of the concept. What Chu Hsi means is that the heart-mind is not a creative ontological *li* reality, although Chu Hsi has claimed that the heart-mind and *li* are one.[42] However, the heart-mind and *li* do have a very close relationship because "without the heart-mind, principle would have nothing in which to inhere."[43] In addition, the heart-mind is a place in which the principle of consciousness and *ch'i* are united together. "As consciousness is always consciousness of something, the way to preserve the heart-mind is not just to contemplate on the heart-mind alone, but rather to investigate principle."[44]

In relation to nature, the heart-mind is a distinct entity but vacuous; whereas nature is a vacuity but consists of concrete *li*. Chu Hsi argues that "nature consists of principles embraced in the heart-mind, and the heart-mind is where these principles are united."[45] Also, "nature is principle. The heart-mind is its embracement and reservoir, and issues it forth into operation."[46] In other words, the heart-mind stores, holds, and manifests principle. The heart-mind is intelligent and nature is substantial. What is called intelligent is that *hsin* is perceptive and conscious.[47] Moreover, Chu Hsi identifies the nature with *t'ai-chi*, while the heart-mind is identified with yin and yang. *T'ai-chi* exists only in the *yin* and *yang*. They are not separated and yet are not intermingled. *T'ai-chi* is still *t'ai-chi* and *yin* and *yang* are still *yin* and *yang*. It is the same in the relation of nature and heart-mind. They are one and yet two, two and yet one.[48]

Furthermore, the essence of the heart-mind is quietude and tranquillity. As Chu Hsi notes, the state before feelings of pleasure, anger, sorrow, and joy is one of equilibrium, which is the nature of every person; and the heart-mind in the state of absolute quiet is the heart-mind of every person.[49] What Chu Hsi means by the heart-mind in the state of absolute quiet is the substance of the heart-mind. For Chu Hsi, the heart-mind is one. But it has substance and function. As Ch'en Ch'un illustrates, "Ch'eng I said, 'The mind is one. Sometimes it is spoken of in terms of its substance. (This is the state of absolute quiet.) Sometimes it is spoken of in terms of its function. (This is that which, when acted on, immediately penetrates all things.)'"[50] Clearly, the substance of the heart-mind for Chu Hsi is the heart-mind in the state of absolute quiet;

and the function of the heart-mind is that which, when acted on, immediately penetrates all things.

In addition, Chu Hsi claims that "the heart-mind means the master."[51] There are two meanings here. First, the heart-mind is the master of the body. As Chu Hsi argues, "nature is the principle of the heart-mind. The heart-mind is the master of the body."[52] Moreover, Ch'en Ch'un elucidates that "the heart-mind is the master of the body. Man's four limbs move, his hands hold things, and his feet step on the ground. He thinks of food when hunger and of drinks when thirsty, of hemp in the summer and fur in the winter. In all cases the heart-mind is the master."[53] Another meaning is that the heart-mind of human beings is the master of the myriad things.[54] Since the heart-mind embraces all of principle, if one enlarges one's heart-mind, one can enter into all things in the world. "It means that the operation of the principle of the heart-mind penetrates all as blood circulates and reaches the entire body."[55] Ch'en Ch'un elaborates on the point that "the capacity of the heart-mind is extremely large. None of the ten thousand principles is not embraced, and none of the ten thousand events not commanded. The ancients often said that in one's learning one wants to be extensive."[56]

In sum, the substance of the heart-mind is the state of absolute quiet. This is the state before the heart-mind is aroused. Once it is active, it can be the master of the myriad things and immediately penetrates all things. This is the state of the function of the heart-mind. Therefore, there are two characteristics of the heart-mind in terms of its active and tranquil aspects or modes. Ontologically speaking, the heart-mind, nature, and *li* share the same characteristic, namely being in the state of tranquillity, and yet the myriad things emerge from them.

To reiterate his concept of Tao heart-mind and the human heart-mind, Chu Hsi, in his Preface to the commentary on the *Doctrine of the Mean*, claims that "In its perspicuity, intelligence, perception, and consciousness, the heart-mind is one. However, it is supposed that there is a difference between "human heart-mind" and "Tao heart-mind". This is because the heart-mind may either be born from the particularity of the physical form and material force, or originated from the perfection of endowed nature and destiny. Because of this difference [in the basis] of perception and consciousness, the same heart-mind may exist in a state of precariousness and instability or in a state of subtlety and obscurity."[57] Also, Chu Hsi refers to a passage in the *Book of Odes*[58] which states that "the human heart-mind is precarious and the Tao heart-mind is subtle. . . . This is the teaching of Yao and Shun."[59] Chu Hsi refers to Ch'eng I's sayings that human heart-mind is human desire, while Tao-heart-mind is the principle of Heaven.[60] What Chu His means by Tao heart-mind is the Principle of Heaven or the perfection of endowed nature and destiny. As Chu Hsi claims, "It is the Principle of Heaven, and is subtle."[61] Or, in other words, it embraces all principles in itself.[62] In addition, Chu Hsi avers that Tao heart-mind emerges from principle and righteousness and is the heart-mind of humanity, righteousness, propriety, and wisdom.[63] That is to say, the heart-mind, which is conscious of principle and righteousness, is Tao heart-mind.[64] In this respect, Tao heart-mind can be called the all-embracing depth of the Principle of Heaven. Viewed from the perspective of humanity, righteousness, propriety, and wisdom, the sense of commiseration, the sense of shame, the sense of deference and compliance, and the sense of right and wrong are aroused by Tao heart-mind.

As the perfection of endowed nature and destiny and the Principle of Heaven, Tao heart-mind is perfectly good. Thus, Chu Hsi claims that what sages have is the Tao heart-mind.[65] What he means here is that sages are thoroughly dependent upon Tao heart-mind in investigating principle to the utmost and in responding to things by following it. Sages still have human heart-mind, but they follow Tao heart-mind, which is the originally good heart-mind, in their moral cultivation.

In regard to the human heart-mind, Chu Hsi claims that it is precarious because it is born from the particularity of physical form and *ch'i*.[66] What is the particularity of physical form and *ch'i*? Chu Hsi illustrates by citing our nature that when humans are hungry, they eat; when humans feel cold, they clothe themselves. These are the particularities of physical form and *ch'i*.[67] Therefore, the human heart-mind "mixes with physical endowment and human desire."[68] As Chu Hsi indicates, "What is called human heart-mind is human desire; it is precarious and also dangerous."[69] For Chu Hsi, human desire is not necessary bad because it is natural that you need food when you hunger and you need clothes themselves when you feel cold. Even sages have these kinds of desire. Therefore, Chu Hsi says, "sages are not without human heart-mind because they have desire to eat when they are hunger and to clothe when they feel cold. Also, wicked people are not without Tao heart-mind. The sense of commiseration is a good example."[70] The major difference between sages and wicked people then is that sages behave in accordance with their Tao heart-mind instead of their human heart-mind because the Tao heart-mind is the Principle of Heaven. In this regard, the heart-mind, which is conscious of human sensual experience, is the human heart-mind.

Furthermore, Chu Hsi argues that the human heart-mind is not thoroughly evil. In other words, human desire itself is not totally evil. As he claims, "Human desire is not thoroughly bad. But it is precarious."[71] Interpreting the phrase "the human heart-mind is precarious" from the *Book of Odes*, Chu Hsi argues that the "human heart-mind is not thoroughly bad. If it is thoroughly bad, the word 'precariousness' should not be used."[72] Further, he claims that the "human heart-mind is consciousness. It is conscious of human sensual experience. It is not bad but it is precarious. If it is bad, there is no reason the word 'precariousness' is used."[73] Therefore, Chu Hsi avers that the "human heart-mind is merely the heart-mind of the physical form and *ch'i*. It can be good, or it can be bad too."[74] This interpretation of the human heart-mind is an innovative twist on the Confucian interpretation of human desires. Although the human heart-mind is born from the particularity of physical form and *ch'i* and is precarious, this does not mean that it is thoroughly evil. Rather, it consists of good as well as evil. The human heart-mind as the heart-mind of physical form and *ch'i* is merely conscious of human sensual experience. There is neither good nor bad in human sensual experience.

Just as the two natures, Tao heart-mind and human heart-mind are not separated, but also not intermingled. Obviously, Tao heart-mind and human heart-mind are different. Originally, Tao heart-mind is born from the perfection of endowed nature and destiny, whereas human heart-mind is born from the particularity of physical form and *ch'i*. In terms of consciousness, Tao heart-mind is conscious of the principle and righteousness, while human heart-mind is conscious of human sensual experience. "Tao heart-mind conforms to the Principle of Heaven, while human heart-mind is that which mixes with physical endowment and human desires."[75] Finally, Tao heart-mind is originally good, but human heart-mind consists of good and bad and is precarious.[76]

Although these two heart-minds are different, it does not mean that humans have two heart-minds. As Chu Hsi clearly affirms, "If Tao heart-mind is the Principle of Heaven and human heart-mind is human desire, then there will be two heart-minds in humans. In fact, humans have only one heart-mind. But it has two kinds of perception. What the heart-mind is conscious of the Principle of Heaven is called Tao heart-mind; and what the heart-mind is conscious of the human sensual experience is called human heart-mind."[77] Here Chu Hsi avers that there is only one, not two, heart-mind. But it has two kinds of perception. It is like one coin with two sides. Although there are two sides, it is still one coin. "You drink when you are thirsty and you eat when you are hungry. This is human heart-mind. In accordance with what circumstances and ways you will drink and eat and in accordance with what circumstances and ways you do not eat and drink. This is Tao heart-mind."[78] Thus, Tao heart-mind and human heart-mind are the same heart-mind, which "may exist in a state of precariousness and instability or in a state of subtlety and obscurity."[79]

Nevertheless, Tao heart-mind and human heart-mind are indeed in conflict with each other, and yet they are interdependent upon each other. Tao heart-mind, as principle and righteousness, needs human heart-mind, which is the physical form and *ch'i*, in which to inhere. Chu Hsi gave an analogy that human heart-mind is like a ship and Tao heart-mind is like a helm. Without the helm, the ship will go anywhere with no direction. Without the ship, the helm is useless.[80] In this respect, Tao heart-mind and human heart-mind coexist. One cannot exist without the other.

Furthermore, in his Preface to the commentary on the *Doctrine of the Mean*, Chu Hsi argues that "Everybody has physical form, so that even the most intelligent cannot but have human heart-mind. Everybody has nature as well, so that even the most foolish cannot but have Tao heart-mind. If these two become confused and cannot be controlled, the precarious one, namely, human heart-mind, will become more precarious and the subtle one, namely, Tao heart-mind, subtler. Finally the selfishness of human desires will no longer be conquerable by the justice of Heavenly Principle."[81] Therefore, Chu Hsi urges us to discern carefully the difference between these two and to keep steadily to the justice of Tao heart-mind. "Strive endlessly until Tao heart-mind becomes the enduring master of the body, with human heart-mind its abiding servant."[82] In so doing, we can "abide by what is right and discern what is wrong, as well as to discard the wrong and restore the right."[83] In this regard, Tao heart-mind becomes the master and human heart-mind acts in accord with it. As Chu Hsi claims, "Tao heart-mind is the heart-mind of principle and righteousness. It can be the master of human heart-mind. And human heart-mind can act in accord with it."[84] On the one hand, Tao heart-mind is the master of human heart-mind; on the other hand, Tao heart-mind needs human heart-mind to adhere to. Thus, they cannot be separated from each other. Instead, they are interdependent upon each other. Actually, they are two sides of the same heart-mind.

Feelings

By his early forties, Chu Hsi completed his theory of feelings.[85] Feelings have a close relationship with nature and mind. Chu Hsi argues that "nature is the state before activity begins, feelings are the state when activity has started, and mind includes both of these states."[86] In the *Yü-lei*, Chu Hsi avers that if there is nature, feelings will be aroused. Due to feelings, we know nature. Because there are feelings today, we know that there is nature originally.[87] Basically, feelings are the state of activity. As Chu Hsi indicates, "It is called destiny in Heaven. It is called nature when it imparts to humans. It is called feelings when it is aroused."[88] Ch'en Ch'un gives his elucidation that "feelings parallel nature; they are nature when aroused. What is in the mind before it is aroused is nature. When it comes into contact with things, it is activated and becomes feelings. The state of absolute quiet is nature, while the state of being acted upon and immediately penetrating all things is feelings."[89] Feelings as the state of activity are not only related to the nature but also in relation to the heart-mind. Feelings are the movements of the heart-mind.

In addition, nature is what has not been aroused, while feelings are what have been aroused. In nature, there are humanity, righteousness, propriety, and wisdom. When they are active, they become the feelings of commiseration, shame and dislike, deference and compliance, and right and wrong.[90] In terms of substance and function, nature is the substance of the heart-mind, while feelings are the function of the heart-mind. "For the heart-mind embraces both nature and feelings."[91] In this respect, feelings are not originally bad. As the function of the heart-mind, feelings can be good or bad. In order to illustrate this point, Chu Hsi compared the heart-mind to water, nature to the tranquillity of still water, feelings to the flow of water, and desires to waves. "Just as there are good and bad waves, so there are good desires . . . and bad desires."[92] Continuously, Ch'en Ch'un argues that "if feelings are not as they should be, they will violate principle. . . . They will then be merely expressions of selfish ideas and human desires."[93] In other words, these are bad desires. However, if feelings enable people to do good, then they are the correct feelings flowing from our nature and are originally all good.[94] Thus, feelings are good and bad. As Ch'en Ch'un clearly argues, "When feelings attain due measure and degree, they issue from the original nature and thus they are good and never evil. Those that do not attain due measure and degree become active when they are affected by material desires, do not issue from the original nature and thus are not good."[95] Further, Ch'en Ch'un says that "when Mencius talked about feelings and treated them as good, he was referring solely to those that are aroused in accordance with the nature."[96] However, the Ch'an Buddhists, on the other hand, treat feelings as evil and "want to exterminate feelings in order to restore nature."[97] Chu Hsi tries to balance these two different viewpoints that feelings are good and evil. "The Four Beginnings of Mencius are spoken of from the point of view of the goodness of nature. Pleasure, anger, sorrow, joy, and the seven feelings are spoken of from the point of view of both good and evil."[98]

Capability (*ts'ai*)

In Mencius, capability is originally good. Chu Hsi argues that capability is originally good. But due to *ch'i*, it can be good or bad.[99] First of all, according to Chu Hsi, capability means natural endowment (*ts'ai-chih*). "Natural endowment refers to the raw material, the stuff that enables one to perform. Here we are talking about substance."[100] In this regard, capability as natural endowment belongs to *ch'i* and has physical form. Second, capability is ability (*ts'ai-neng*). "Ability means the capacity to do something. The thing may be the same, but some people can bring their skill into full play and others cannot do it at all. That is because their capabilities are different. Here we are talking about function."[101] Further, Chu Hsi claims that capability is the ability of the heart-mind.[102] In other words, capability is the function of the heart-mind. Once again, Chu Hsi compares heart-mind to water. Nature is the principle of water; therefore it is the tranquillity of water. Feelings are the flowing of water; therefore they are activity. And capability is the energy of the flowing water flow. Because of different capabilities, there is rapid water and smooth-running water.[103] Thus, speaking in terms of substance and function, capability as substance is natural endowment and capability as function is ability.

Since capability is natural endowment and ability, it can be good or bad. As Chu Hsi mentions, "the capacity to do something good is capability, and the capacity to do something bad is capability as well."[104] What Chu Hsi means is that nature is originally good and capability is aroused by nature, therefore it is not bad. However, capability is natural endowment, it belongs to physical form and *ch'i*. If one's *ch'i* is clear, one's capability is clear. But if one's *ch'i* is turbid, one's capability is turbid too. Mencius considers capability to be good because he regards capability as issuing from the great basis of the goodness of human nature; whereas Chu Hsi considers capability to be good or bad because he regards capability as physical form and *ch'*i.[105]

The Relation between Heart-Mind, Nature, and Feelings

Chu Hsi applauds Chang Tsai's doctrine that "the heart-mind commands human nature and feelings (*Hsin t'ung Ch'ing Hsing*)." This is a great contribution in understanding the relation between heart-mind, nature, and feelings.[106] Chu Hsi takes *t'ung* to have two meanings. First, it means inclusion. Chu Hsi claims that "Nature is the state before activity begins, the feelings are the state when activity has started, and the heart-mind includes both of these states."[107] Another meaning is control or command. Chu Hsi states the heart-mind is the master. "By master is meant an all-pervading control and command existing in the heart-mind by itself."[108] With these understandings, Chu Hsi avers that "nature as principle is substance. Feelings are function. Both nature and feelings are included in the heart-mind, therefore the heart-mind can command them."[109]

By his early forties, Chu Hsi revised his theory of the Unaroused Equilibrium and the Aroused Harmony of the Doctrine of the Mean. Using this theory, Chu Hsi explained the relation between heart-mind, nature, and feelings. Before this period, Chu Hsi treated Unaroused

Equilibrium as nature and Aroused Harmony as heart-mind. However, with his new theory, Chu Hsi treats Equilibrium and Harmony as the tranquil and active states of heart-mind respectively.[110] Therefore, Chu Hsi states that "nature is the heart-mind before it is aroused, while feelings are the mind after it is aroused."[111] Moreover, Chu Hsi avers that nature consists of principles. Humanity, righteousness, propriety, and wisdom are the principles of nature. These are principles in the heart-mind before it is aroused. Commiseration, shame and dislike, deference and compliance, and right and wrong are feelings in the heart-mind after it is aroused.[112] In this respect, before it is aroused, the heart-mind is the Four Virtues; after it is aroused, the heart-mind is the Four Beginnings. The former is nature and the latter is feelings, and both are included by the heart-mind.

In terms of his concept of tranquillity and activity, Chu Hsi argues that nature is the tranquillity of the heart-mind, while feelings are the activity of the heart-mind. That is to say, "the heart-mind involves both tranquillity and activity."[113] Tranquillity is what has not been aroused and activity is what has been aroused. Before the feelings of pleasure, anger, sorrow, joy are aroused, the state of tranquillity exists. After they are aroused, the state of activity exists. Regardless of the state of activity or tranquillity, the heart-mind is the master. "It is master whether in the state of activity or in the state of tranquillity. . . . By master is meant an all-pervading control and command existing in the heart-mind by itself."[114] In this respect, the heart-mind commands nature and feelings.

Furthermore, "the heart-mind has substance and function. What has not been aroused is the substance of the heart-mind, while what has been aroused is the function of the heart-mind."[115] Ch'en Ch'un elaborates that "being in the state of absolute quiet is substance, and immediately penetrating all things when acted on is function. The substance of the heart-mind is nature, referring to its state of tranquillity, and the function of the heart-mind is feeling, referring to its state of activity."[116] The heart-mind embraces all principles. When it is in the state of tranquillity, it is nature. It "is eminently empty like the mirror and level like the balance, being calm there all the time."[117] When active, the heart-mind is aroused and becomes feeling. Feeling refers to the function of the heart-mind. In relation to the heart-mind, nature and feelings are in the heart-mind. In other words, there is only one heart-mind. "Sometimes it is spoken of in terms of its principle. . . . Sometimes it is spoken of in terms of its function."[118] The former is nature and the latter is feeling. And the heart-mind commands and unites them. Thus, Chu Hsi avers that "the nature is the principle of the heart-mind. Feelings are the function of the heart-mind. And the heart-mind is the master of feelings and nature."[119]

In his concept of nature, heart-mind, and feelings, Chu Hsi divides human nature into the nature of Heaven and Earth and physical nature; and the heart-mind into Tao heart-mind and human heart-mind. Based upon his concept of *li* and *ch'i*, the nature of Heaven and Earth and Tao heart-mind belong to *li*, while the physical nature and human heart-mind belong to *ch'i*. Since *li* is incorporeal, eternal, unchanging, the essence of myriad things, and always good, the nature of Heaven and Earth and Tao heart-mind are good and in a state of tranquillity. In other words, they are the principle that is received from Heaven and possessed by humans. Therefore, they are the Principle of Heaven. However, as *li* attaches itself to *ch'i* to operate, the nature of Heaven and Earth attaches itself to the physical nature and Tao heart-mind attaches itself to human heart-mind. Since *ch'i* is corporeal, transitory, changeable, physical form, and involves both good and evil, the physical nature and human heart-mind mix with physical endowment and human desires. Although they are not necessarily evil, the desires are precarious and liable to make mistakes. Therefore, for Chu Hsi, the purpose of human self-cultivation is to transform what humans are into what humans ought to be. In other words, humans are essentially good and received their nature and heart-mind from Heaven. But existentially, humans are precarious due to their physical endowment and desires, which are responsible for wrongdoing. This is our human predicament. In order to resolve this human predicament, Chu Hsi provides his idea of humanity (*jen*).

Notes

1. See Chan, *A Source Book in Chinese Philosophy*, 115.

2. A. C. Graham, "What Was New in the Ch'eng-Chu Theory of Human Nature?" in *Chu Hsi and Neo-Confucianism*, ed. Wing-tsit Chan (Honolulu: University of Hawaii Press, 1986), 138.

3. Chan, *A Source Book in Chinese Philosophy*, 474.

4. Ibid., 511.

5. Ibid., 528.

6. Wing-tsit Chan, 宋明理學之概念與歷史 [The Concept and History of the School of Principle in Sung and Ming], 8.

7. A. C. Graham argues that by inserting the concept of *li* into the theory of human nature Ch'eng-Chu made what Thomas S. Kuhn called a paradigm shift in the history of Chinese history. See A. C. Graham, "What Was New in the Ch'eng-Chu Theory of Human Nature?" 139.

8. Ch'en Ch'un, *Neo-Confucian Terms Explained*, 46-7.

9. Chan, *A Source Book in Chinese Philosophy*, 623.

10. *Yü-lei*, ch. 94, sec. 24, 2371.

11. Chan, *A Source Book in Chinese Philosophy*, 640.

12. Ibid., 614.

13. *Yü-lei*, ch.5, sec. 5, 82.

14. Chan, *A Source Book in Chinese Philosophy*, 614.

15. Ibid., 621.

16. Ibid.

17. Ibid., 622.

18. Ibid.

19. *Yü-lei*, ch.4, sec.

20. In his *A New Anthology and Commentary on Chu Hsi's Philosophy*, Ch'ien Mu argues that before the age of sixty Chu Hsi stressed the distinction between nature and vital force; but after sixty he combined nature with vital force. See Ch'ien Mu, 朱子新學案 [*A New Anthology and Commentary on Chu Hsi's Philosophy*], vol. 1 (Taipei: San-min shu-chü, 1971), 445-461.

21. Chan, *A Source Book in Chinese Philosophy*, 511. Chan translates *t'ien-ti chih hsing* as the original nature endowed by Heaven and Earth and *ch'i-chih chih hsing* as physical nature. In fact, *t'ien-ti chih hsing* can also be called original nature (*pen-jan chih hsing*), while *ch'i-chih chih hsing* can be translated as the nature which is *ch'i* and matter.

22. Chan, *A Source Book in Chinese Philosophy*, 527.

23. Ibid., 567.

24. *Yü-lei*, ch.4, sec. 38, 63.

25. Chan, *A Source Book in Chinese Philosophy*, 624.

26. *Yü-lei*, ch.4, sec. 48, 67.

27. Chan, *A Source Book in Chinese Philosophy*, 624.

28. Ibid.

29. Ibid., 625.

30. *Yü-lei*, ch. 4, sec. 50, 68.

31. Chan, *A Source Book in Chinese Philosophy*, 624.

32. Ibid.

33. *Yü-lei*, ch. 4, sec. 46, 67.

34. *Yü-lei*, ch. 4, sec. 50, 68.?

35. See John H. Berthrong, *All Under Heaven*, 90-91.

36. *Hsin* has been translated as the mind by Wing-tsi Chan in his *Source Book*, the mind-and heart by Wm. Theodore de Bary, and the heart-mind by Tu Wei-ming. Here the author follows Tu's translation because *hsin* is both cognitive and sensitive, or rational and experiential. See Wm. Theodore de Bary, *Neo-Confucian Orthodoxy and the Learning of the Mind-and-Heart* (New York:

Columbia University Press, 1981) and Tu Wei-ming, "Confucianism," in *Our Religions*, ed. Arvind Sharma (San Francisco: Harper and Row, 1993), 137-227. In addition, *Tao hsin* and *jen hsin* have been translated by Shu-Hsien Liu as moral mind and human mind respectively. See Shu-Hsien Liu, "The Function of the Mind in Chu Hsi's Philosophy," *Journal of Chinese Philosophy*, 5 (1978): 195-208. However, following the above translation of *hsin*, the author translates *Tao hsin* and *jen hsin* as Tao heart-mind and human heart-mind respectively.

37. *Yü-lei*, ch.4, sec. 45, 67.

38. *Yü-lei*, ch.5, sec. 28, 85.

39. Allen Wittenborn, *Further Reflections on Things at Hand: A Reader,* 32.

40. Chan, *A Source Book in Chinese Philosophy*, 606.

41. Ibid.

42. *Yü-lei*, ch.5, sec. 32, 85.

43. Chan, *A Source Book in Chinese Philosophy*, 628.

44. Shu-Hsien Liu, "The Function of the Mind in Chu Hsi's Philosophy," 197.

45. Chan, *A Source Book in Chinese Philosophy*, 631.

46. Ibid.

47. *Yü-lei*, ch16, sec. 51, 323.

48. Chan, *A Source Book in Chinese Philosophy*, 630.

49. *Yü-lei*, ch. 95, sec. 2, 2415.

50. Ch'en Ch'un, *Neo-Confucian Terms Explained*, 60.

51. Chan, *A Source Book in Chinese Philosophy*, 631.

52. *Yü-lei*, ch. 5, sec. 60, 90.

53. Ch'en Ch'un, *Neo-Confucian Terms Explained*, 56.

54. *Yü-lei*, ch. 12, 10, 199.

55. Chan, *A Source Book in Chinese Philosophy*, 629.

56. Ch'en Ch'un, *Neo-Confucian Terms Explained*, 59.

57. James Legge, *The Chinese Classics*, vol. 3 (Oxford: Clarendon Press, 1893), 61.

58. This is one of the Five Classics of Chinese History. The others fours are the *Book of History* , *Book of Changes*, *Book of Rites* and the *Spring and Autumn Annals*.

59. *Yü-lei*, ch. 58, sec. 18, 1361.

60. *Yü-lei*, ch. 78, sec. 110, 2014.

61. *Yü-lei*, ch. 78, sec. 89, 2010.

62. *Yü-lei*, ch. 78, sec. 107, 2013.

63. *Yü-lei*, ch. 78, sec. 123, 2018.

64. *Yü-lei*, ch. 78, sec. 85, 2009.

65. *Yü-lei*, ch. 78, sec. 88, 2010.

66. James Legge, *The Chinese Classics*, vol. 3 (Oxford: Clarendon Press, 1893), 61.

67. *Yü-lei*, ch. 78, sec.

68. Shu-Hsien Liu, "The Function of the Mind in Chu Hsi's Philosophy," 198.

69. *Yü-lei*, ch. 78, sec. 121, 2017.

70. *Yü-lei*, ch. 78, sec. 91, 2011.

71. *Yü-lei*, ch. 78, sec. 88, 2010.

72. *Yü-lei*, ch. 78, sec. 89, 2010.

73. *Yü-lei*, ch. 78, sec. 107, 2013.

74. *Yü-lei*, ch. 78, sec. 106, 2013.

75. Shu-Hsien Liu, "The Function of the Mind in Chu Hsi's Philosophy," 197-8.

76. See Li-wen Chang, 朱子思想研究 [A Study of Chu Hsi's Thought], 504-5.

77. *Yü-lei*, ch. 78, sec. 89, 2010.

78. *Yü-lei*, ch. 78, sec. 93, 2011.

79. James Legge, *The Chinese Classics*, vol. 3 (Oxford: Clarendon Press, 1893), 61.

80. *Yü-lei*, ch. 78, sec. 86, 2009.

81. Tsai-chun Chung, *The Development of the Concepts of Heaven and of Man in the Philosophy of Chu Hsi*, 240.

82. Ibid.

83. Chan, *A Source Book in Chinese Philosophy*, 603.

84. *Yü-lei*, ch. 62, sec. 41, 1488.

85. See Li-wen Chang, 朱子思想研究 [A Study of Chu Hsi's Thought], 507.

86. Chan, *A Source Book in Chinese Philosophy*, 631.

87. *Yü-lei*, ch. 5, sec. 56, 89.

88. *Yü-lei*, ch. 5, sec. 58, 90.

89. Ch'en Ch'un, *Neo-Confucian Terms Explained*, 62.

90. *Yü-lei*, ch. 5, sec. 66, 92.

91. Chan, *A Source Book in Chinese Philosophy*, 631.

92. Ibid.

93. Ch'en Ch'un, *Neo-Confucian Terms Explained*, 63.

94. Chan, *A Source Book in Chinese Philosophy*, 631.

95. Ch'en Ch'un, *Neo-Confucian Terms Explained*, 63.

96. Ibid.

97. Ibid.

98. Ibid.

99. Here Chu Hsi tries to deal with the difference between Mencius and Ch'eng I. For Ch'eng I, capability is endowed with *ch'i*. But Mecius relates capability merely to nature. See Liu Shu-hsien, 朱子哲學思想的發展與完成 [Development and Completion of Chu Hsi's Philosophical Thought], 221-226.

100. Ch'en Ch'un, *Neo-Confucian Terms Explained*, 64.

101. Ibid.

102. *Yü-lei*, ch. 5, sec. 91, 97.

103. Ibid.

104. Ibid.

105. Ch'en Ch'un, *Neo-Confucian Terms Explained*, 64. Also see Liu Shu-hsien, 朱子哲學思想的發展與完成 [Development and Completion of Chu Hsi's Philosophical Thought], 221-226.

106. Chan, *A Source Book in Chinese Philosophy*, 631.

107. Ibid.

108. Ibid.

109. *Yü-lei*, ch. 98, sec. 41, 2513.

110. Tsai-chun Chung, *The Development of the Concepts of Heaven and of Man in the Philosophy of Chu Hsi*, 119-120.

111. Chan, *A Source Book in Chinese Philosophy*, 631.

112. *Yü-lei*, ch. 5, sec. 67, 92.

113. Chan, *A Source Book in Chinese Philosophy*, 629.

114. Ibid., 631.

115. *Yü-lei*, ch. 5, sec. 61, 90.

116. Ch'en Ch'un, *Neo-Confucian Terms Explained*, 58.

117. Ibid.

118. Ibid., 60.

119. Ibid., 60.

CHAPTER EIGHT
Chu Hsi's Concept of *Jen*

Jen in Confucian Tradition

Jen is the pivotal concept of Chinese religious thought. Confucians, Taoists, and Buddhists have used *jen* in their texts. Although both Taoists and Buddhists regard *jen* as a cardinal virtue, *jen* is the symbol or keystone of Confucianism.[1] It "is treated as the religious and moral principle or substance of the universe, which has a specific relation to the Confucian political ideal, its philosophical exploration and religious pursuit."[2] Originally, as Chan indicates, *jen* can be traced back to the later portions of the *Book of Odes*, the *Book of History*, and the *Book of Changes*.[3] However, *jen* was not a significant concept in Chinese philosophic thought until the time of Confucius (551-479 B.C.E.). He uses the concept of the ancient classics and reinterpreted it as the highest virtue, which unites Heaven and human beings. He treats *jen* as not only human excellence but transcendental principle as well.[4] In the *Analects*, *jen* appears 105 times, and 58 out of the 499 sections directly discuss its meaning, function, or practice.[5] Generally speaking, Confucius depicts *jen* as the underlying principle and substance, inherent in all human beings. Particularly, in the human social level, *jen* is defined as love.[6] Due to *jen*, the Confucian Golden Rule[7] has its positive aspect as the method of achieving *jen*.[8] Since Confucius defines *jen* as love, *jen* then becomes a very controversial concept from his time on.

Mencius criticizes Mo Tzu (468-376?) for defining love in a universal context without any distinctions.[9] For Mencius, *jen* as love must be in accordance with an order, a gradation, or distinction, starting with filial piety. Moreover, he links love with righteousness. In so doing, the nature and the application of *jen* are equally stressed. "It is love that embraces all relations, but it is righteousness that distinguishes them."[10] In this respect, *jen* as love has both universality and particularity. That is to say, not only is *jen* the cultivation of the inner life, but it also consists in proper external conduct.[11] In addition, Mencius defines *jen* as the heart-mind of human beings. In his concept of the Four Beginnings, Mencius claims that the sense of commiseration is the beginning of *jen*. What he means is that "all men have the mind which cannot bear [to see the suffering of] others."[12] In this regard, *jen* and righteousness are two aspects of one human heart-mind. "Humanity is man's mind and righteousness is the man's path;"[13] and "Humanity is the peaceful abode of human beings, while righteousness is his straight path."[14] Furthermore, Mencius even extends his identification of *jen* to the macrocosmic level. Essentially, the cosmos and humans are united by *jen*. Being the essence of humans as well as of the cosmos, *jen* "functions as a governing principle and supportive substance, motivates the unity and variety of the universe, underlies all forms of action and expresses itself in the nature of all beings."[15] Because humans share the same principle with the cosmos and the myriad things, humans can extend their *jen* to the myriad things and even to the whole cosmos. Mencius was the first Confucian to explore the theory of *jen* systematically, defining it as the active force driving human beings to strive for the unity between themselves and the universe.[16]

Before the Five Masters of the Northern Sung, HanYü (768-824) defined the idea of *jen* as *po-ai* (universal love). As he claims, "universal love is called humanity. To practice this in the proper manner is called righteousness. To proceed according to these is called the Way."[17] Han Yü's concept of *po-ai* is not concerned with whether love must have distinctions, because this question had been settled long time before. Rather, his concept is basically a refutation of Buddhist and Taoist ways of non-activity in love. In contrast to Buddhist nihilism and Taoist quietism, Han Yü contends that love is universal and its way is a way of action guided by what is proper.[18] Therefore, his concept of love as universal love is totally different from that of Mo Tzu.

Chou Tun-i (1017-1073) does not mention *jen*; instead, he substitutes for it impartiality (*kung*). He argues that "the way of the sage is nothing other than absolute impartiality."[19] Replacing *jen* with impartiality, Chou Tun-i contends that not only is impartiality an ethical quality, involving an equal consideration for self and others, but also there is no separation between the internal and the external metaphysically.[20] Furthermore, Ch'eng I distinguishes impartiality from *jen* by defining impartiality as the principle of *jen* and insisting that impartiality must be practiced or embodied in action.[21]

Among the Five Masters of the Northern Sung, Chang Tsai provides a metaphysical explanation for the doctrine of *jen*. In his Western Inscription, Chang Tsai contends that "Heaven is my father and Earth is my mother, and such a small creature as I find an intimate place in their midst. . . . All people are my brothers and sisters, and all things are my companions."[22] This universal aspect of *jen* emerged from Chang's concept of *li-i fen-shu* (the principle is one but its manifestations are many). In this regard, for Chang Tsai, due to the principle of the many, love cannot be without distinctions. However, on the other hand, due to the principle of the one, love is extended to encompass the entire universe.[23]

The Ch'eng brothers provide a significant contribution to the redefinition of the concept of *jen*. Ch'eng Hao defines *jen* as life force. *Jen* is not merely a virtue, but also the vital force. That is to say, *jen* is the dynamic element behind all life and productivity.[24] This is an innovation making *jen* and productivity synonymous. As Ch'eng Hao contends, "The great characteristic of Heaven and Earth is to produce. . . . This is what is meant by origination being the chief quality of goodness. This is *jen*."[25] In addition, Ch'eng I elaborates on this idea by identifying *jen* with seeds. He claims that "the heart-mind is comparable to seeds of grain. The nature of growth is *jen*."[26] In this respect, *jen* is the source of virtue due to its characteristic of growth and life giving force. It is also "the chief character of the universe."[27] Furthermore, Ch'eng I identifies love with feelings and *jen* with nature. "The feeling of commiseration is of course [an expression of] love. But love is feeling whereas humanity is nature."[28] Ch'eng I argues that the Mencian idea of the feeling of commiseration is merely the beginning of humanity. It is not *jen*. Therefore, Han Yü is wrong to define *jen* as universal love. "A man of humanity of course loves universally. But one may not therefore regard universal love as humanity."[29]

One of the students of the Ch'eng brothers, Hsieh Liang-tso

(1050-1103), depicts *jen* as consciousness. "*Jen* is the awareness of pain [in the case of illness]. The Confucians call it *jen*, while the Buddhists call it consciousness."[30] Defining *jen* as consciousness, Hsieh is later criticized by Chu Hsi because his concept departs from the Confucian concept of *jen*. Another student, Yan Kuei–shan (1053-1135) defines *jen* as forming one body with things. For him, the myriad things and I are united as one body in the substance of *jen*.[31] However, Chu Hsi criticizes him because his definition of *jen* is too loose.

From the above discussion, we see that *jen* is the kernel of Confucianism. It has been defined as (1) benevolence, (2) perfect virtue, (3) love, (4) more specifically, affection, (5) more emphatically, universal love, (6) human heart-mind, (7) impartiality, (8) vital force, (9) consciousness, and (10) forming one body with things. As a great synthesizer, Chu Hsi blends all these various concepts into his systematic theory. In analyzing his concept of *jen*, all these concepts will be reiterated.

Chu Hsi's Treatise of *Jen*

After establishing his new doctrine of equilibrium and harmony at the age of forty, Chu Hsi wrote "A Treatise on *Jen*" (*Jen-shou*). The date of this treatise is very controversial, and yet it was surely written after his fortieth birthday.[32] It is an important treatise for us to understand his idea of *jen*. In this treatise, Chu Hsi uses only 824 characters and divides the text into two sections, namely, *jen* as the character of the heart-mind and *jen* as the principle of love. As Wing-tsit Chan indicates, the reasons for Chu Hsi writing this treatise are that the different contemporary doctrines of *jen* needed to be corrected. Hsieh Liang-tso in particular treats *jen* as consciousness and Yan Kuei–shan defines *jen* as forming one body with all things. Moreover, Chu Hsi claims that *jen* as love is based upon the concept of the heart-mind of Heaven and Earth is to produce things. Finally, in his concept of *jen*, Chu Hsi argues that substance and function are not two different things, but one.[33]

In his first sentence of the treatise, Chu Hsi quotes from the Ch'eng brothers that "the heart-mind of Heaven and Earth is to produce things."[34] Chu Hsi writes, "In the production of man and things, they receive the heart-mind of Heaven and Earth as their heart-mind. Therefore, with reference to the character of the heart-mind, although it embraces and penetrates all and leaves nothing to be desired, nevertheless, one word will cover all of it, namely, *jen*."[35] Clearly, Chu Hsi argues that the foundation of *jen* is the heart-mind of Heaven and Earth. Following Ch'eng I's view of that the heart-mind of Heaven and Earth is to produce things, Chu Hsi avers that humans and the myriad things are endowed with *jen* by receiving the heart-mind of Heaven and Earth. Further, referring to the relation of substance and function, Chu Hsi argues that *jen* is both substance and function. As the heart-mind of humans has its substance and function, the heart-mind of Heaven and Earth has its substance and function as well.

Defining *jen* as the character of heart-mind and the principle of love is Chu Hsi's creative synthesis of the Confucian tradition. Besides this treatise, these two phrases have occurred elsewhere in Chu Hsi's writings and conversations.[36] Basically, these two phrases are the main idea of his doctrine of *jen*. Nevertheless, how Chu Hsi develops these two phrases is very controversial, i.e., whether they are originally from Chu Hsi, or whether Chu Hsi borrows from others. Some Japanese scholars argue that Chu Hsi borrowed these two phrases from Buddhism or from Chang Shih (1133-1180); but some regard these phrases as Chu Hsi's own idea.[37] Hoyt C. Tillman argues that even though these phrases are not from Chang Shih, he still was an important colleague who enriched Chu's evolving synthesis on *jen* as the character of heart-mind and the principle of love.[38]

The Character of the Heart-Mind

Hu Hung (1106-1161) defines *jen* as the way of the heart-mind. Hu Hung's concept of the heart-mind is wondrously transcendent. Not only can the heart-mind comprehend all things under Heaven, but also can command them. The heart-mind is broad and inexhaustible. Therefore, the Hunan school criticizes Chu Hsi's idea of the heart-mind of Heaven and Earth as one that represents a narrow view. It limits and undermines the all pervasiveness of the substance of *jen*.[39] However, Chu Hsi responds that the Hunan concept of the wondrous heart-mind would result ultimately in Buddhist emptiness and Taoist quietism. He warns that the Hunan concept of the heart-mind is something transcendental and lofty. And the followers of Hu Hung "do not understand that what Heaven and Earth focus on as their heart-mind is none other than the production of things."[40] Chu Hsi does not only disagree with their view of the heart-mind of Heaven and Earth, but also affirms that "when Heaven and Earth endow human beings and things with the heart-mind of productiveness, this becomes the heart-mind of human beings and things as well."[41]

For Chu Hsi, as the character of the heart-mind, *jen* has the quality of *sheng*, to produce or to give life.[42] *Jen* as the character of the heart-mind can be traced back to Ch'eng I's concept that "the heart-mind is comparable to seeds of grain. The nature of growth is *jen*."[43] By following Ch'eng I's pictorial image of a seed of grain, Chu Hsi argues that the process of growth is present in the heart-mind as potentiality. And *jen* as the principle of life lies dormant in the plant during winter or hidden in the seed before branches and leaves blossom forth.[44] Based upon Ch'eng I's idea of *sheng-sheng* (production and reproduction, perpetual renewal of life), Chu Hsi argues that *jen* has the character of production. Therefore, as Ch'en Ch'un illustrates, "humanity is the totality of the heart-mind's principle of production. It is always producing and reproducing without cease."[45]

Since *jen* has this idea of growth, it embraces the Four Virtues, humanity, righteousness, propriety, and wisdom. In Mencian thought, there are four characters of the heart-mind, namely, humanity (*jen*), righteousness, propriety, and wisdom. And correspondingly, there are Four Beginnings, namely, commiseration, deference and compliance, shame and dislike, and right and wrong. In this regard, *jen*, for Mencius, is the feelings of commiseration.[46] Following Ch'eng I's thought, Chu Hsi argues that *jen* is not merely the feelings of commiseration, but also is *yüan* (origination). In the treatise. Chu Hsi claims that "the moral qualities of the heart-mind of Heaven and Earth are four: origination, flourish, advantages, and firmness. And the principle of origination unites and controls them all. . . . Therefore in the heart-mind of man there are also four moral qualities—namely, *jen*, righteousness, propriety, and wisdom—and *jen* embraces them all."[47] By identifying *jen* as origination, Chu Hsi indicates that *jen* is the beginning of life and the first stage in the process of growth. It unites and controls all virtues of the human beings. When Ch'en Ch'un asks Chu Hsi that if *jen* is the character of the heart-mind, are righteousness, propriety, and wisdom also characters of the heart-mind? Chu Hsi answered him that all of them are the character of the mind, however, *jen* alone embraces them all.[48] Individually speaking, *jen* is one of the Four Virtues. However, collectively speaking, the Four Virtues are qualities of the heart-mind but *jen* is the master of them.[49] In the *Yü-lei*, Chu Hsi clarifies that "as the character of the heart-mind, *jen* possesses all the other three. . . . What is called the character of the heart-mind here is similar to what Master Ch'eng meant by 'collectively, it embraces all four.'"[50]

Furthermore, Chu Hsi elaborates that the character of the heart-mind is the substance of *jen*.[51] For this reason, Chu Hsi does not follow Ch'eng I's idea of *jen* as the correct principle of the world because it is too broad or too vague. For him, not only is the correct principle *jen*, but so is righteousness and even propriety.[52] Thus, Chu Hsi claims that "*jen* is the complete character of the original heart-mind, if the innate heart-mind of the Principle of Heaven as it naturally is has been preserved and not lost, whatever one does will be orderly and harmonious."[53] In this respect, *jen* as the complete character of the heart-mind is already existent even before the feelings are aroused. And its function is infinite after the feelings are aroused. "If we can truly practice love and preserve it, then we have in it the spring of all virtues and the root of all good deeds."[54] If we do preserve, practice, and not lose the character of the heart-mind, then it will be present everywhere and its functions will always be operative.[55]

In order to preserve and not to lose the character of the heart-mind, Chu Hsi argues that as long as one preserves *jen* as the character of the heart-mind, there will be nothing but *jen*. Confucius says "to master oneself and return to propriety" means that after eliminating selfish desires, *jen* will then be preserved forever.[56] In practice, Ch'en Ch'un explicates Chu Hsi's concept of *jen* as the character of the heart-mind, such that *jen* is the complete virtue of the heart-mind, embracing and controling the Four Virtues. It is impossible that righteousness, propriety, and wisdom exist without *jen*. For *jen* is the principle of production in the heart-mind. It is operating, producing and reproducing ceaselessly, and remains from the beginning to the end without interruption.[57] Once there is actual practice, there is the principle of production and reproduction, namely, *jen*.

Principle of Love

In his idea of the principle of love as *jen*, Chu Hsi pictures *jen* as the root and love as the sprout. If the love of *jen* is the sweetness of sugar and the sourness of vinegar, then love is the taste.[58] Since *jen* is the root and love is the sprout, they cannot be confused. However, the sprout is grown from the root.[59] Also Ch'en Ch'un notes that "*jen* is the root of love, commiseration the sprout from the root, and love the sprout reaching its maturity and completion."[60] Based upon Chu Hsi's concepts of what has been aroused and what has not been aroused, love is the former and *jen* is the latter.[61] What Chu Hsi means by love is the principle of *jen* in the heart-mind. *Jen* is the principle in the heart-mind, while filial piety and brotherly respect are feelings, which are the expression of the heart-mind. In this respect, filial piety and brotherly respect belong to *jen*. "But these feelings are aroused, what is preserved in the heart-mind is only the principle of love."[62] In characterizing *jen* as the root and love as the sprout, Chu Hsi depicts the relation between the state of tranquillity and the state of activity. In tranquillity, the life force is hidden like a seed in winter. In activity, it becomes manifest like a springtime bud.[63]

Furthermore, as the state of what has not been aroused, *jen* is an a priori principle, and does not depend upon anything else. As an a priori principle, *jen* is the inner nature rather than either feelings or the heart-mind.[64] As Chu Hsi claims, "What is called *jen* is the nature and nature is merely principle."[65] Humanity, righteousness, propriety, and wisdom are nature. Once they are manifested, they become the feelings of commiseration, of deference and compliance, of shame and dislike, and of right and wrong. Therefore, "the Four Beginnings come into being only when nature is aroused, but cannot be seen before it is aroused."[66] In this regard, *jen* is nature, while the feeling of commiseration as the beginning of *jen* is love.

In terms of substance and function, *jen* is the principle of love as substance, while love is function.[67] Chu Hsi explains that "*jen* is the principle of love, while love is the function of *jen*. It is simply called *jen* before it is activated, when it has neither shape nor shade. It is called love only after it is activated, when it has shape and shadow."[68] As substance and function cannot be separated, neither can *jen* and love be separated, although they are two different states. Before it is aroused, *jen* embraces righteousness, propriety, and wisdom because it is the principle of the production of the heart-mind. Correspondingly, after it is aroused, it becomes the feeling of commiseration and embraces the feelings of deference and compliance, of shame and dislike, and of right and wrong.[69] Using the images of root and sprout, "*jen* is the root of love, commiseration the sprout from the root, and love the sprout reaching its maturity and completion."[70] In addition, Ch'en Ch'un avers that "*jen* is the principle of love. . . . When love is manifested externally, it is the function of humanity, but the principle of love is in it."[71]

In the relation of *jen* and love, Chu Hsi treats love as the state of activity and the force of production. Before it is aroused, love is nature, the substance of *jen*, and embraces the Four Virtues. After it is aroused, it is feeling and embraces the Four Beginnings. However, the nature and feelings as well as substance and function are not separated. They are not bifurcated.[72] One cannot exist without the other. *Jen* as the principle of love has priority over other virtues because *jen* is the ground of other virtues and operates completely in accord with the Principle of Heaven.[73] And it "consists of the fact that the heart-mind of Heaven and Earth to produce things is present in everything."[74]

The Character of the Heart-Mind and the Principle of Love

Before further discussing these two phrases, it is necessary to clarify two things. First, since the character of the heart-mind and the principle of love are used by Chu Hsi to define the concept of *jen*, they cannot be separated from each other. In fact, they are not two different things; rather they are two aspects of *jen*. In many ways, Chu Hsi uses them together to elucidate his idea of *jen*. Second, although Chu Hsi defines *jen* as the character of the heart-mind and the principle of love, it does not mean that *jen* is the heart-mind or love, or even both. In the *Yü-lei*, Chu His lucidly notes that "love is not *jen*; the principle of love is *jen*. The heart-mind is not *jen*, the character of the heart-mind is *jen*."[75] For Chu Hsi, *jen* is nature and nature is principle; therefore, *jen* cannot be love, which is feeling, or the heart-mind.

The relation between the character of the heart-mind and the principle of love is that the former is the cause and the latter is the effect. Due to the fact that *jen* is the principle of love, *jen* then is the character of the heat-mind.[76] "Love is commiseration and commiseration is feeling. Its principle is *jen*. In the phrase 'the character of the heart-mind,' the character is also love. What is called the character of the heart-mind is the root of love."[77] Principle is the state of tranquillity. It is not active but it is the foundation of what things emerge. Therefore, speaking in terms of the principle of love, *jen* is used to describe the root of things, or the grounds of things. On the other hand, the heart-mind is active and productive. Speaking in terms of the character of the heart-mind, *jen* is pointing to the sprout of things, or the production or function of things. In this respect, in the relation between these two phrases, the principle of love can be regarded as cause and the character of the heart-mind as effect. Ch'en Ch'un suggests that when Chu Hsi treats *jen* as the character of the heart-mind and the principle of love together, he is speaking in terms of principle.[78] That is to say, when Chu Hsi claims *jen* as the character of the heart-mind and the principle of love, he is saying that *jen* is the foundation or ground of things.

Furthermore, for Ch'eng I, "separately speaking, *jen* is one of the Four Virtues; but collectively speaking, *jen* embraces all four."[79] Following this view, Chu Hsi argues that "the principle of love is spoken of separately as one thing, while the character of the heart-mind is spoken of collectively as including the four."[80] All Four Virtues are the character of the heart-mind, and *jen* is the master because "the Principle of heaven embodied in the human heart-mind is totally *jen*."[81] As one of the Four Virtues, *jen* is the principle of love, just as righteousness is the principle of appropriateness, propriety is the principle of respect and reverence, and wisdom the principle of right and wrong.[82] In this respect, Ch'en Ch'un claims that "when [these] four are viewed horizontally, they are four parallel moral principle, but when humanity is viewed alone, it is broader and can combine all four. Hence humanity is the character of the heart-mind."[83]

In terms of substance and function, the character of the heart-mind is substance before it is activated and is function after it is activated. As the principle of love, *jen* is substance and love is function.[84] Further, Ch'un Ch'en avers that "the character of the heart-mind refers, collectively, to substance, while the principle of love refers, separately, to function."[85] Although *jen* can be defined in terms of substance as the character of the heart-mind, or function as the principle of love, *jen* cannot be divided into two, just as substance and function cannot be separated. Actually, there is only one *jen* but has two aspects. As the character of the heart-mind, *jen* is the heart-mind of Heaven and Earth to produce things. As the principle of love, *jen* is comparable to the root. Viewed from the concept of vital force (*ch'i*), the heart-mind of Heaven and Earth is revealed from its root, and love is the sprout reaching its maturity and completion. However, "both the character of the heart-mind and the principle of love are forces of life."[86] *Jen* as substance is the ground of the life, while *jen* as function is the active force by which the life is produced.

In short, *jen* as the character of the heart-mind is comparable to the seed of grain because of the generative character of *jen*. It also implies that humans receive the heart-mind of Heaven and Earth as their heart-mind, and this heart-mind has its generative character. It is always producing and reproducing without ceasing. Moreover, *jen* as the principle of love is human nature. It is not love. What is called love is *jen* that has been activated. In this respect, *jen* is nature, while love is feeling. *Jen* is principle, while love is vital force.[87] Speaking in terms of substance and function, *jen* as substance is the universal nature of the human heart-mind. Once it functions, it generates all virtues, embracing righteousness, propriety, and wisdom. Spoken of collectively, not only is *jen* the totality of all virtues, but it is also the generative force that makes virtues real, social, and dynamic. In other words, *jen* is the process of production.[88]

The Role of *Ch'eng*

Jen is principle, the universal nature, and substance. It is depicted as "the ideal moral virtue as the intentionality of an individual that gives unity of human purpose to all human conduct."[89] But still, *jen* is an ideal concept in Chu Hsi's thought. In other to actualize it in the reality, the other concept Chu Hsi needs to mention is *ch'eng* (self-actualization). *Ch'eng* is depicted as what the process should be and points to the ideal foundation of all actuality. It is the direction of the actualization of principle in the formation of human virtue and a participant in the creation of a just social order.[90] In this regard, not only is *ch'eng* a process of self-actualization, but it is also "a statement of what this process of becoming ought to be, a normative value embedded in the person."[91]

Conventionally, *ch'eng* means to be sincere. Chu Hsi still holds this understanding of *ch'eng*. But for him there is another meaning of *ch'eng*, the self-realization of the norms of human excellence. These two meanings are equally important. One cannot exist without the other. With these meanings, Chu Hsi claims that *ch'eng* is the real principle. It is solid and real and also it is principle.[92] Basically, what Chu Hsi means is that *ch'eng* includes values and is the focus of dynamic reality.[93] As the real principle, *ch'eng* manifests itself without depending upon any manipulation. It is "the natural manifestation of the true principle endowed by Heaven in all."[94]

Furthermore, Chu Hsi distinguishes *ch'eng* from principle by referring to the relation between *ch'eng* and nature. Chu Hsi argues that "nature is the real or the solid, while *ch'eng* is void. What is called nature is principle, while what is called *ch'eng* is excellence. If nature is like a fan, then *ch'eng* is comparable to this fan being well made."[95] In this respect, *ch'eng* can be depicted as the concept of complete perfection without deficiency.[96] In terms of principle, *ch'eng* can be delineated as the beginning and end of things.[97] As the beginning, *ch'eng* is the true principle endowed by Heaven. On the other hand, as the end, *ch'eng* is the complete perfection of self-realization.

In addition, as self-realization, *ch'eng* is the mode of self-actualized perfection, a model for how things ought to be. In relating to reverence as avoiding disrespect, *ch'eng* is sincerity, the action of not disregarding one's conscience.[98] In other words, reverence is respectfulness, while *ch'eng* is the normative state of being a sage. In this regard, not only is *ch'eng* the manifestation of virtue, but the principle informing perfected ethical action as well.[99] As Ch'un Ch'en indicates, "When ancients established the meaning [of sincerity], sometimes they had effort in mind. As to perfect *ch'eng*, it is on the level of the sage's moral nature."[100]

Furthermore, Chu Hsi compares *ch'eng* to *hsin* (faithfulness or truthfulness). "*Ch'eng* refers to natural or spontaneous, while *hsin* refers to human effort."[101] The former describes a sage and the latter describes a common person. Ch'en Ch'un elaborates that "*ch'eng* is a matter of principle while truthfulness is a matter of the heart-mind, *ch'eng* is the Way of Heaven while truthfulness is the way of man."[102] Basically, *ch'eng* and *hsin* are different. "Truthfulness cannot be defined as *ch'eng* as love cannot be defined as *jen*."[103] Only sages have self-actualized perfection, namely, *ch'eng*, and all the common people are in the state of *hsin*.

Compared with *chung* (steadfastness), "*ch'eng* refers to the complete essence of the heart-mind, while steadfastness refers to the heart-mind's response to events and its coming into contact with things."[104] In this regard, *ch'eng* is the fullness of the process of self-determination.[105] It is the level of the sage's moral nature. "Only when all principles are perfectly true and real without an iota of insincerity can one deserve the description."[106] Ch'en Ch'un argues that *chung* and *hsin* are close to *ch'eng* in meaning. All of them can mean being real. However, in *ch'eng* being real comes naturally, while in *chung* and *hsin* being real comes about in human performance of a task.[107]

In addition, not only is *ch'eng* self-actualized perfection or the fundamental principle of normative action, but also it has its dynamic aspect. "*Ch'eng* is a principle of order that regulates the production of things as the decree of the way."[108] It "always operates and manifests itself in one's daily life, except that one is not aware of it."[109] In other words, *ch'eng* is the ideal goal for humans, and also manifests through one's daily activity with *hsin* and *chung* as its guide. "This is what human effort should be, and that is the way of man."[110] Whenever the heart-mind reaches its totality as honest action, it is then *ch'eng*. Similarly, "when one's word and act is true, that is also *ch'eng*."[111] In this sense, *ch'eng* is human normative moral principle, and manifests itself in our daily life through our effort to maintain *hsin* and *chung*. Once our self-actualization reaches perfect truth without an iota of insincerity, then it is *ch'eng*.[112]

In short, *ch'eng*, on the one hand, is the human normative moral principle and the self-realization of the norms of human excellence. It is the dynamics of actualization. However, on the other hand, it is one of the elements of this dynamic process. *Ch'eng* is the Way of Heaven and the natural principle of self-realization. To achieve *ch'eng* is the way of *jen*. *Ch'eng* carries out its real principle and makes an effort to achieve it. It "is the foundation of the sage, the beginning and the end of things and the Way of the Decree."[113] In relation to *jen*, *ch'eng* is *ch'eng* and *jen* is *jen*. Viewed from the utmost viewpoint, you will clearly understand.[114] In other words, when human self-realization is perfectly completed, *ch'eng* is *jen* and *jen* is *ch'eng* because in that moment, what is human nature as principle is freely expressed without an iota of insincerity. Thus, that is to say, "there is the way of Heaven, the way of humanity and their mediation through the process of *ch'eng* ending in *jen*."[115]

Finally, we turn to Chu Hsi's Diagram on the "*Jen-shuo*" [Treatise on Humanity] in order to summarize his view. In his Diagram, Chu Hsi avers that *jen* is the heart-mind of Heaven and Earth effective in the production of things, and Origination, Flourishing, Advantage, and Firmness are the heart-mind of Heaven and Earth. Humans receive this heart-mind as their heart-mind. Before manifestation has taken place, the Four Virtues are present, but only humanity embraces all four; therefore, *jen* cherishes and nourishes them completely without any differentiation. It unites and commands all. After manifestation takes place, The Four Beginnings are prominent, but only *jen* penetrates all four; therefore, commiseration operates everywhere and goes through everything. There is nothing it does not penetrate. *Jen* is inborn and is called nature. As nature, *jen* is the principle of love. But when it is activated, it becomes feeling, which is love. In this respect, *jen* is substance and function. Collectively speaking, the state before manifestation is substance. However, separately speaking, the state after manifestation is function. The former is called *jen* and the latter is called commiseration. In addition, impartiality is the way personally to realize humanity, as in the saying, "To master oneself and return to propriety is humanity," for impartiality leads to humanity, and humanity leads to love.[116]

Throughout this process, *ch'eng* is the beginning and the end. That is to say, to be human is to be sincere in your nature that is received from Heaven and Earth. In the beginning, the essence of human nature is the nature of Heaven and Earth. However, due to *ch'i*, physical nature emerges. Although it is not necessarily evil, it is precarious and liable to make mistakes. In order to transform the physical nature into the original nature of Heaven and Earth, humans need *ch'eng* as a human normative moral principle and the self-realization of the norms of human excellence. When one reaches to the perfectly true and real without an iota of insincerity, there is *ch'eng* as well as *jen*. Then one will be called a sage. This is also what we call the resolution of human estrangement.

Notes

1. Wing-tsit Chan, "The Evolution of the Confucian Concept *Jen*," in *Neo-Confucianism, Etc.: Essays by Wing-tsit Chan*, ed. Charles K. H. Chen, (Hanover, NH: Oriental Society, 1969), 1-2.

2. Xinzhong Yao, *Confucianism and Christianity: A Comparative Study of Jen and Agape*, (Brighton, UK: Sussex Academic Press, 1996), 69.

3. Chan, "The Evolution of the Confucian Concept *Jen*," 2.

4. Xinzhong Yao, *Confucianism and Christianity: A Comparative Study of Jen and Agape*, 69.

5. Chan, "The Evolution of the Confucian Concept *Jen*," 2.

6. Ibid., 6.

7. The Golden Rule of Confucius is "do not do to others what you do not want others to do to you." It is in the *Doctrine of the Mean* ch. 13, the *Analects* 12:2; 15:23. See Chan "The Evolution of the Confucian Concept *Jen*," 7.

8. Chan, "The Evolution of the Confucian Concept *Jen*," 8.

9. For Mo Tzu, love is universal without any distinctions. Therefore, he calls it *chien-ai* (universal love). See Chan, *A Source Book of Chinese Philosophy*, 211-213.

10. Chan, "The Evolution of the Confucian Concept *Jen*," 11.

11. Ibid.

12. Chan, *A Source Book of Chinese Philosophy*, 65.

13. Ibid., 58.

14. Ibid., 74.

15. Xinzhong Yao, *Confucianism and Christianity: A Comparative Study of Jen and Agape*, 111.

16. Ibid., 111-2.

17. Chan, *A Source Book of Chinese Philosophy*, 454.

18. Chan, "The Evolution of the Confucian Concept *Jen*," 13.

19. Chan, *A Source Book of Chinese Philosophy*, 479.

20. Chan, "The Evolution of the Confucian Concept *Jen*," 24.

21. Ibid., 25.

22. Chan, *A Source Book of Chinese Philosophy*, 497. Also Chan, "The Evolution of the Confucian Concept *Jen*," 16.

23. Chan, "The Evolution of the Confucian Concept *Jen*," 19.

24. Ibid., 27.

25. Chan, *A Source Book of Chinese Philosophy*, 539. Also Chan, *Chu Hsi: Life and Thought*, 119-120.

26. Chan, *A Source Book of Chinese Philosophy*, 560.

27. Chan, *Chu Hsi: Life and Thought*, 119.

28. Chan, *A Source Book of Chinese Philosophy*, 559.

29. Ibid.

30. Chan, "The Evolution of the Confucian Concept *Jen*," 26.

31. Chan, 宋明理學之概念與歷史 [The Concept and History of the School of Principle in Sung and Ming], 55.

32. Mou Tsung-san argues that Chu Hsi finishes the final draft of *A Treatise on Jen* after he was forty-three years old. However, Wing-tsit Chan disagrees with Mou. Chan avers that the final draft was finished when Chu Hsi was forty-two. See Mou Tsung-san, 心體與性體 [Substance of the mind and substance of nature], vol. 3, (Taipei: Cheng-chung Book Co., 1969), 229; and also Wing-tsit Chan, *Chu Hsi: New Studies*, (Honolulu: University of Hawaii Press, 1989), 156-7.

33. Chan, *Chu Hsi: New Studies*, 153.

34. Chan, *A Source Book of Chinese Philosophy*, 593.

35. Ibid., 593-4.

36. These two phrases are used more than ten times in his commentary on the *Analests* and the *Book of Mencius*, and many places in the *Yü-lei,* such as chapter 19. See Chan, *Chu Hsi: New Studies*, 157.

37. See Chan, *Chu Hsi: New Studies*, 157-9.

38. Hoyt C. Tillman, *Confucian Discourse and Chu Hsi's Ascendancy*, (Honolulu: University of Hawaii Press, 1992), 72-73.

39. Sato Hitoshi, "Chu Hsi's 'Treatise on Jen'," in *Chu Hsi and Neo-Confucianism*, ed. Wing-tsit Chan, (Honolulu: University of Hawaii Press, 1986), 219.

40. Ibid.

41. Hoyt C. Tillman, *Confucian Discourse and Chu Hsi's Ascendancy*, 75.

42. Chan, *Chu Hsi: New Studies*, 159.

43. Chan, *A Source Book of Chinese Philosophy*, 560.

44. Donald J. Munro, *Images of Human Nature: A Sung Portrait*, (Princeton: Princeton University Press, 1988), 121.

45. Ch'en Ch'un, *Neo-Confucian Terms Explained*, 71.

46. Chan, *A Source Book of Chinese Philosophy*, 54.

47. Ibid., 594.

48. *Yü-lei*, ch. 20, sec. 95, 465. See also Chan, *Chu Hsi: New Studies*, 159.

49. *Yü-lei*, ch. 20, sec. 103, 466.

50. *Yü-lei*, ch. 20, sec. 102, 466. See also Chan, *Chu Hsi: New Studies*, 159.

51. *Yü-lei*, ch. 20, sec. 104, 466.

52. *Yü-lei*, ch. 25, sec 23, 606.

53. *Yü-lei*, ch. 25, sec. 22, 606. See also Chan, *Chu Hsi: New Studies*, 160.

54. Chan, *A Source Book of Chinese Philosophy*, 594.

55. Ibid.

56. Chan, *Chu Hsi: New Studies*, 161.

57. Ch'en Ch'un, *Neo-Confucian Terms Explained*, 75-6.

58. *Yü-lei*, ch. 20, sec. 87, 464. See also Chan, *Chu Hsi: New Studies*, 161.

59. *Yü-lei*, ch. 20, sec. 88, 464.

60. Ch'en Ch'un, *Neo-Confucian Terms Explained*, 71.

61. *Yü-lei*, ch. 20, sec. 89, 464.

62. *Yü-lei*, ch. 20, sec.127, 475. See also Chan, *Chu Hsi: New Studies*, 161.

63. Donald J. Munro, *Images of Human Nature: A Sung Portrait*, 124.

64. Hoyt C. Tillman, *Confucian Discourse and Chu Hsi's Ascendancy*, 76.

65. *Yü-lei*, ch. 20, sec. 87, 464

66. Ch'en Ch'un, *Neo-Confucian Terms Explained*, 74.

67. *Yü-lei*, ch. 20, sec. 90, 464.

68. *Yü-lei*, ch. 20, sec. 93, 465. See also Chan, *Chu Hsi: New Studies*, 163.

69. *Yü-lei*, ch. 20, sec. 93, 465.

70. Ch'en Ch'un, *Neo-Confucian Terms Explained*, 71.

71. Ibid., 70.

72. Chan, *Chu Hsi: New Studies*, 163.

73. Ch'en Ch'un, *Neo-Confucian Terms Explained*, 77.

74. Chan, *A Source Book of Chinese Philosophy*, 594.

75. *Yü-lei*, ch. 20, sec. 124, 474. See also Chan, *Chu Hsi: New Studies*, 163.

76. Chan, *Chu Hsi: New Studies*, 164. Also *Yü-lei*, ch. 20, sec.97, 465.

77. *Yü-lei*, ch. 20, sec. 99, 465.

78. Ch'en Ch'un, *Neo-Confucian Terms Explained*, 84.

79. Chan, *Chu Hsi: New Studies*, 164.

80. *Yü-lei*, ch. 20, sec. 103, 466.

81. Ch'en Ch'un, *Neo-Confucian Terms Explained*, 70.

82. *Yü-lei*, ch. 20, sec. 103, 466.

83. Ch'en Ch'un, *Neo-Confucian Terms Explained*, 70.

84. *Yü-lei*, ch. 20, sec. 104, 466.

85. Ch'en Ch'un, *Neo-Confucian Terms Explained*, 84.

86. Chan, *Chu Hsi: New Studies*, 165.

87. *Yü-lei*, ch. 20, sec. 111, 470.

88. Chan, "The Evolution of the Confucian Concept *Jen*," 31.

89. Berthrong, *All Under Heaven*, 87.

90. Ibid.

91. Berthrong, "Master Chu's Self-Realization: The Role of *Ch'eng*," *Philosophy East and West*, vol. 43, no. 1 (January) 1993: 43.

92. *Yü-lie*, ch. 6, sec. 26-27, 102.

93. Berthrong, "Master Chu's Self-Realization: The Role of *Ch'eng*," 45-6.

94. Ch'en Ch'un, *Neo-Confucian Terms Explained*, 98-9.

95. *Yü-lei*, ch. 6, sec. 29, 102-3. See also Berthrong, "Master Chu's Self-Realization: The Role of *Ch'eng*," 46.

96. Berthrong, "Master Chu's Self-Realization: The Role of *Ch'eng*," 46.

97. Ch'en Ch'un, *Neo-Confucian Terms Explained*, 99.

98. *Yü-lei*, ch. 6, sec. 33, 103. See also Berthrong, "Master Chu's Self-Realization: The Role of *Ch'eng*," 46.

99. John Berthrong, "Chu Hsi's Ethics: *Jen* and *Ch'eng*," *Journal of Chinese Philosophy*, 14 (1987):169.

100. Ch'en Ch'un, *Neo-Confucian Terms Explained*, 99.

101. *Yü-lei*, ch. 6, sec. 35, 103.

102. Ch'en Ch'un, *Neo-Confucian Terms Explained*, 100.

103. *Yü-lei*, ch. 6, sec. 36, 103.

104. *Yü-lei*, ch. 6, sec. 37, 103. See also Berthrong, "Master Chu's Self-Realization: The Role of *Ch'eng*," 47.

105. Berthrong, "Master Chu's Self-Realization: The Role of *Ch'eng*," 47.

106. Ch'en Ch'un, *Neo-Confucian Terms Explained*, 99.

107. Ibid., 87.

108. Berthrong, "Master Chu's Self-Realization: The Role of *Ch'eng*," 47.

109. Ch'en Ch'un, *Neo-Confucian Terms Explained*, 98.

110. Ibid., 99.

111. Ibid.

112. Ibid.

113. Berthrong, "Master Chu's Self-Realization: The Role of *Ch'eng*," 49.

114. *Yü-lei*, ch. 6, sec. 39, 104.

115. Berthrong, "Chu Hsi's Ethics: *Jen* and *Ch'eng*" 171.

116. Chan, *Chu Hsi: New Studies*, 281. Here Wing-tsit Chan translates the Diagram into English and the author is describing it in a written form.

PART THREE
A Confucian-Christian Dialogue

After describing the thought of Paul Tillich and Chu Hsi in the previous two parts, we now come to a dialogue between two different systems of thought. In the ninth chapter, the methodology of this comparative study will be discussed. Three categories, namely unity, activity, and reunification, will be developed for the sake of comparison. Then in the following three chapters, I will analyze the similarities as well as differences between Chu Hsi's and Tillich's views on unity, activity, and reunification. Unity is the fundamental structure of the way human beings are and behave. Activity is understood as the way human beings are activated from their ontological structure and this activity leads to their existential estrangement. Reunification means reuniting the human with their ground of being, with others, and even with themselves.

CHAPTER NINE
Methodology

The comparative theological method employed here is derived from a close hermeneutical reading of Tillich. Based on Tillich's systematic theology, three vague comparative terms are suggested for the task of comparison, namely, unity, activity, and reunification. Although these three comparative categories are generated from the fertile matrix of Tillich's thought, they are designed to deal with a problem and its resolution common to Chu's thought as well.

Generally speaking, categories are the common nature of things and the formal representations of them. A vague category is an abstract category, often suitable for the comparison of more specific terms. Whenever a vague category applies to a thing, it needs further specifications. The function of a vague category, then, is to provide a context in which different things with different meanings in different cultural contexts might be compared.

Unity as the first category is the fundamental structure of the whole human reality. Activity as the second category is understood as the fact that once human beings are activated or move out from their statically fundamental structure, their original nature will be distorted and selfishness will emerge. Reunification, the third category, does not mean that humans return to where they were before. Once humans are dislodged from their statically ontological structure, there is no way they can return to where they were before being activated. Reunification means to overcome human estrangement so as to reunite human reality as a whole.

Needless to say, the presuppositions of traditional Western metaphysical speculation, beginning from Plato and Aristotle, through the medieval world into the Enlightenment, are quite different from those of classical Chinese thinking. From a Confucian perspective, Chung-ying Cheng provides an elucidation of these cultural orientations by suggesting that the basic orientations of Chinese thought is to harmonize human experience with human thinking, whereas the goal of Western thought is to overcome human experience by human rationalistic thinking.[1] In Western philosophy, two modes of origination and orientation are rational rationalization and divine transcendentalization. According to Cheng, "rationalization is the process of achieving rational knowledge of reality and performing rational action according to this rational knowledge of reality."[2] Thus, rational rationalization is "to make rationalization an exclusive ideal and goal in all aspects of life and therefore to make reason and rationality a systematic pursuit and absolute value."[3] Therefore, rational rationalization can be "regarded as a radical development of reason and rationality."[4] Moreover, divine transcendentalization is to look "for a transcendent subject and object as ultimate goal or source of values. The transcendent subject or object is conceived as qualitatively different from the mundane world and yet is the ultimate cause or source of meaning and value in things in the world."[5]

In contrast with Western philosophical orientations, Chinese philosophical orientations emphasize naturalization and human immanentization. According to Cheng, "naturalization presents a process of harmonization, balancing, and totalization of elements in the world;"[6] it is a process of transforming and interpreting what is transcendent and external into what is immanent and internal. In this process, Heaven, Earth, and humans are regarded as united in terms of their essential natures. Thus, naturalization provides "a naturalistic mode of thinking and represents a naturalistic form of experience."[7] In addition, human immanentization means that there are "the inherent source and resources of creation and creativity in the nature of human beings as well as in the nature of the world for the meaningful fulfillment of human life and for the valid explanation and justification of existence and value of the world."[8] In other words, the nature of human beings and the world can be treated as "the immanent source and resources of existence and the value of humanity or the world."[9]

From these orientations, Chinese thought has developed: 1) naturalization in the *Book of Change* and *the Tao Te Ching*, 2) humanization in classical Confucianism, and 3) the interplay of naturalization and humanization in Neo-Confucianism. In Western thought, there are: 1) rationalization in Greek philosophy, 2) transcendalization in Judeo-Christianity, and 3) the interplay of rationalization and transcendentalization in modern science and rationalistic philosophy.[10] Although these descriptions may be too general, they still help us to perceive how Chinese thinking is incommensurable with most speculative thinking in the West

In this respect, David L Hall and Roger T. Ames warn us that there is no way to understand the Chinese mode of thinking by means of the exclusive use of Western concepts or vice versa. Each cultural tradition has its historical continuity.[11] In other words, we cannot translate Chinese concepts from the Western perspective exclusively or vice versa. Otherwise, the translation will be like Ludwig Wittgenstein's Duck-Rabbit figure. That is, the Chinese draws a duck, but the Westerner sees it as a rabbit. If this is the case, how can we do a comparative work of two different cultural traditions? In answering this question, Alasdair MacIntyre argues that in order to do comparative work, we have to understand our own standpoint from both a practical and a theoretical perspective. Hence, there is no neutral or independent standpoint in a comparative work.

From MacIntyre's argument, we can deduce three ways of comparing Confucianism with Christianity. We may compare Confucianism and Christianity from a Confucian standpoint, or from a Christian standpoint; or we may compare them from the third totally different standpoint, such as from the Buddhist or Taoist standpoint. But we cannot do any comparative work without the context of a specific point of view.[12] Therefore, the comparative theological method employed here starts from a close hermeneutical reading of Tillich so as to derive three vague comparative categories for the task of comparison, namely unity, activity, and reunification.

In regard to comparative categories, Robert C Neville provides an insightful theory that "fundamental comparative categories must be elements of a responsible system of abstractions."[13] Neville argues that there are three features of the abstract metaphysical categories. First, categories must be "logically formed so that their consistency, coherence, and possible exemplifications are apparent."[14] Second, each category must be "dialectically distinguished from its logical alternative."[15] That is to say, each category must be different from other categories of the system. Basically, these two features are the Cartesian clarity and distinctness rules of metaphysical systems. Third, categories must be related to the concrete items that exemplify them.[16] Regarding these three features, Neville elucidates two kinds of abstractions, namely, general and vague.[17] What he means by a general abstraction is that "it applies immediately to its instances without any further definition."[18] For instance, due to the fact that every human being is mortal Socrates is mortal. On the contrary, a logically vague abstraction is such that it "cannot be applied to the subject matter without intermediate specifications."[19] For instance, the category of human being is vague unless more specific notions of human nature, such as soul, mind, body, and so forth, are used as specification. Further, specifications, such as soul, mind, and body, also need further specification. In this respect, "no categories apply to a concrete person except by assuming specifications."[20] Thus, in regard to a comparison between two different religious traditions, vague categories will be very useful because of their generality and ability to cluster similar insights.

Generally speaking, categories are not only the common nature of things, but also the formal representations of them. They can be possibly realized in actual things. "They relate to one another horizontally as interconnected, and vertically as vaguer and more specific."[21] Moreover, the vagueness of the category, for Neville, is "the category does not dictate the law of excluded middle to its potential specifications."[22] As a vague category of human being, it does not determine anything without a further specification. In this sense, not only does the human being need an intermediate category to specify it, but it also "tolerates all sorts of relations among the categories that are candidates of specifications."[23] Even those intermediate categories may not be determinate or commensurate with one another. In addition, the function of a vague category "is to provide a context in which different things, with different self-expressions, might be compared."[24] To formulate a vague category is to enhance one's language and expand one's synoptic vision in order to compare all the specifications with other metaphysical systems. Therefore, the fundamental comparative categories are "purified and abstracted so that they perhaps can be seen to represent other traditions."[25] In other words, they are logically vague so that they can be specified by more than one tradition. Thus, not only can we find real resemblances in two different metaphysical traditions, but also we can stipulate some clear differences between certain ideas of that seem to resemble each other only superficially.

The three comparative categories of unity, activity, and reunification, although generated from the fertile matrix of Tillich's thought, are directed towards the hermeneutic reading of the problem of human nature and not the technical details of Tillich's own answer to the question of general religious ontology and human finitude. Thus, we are able to compare Tillich's view on human nature with Chu's analogous Neo-Confucian formulation of the human predicament based on these vague comparative categories.[26]

By developing three vague comparative theological categories, namely, unity, activity, and reunification, this study suggests that, although these two great thinkers came from two radically different religious traditions and cultures, Chu and Tillich articulated similar views of the unity of human reality and the problem of human existence. Furthermore, they proposed remarkably parallel strategies to resolve the tensions of finite human existence in searching for a reunification of human nature with its root in divine reality.

The first category is unity. It is the fundamental structure of the whole human reality. In other words, there is essentially order instead of chaos. In this respect, every particular thing has its own place and role in relation to the others within this structure. With these understandings, we can argue that both Chu Hsi and Tillich have a similar view on the unity of the whole human reality. The fundamental categories of Chu Hsi and Tillich are *principle* and *being* respectively. Both *principle* and *being* are delineated as the common structure and common ground of the human reality. They penetrate into all things and are what things emerge from. In the fundamental structure, there are five aspects by means of which Chu Hsi's and Tillich's thought resemble one another.

First, both Chu Hsi and Tillich agree that humans are inter-related with the world, and the objective world cannot be self-sufficient because it is always a projection or construct of the self. In this respect, human self and the world are interrelated. One cannot exist without the other. Second, what makes humans different from the other things is the source they share. For Chu Hsi, the source is the heart-mind, whereas for Tillich, it is human reason. Both the heart-mind and reason enable humans to grasp and shape reality. Both control the whole human being and have the characteristic of transcendence.

Third, humans are both individual and communal or social. To be an individual person is to be a communal person and to participate in the objective world. Fourth, humans are creative beings due to their vitality. As an individual with creative power, a human being can be defined as a free being. But, fifth, humans are not absolutely free in the sense that they are bounded by their destiny. They are bounded by their conditions in the self-world structure. Furthermore, although Chu Hsi's religiosity is humanistic and naturalistic while Tillich's religiosity is theistic, both Chu Hsi and Tillich agree that humans can experience the Transcendent because of their capacity for self-transcendence.

The second category, activity, is understood such that once human beings are differentiated from their statically fundamental structure, their original nature will be distorted and selfishness will emerge. By means of the category of activity, we indicate that, on the one hand, although both Chu Hsi and Tillich agree that human original nature is good, it is merely human potential nature. The human original nature is prior to the actualization of human beings and refers to the nature that precedes actual existence. On the other hand, both Chu Hsi and Tillich agree that once humans actualize their nature in existence, their original nature then will be distorted. After humans have broken with their original status of their fundamental structure, the perversion of the principle in human life will occur. If the principle of human fundamental structure is violated, then human desires will be uncontrollable. Selfishness will emerge and prevent humans from doing what they ought to do.

Furthermore, both Chu Hsi and Tillich affirm that human distortion is the passage from potentiality to actuality. Once human nature has abandoned the primal unity of human essential reality, humans are estranged from their ground, others, and even themselves. In this respect, humans fall into the existential distortion because of the very nature of the self. The fall is a universal fact of our humanity, but also a personal act for us. Thus, human existential estrangement is not necessary but it is inevitable. Following this concept of human distortion, we finally contend that both Chu Hsi and Tillich agree that selfishness or sin is motiveless because it is the problem of human existence, and humans have no motive for being selfish. In other words, the distortion from the original nature to the existential nature of human beings is an ontological, not a moral, issue.

The third category is reunification. It is the resolution of actual human existential distortion. Reunification means sanctification in the Christian sense, or humanization in the Confucian sense. In both traditions, the way to resolve the human existential problem is to return to what humans ought to be. Reunification then means to overcome the distortion of finite actualization by reunifying the whole human reality. That is to say, humans are reunited with what they are estranged from, namely, the ground of their being, others, and even themselves. By employing the category of reunification, we argue that both Chu Hsi's Confucian *jen* and Tillich's Christian love are the resolution of the concrete human existential problem. Both *jen* and love are similar in the sense that they are regarded as the principle and the drive toward the unity of the whole human reality, the restoration of what humans truly ought to be.

Both Chu Hsi and Tillich provide innovative meanings for their categories, *jen* and love respectively. Traditionally, Confucianism regards *jen* as one of the cardinal virtues and Christianity regards love as an emotional and ethical concept. However, both Chu Hsi's *jen* and Tillich's love are not merely understood ethically, but also in ontologically. They are the principle and the drive. Vertically speaking, Chu Hsi's *jen* and Tillich's love are the source and path for humans to reunite with their ground of being. That is to say, both of them have the ontological dimension toward the Transcendent, although the understandings of the Transcendent in the thought of Chu Hsi and of Tillich are radically different.

In the ethical dimension, both *jen* and love embrace all other forms of virtue or of love respectively, and are their ultimate criteria. *Jen* brings the other forms of virtue into their completeness, whereas love as *agape* fulfils the other forms of love. Moreover, both *jen* and love have the power to overcome alienation between humans. Hence, *jen* has *ch'eng* as self-actualization and love needs justice to direct their work. Both *jen* and love are the dynamic resolution of human estrangement, and function as a unifying force. They are no longer the principle, but the active force. Thus, *jen* needs *ch'eng* as self-actualization and love needs faith to sustain their notions of the dynamic resolution of the problem of human existence. In fact, both *jen*/*ch'eng* and love/faith are but the two sides of the same coin.

In the following three chapters, I analyze similarities within differences between Chu Hsi's and Tillich's views on these three comparative vague categories.

Notes

1. Some other Confucian scholars, such as Tu Wei-ming and Liu Shu-hsien, have views similar to Cheng's. See Tu Wei-ming, *Confucian Thought: Selfhood as Creative Transformation*, (Albany: State University of New York, 1985); see also Shu-hsien Liu, "Toward a New Relation Between Humanity and Nature: Reconstructing," *Zygon*, vol. 24, no. 4 (December 1989): 457-468.

2. Chung-ying Cheng, *New Dimensions of Confucian and Neo-Confucian Philosophy*, (Albany: State University of New York Press, 1991), 5.

3. Ibid.

4. Ibid.

5. Ibid., 8.

6. Ibid., 11.

7. Ibid., 13.

8. Ibid., 16.

9. Ibid., 17.

10. Ibid., 5.

11. David L. Hall and Roger T. Ames, *Thinking Through Confucius* (Albany: State University of New York Press, 1987), 99; see also David L. Hall and Roger T. Ames, *Anticipating China*, (Albany: State University of New York Press, 1995).

12. Alasdair MacIntyre, "Incommensurability, Truth, and the Virtues," in *Culture and Modernity: East-West Philosophic Perspectives*, ed. Eliot Deutsch, (Honolulu: University of Hawaii Press, 1991), 121.

13. Robert C. Neville, *Behind the Masks of God: An Essay Toward Comparative Theology,* (Albany: State University of New York Press, 1991), 159.

14. Ibid., 160.

15. Ibid.

16. Ibid.

17. Originally, the distinction between general and vague abstractions is illustrated by Charles Peirce. See Robert C. Neville, *Behind the Masks of God*, 160. And also Robert C. Neville, *Normative Cultures*, (Albany: State University of New York Press, 1995), 62.

18. Neville, *Behind the Masks of God*, 160.

19. Neville, *Normative Cultures*, 62.

20. Ibid.

21. Ibid., 64.

22. Ibid., 62.

23. Ibid., 63.

24. Ibid., 64.

25. Neville, *Behind the Masks of God*, 167.

26. In his *Escape from Predicament*, Thomas A. Metzger has done a good analysis of the Neo-Confuian predicament. See Thomas A. Metzger, *Escape from Predicament: Neo-Confucianism and China'Evolving Political Culture*, (New York: Columbia University Press, 1977)

CHAPTER TEN
Unity

Unity is the fundamental structure of the whole human reality. The human reality has its order, and within this order, every particular thing has its own place and role in relation to the others.[1] In this fundamental structure, humans are not merely in relation to the other things immanently, but also to the ground of the whole reality transcendently. That is to say, the whole human reality is the order of things in which things are not merely in relation to themselves, but also to the foundation or basis of this order, that is, the infinite ground of this structure. Since all things have their own places and roles in relationship, the whole reality is united in a harmonious state. Thus, unity is understood as the essential structure of the whole. In this structure, what are the ontological elements of human beings? What are the proper relations of humans to their ground, to the others, and even to themselves? What are the categories that Tillich or Chu Hsi uses to delineate this unity? In the following section, we compare Chu Hsi's and Tillich's ideas about this fundamental structure.

The Fundamental Categories: Being and Principle

Since Chu Hsi and Paul Tillich are from two radically different traditions, they are indeed different in their systems of thinking. And yet they have similar ideas of unity, that is, the fundamental structure of the whole human reality. For Tillich, being is a category that penetrates below the distinction of object and subject, of matter and spirit, and of inorganic reality and organic and psychological reality. Therefore, being refers to the common structure and the common ground of subjects and objects, world and self. This definition of being is quite different from the general Western definition of being as "an abstraction from the varied objects of our sensory experience and so of our knowledge."[2]

Similarly, *li* as principle, for Chu Hsi, is a category that refers to "the Way, which exists before physical form [and is without it] and is the root from which all things are produced."[3] In addition, it is "incorporeal, one, eternal and unchanging, uniform, constituting the essence of things, indestructible, the reason for creation, and always good."[4] As Tillich's being, principle penetrates into all things. But principle is also prior to everything, at least in analysis, and is the root from which all things are produced. All things partake of principle; everything, whether it is living or non-living, natural or artificial, has been patterned by principle.

In order to understand unity, Tillich uses being as the fundamental category, while Chu Hsi uses the category of principle. Both of these categories are used to delineate fundamental unity. They penetrate into all things and are what things emerge from. In this respect, everything has its own being as well as principle. Here Chu Hsi and Tillich share similar fundamental categories of unity. So we turn to the resemblance of the ontological structure in Chu Hsi's and in Tillich's thought.

The Ontological Structure

Self-World

Both Tillich and Chu Hsi have a similar view that humans have to be defined in relation to the world. The isolated self does not really help in defining what a human being is. For Tillich, being is the fundamental category of the unity of the human reality and penetrates into all things. Since everything has its own being, humans then also have their own being. Objectively, humans can know about a tree, for instance, but they cannot know what it means to be a tree.[5] By the same token, humans can know what it means to be humans because they experience their being from the inside. In this experience, humans are aware not only of themselves but also of what they are separated from. In this regard, they realize the structure of human reality, the relation of self and world. In other words, in their experience of their own being, humans realize that being manifests its characters around us.[6] In this regard, humans can experience themselves as having a world to which they belong. When one becomes conscious of the self, one simultaneously becomes aware of something other than the self. To be a self means to be separated from everything else. By the same token, however, one's self is aware that a self belongs to that from which it looks. That is to say, "every self has an environment in which it lives, and ego-self has a world which it lives."[7]

Correspondingly, Chu Hsi also has this self-world structure. According to him, principle is one, but its manifestations are many. In order to illustrate this concept, Chu Hsi uses the analogy of the moon and its beams. There is only one moon, as there is only one principle. When moonlight scatters upon the myriad things, it produces myriad reflections. Similarly, everything has a principle that makes it what it is, and that represents the same principle, namely, the ontological principle. However, when principle is diversified into different types and orders of things, it can manifest itself in the order, structure, and law of things, the ordering and analytical-synthetic activities of heart-mind, the ideas and concepts in heart-mind, the design of artifacts, and the conduct-pattern of moral conduct and correct social behavior.[8] To understand one's self is to understand the structure of one's reality. Not only does everything and every person share the same ontological principle in this structure, but also each of them is a part of the whole ontological structure.

Furthermore, in this self-world structure, the objective world cannot be self-sufficient because it is always a projection or construction of the self.[9] Tillich argues that humans grasp and shape their environment into a world. Hence, "world-consciousness is possible only on the basis of a fully developed self-consciousness."[10] That is to say, humans know the structure of the objective world through the power, the capacities, and the intentions of human reason. In this respect, in the self-world structure, the objective world is known because the self grasps the order of the world and then shapes the world. This is due to self-transcendence, self-consciousness, and then world-consciousness.[11]

In Chu Hsi's thought, what is meant by nature does not merely indicate human nature, but also the nature of things. Nature consists of principles, which is created by Heaven. When principle dwells in humans, it becomes human nature; when principle dwells in things, it becomes the nature of things. Thus, the natures of humans and things are originally the same because they receive the same principle from Heaven, but due to different vital forces (*ch'i*), their natures are different. Therefore, in order to understand the world, the self has to understand the principle of things. That is what Chu Hsi explains as "investigation of things" in the *Great Learning*. After investigating the principle of things, humans can know the ultimate principle, and then they can shape the ontological reality of the world.

In their ideas of the fundamental structure, Chu Hsi and Tillich affirm that humans cannot be considered as isolated selves. In Tillich's view, the self is empty without correlation with its world. And in Chu Hsi's view, the self is only part of the whole fundamental structure. However, although both of them affirm the self-other structure as the primordial structure, they still agree that the human self is different from others. According to Tillich, humans still are fully developed and completely centered selves and possesses themselves in the form of self-consciousness.[12] That is to say, in this inseparable relationship between self and others, there is still the individual self and also others. They are not intermingled with each other. In Chu Hsi's thought, the difference between the individual self and others is due to the different degrees of purity of vital force (*ch'i*) that they have as well as their specific principle. The vital force of animals is different from that of humans. Due to different vital forces, there are the different shapes and forms of the myriad things. Although the myriad things have the same ontological principle, they still have their uniqueness because of the different degrees of purity of vital force in different things.

Reason and Heart-Mind

What makes humans different from others is the source they possess. Reason for Tillich is the source of humanity. It is a key concept in Tillich's thought. As Tillich says, "reason makes the self a self, namely, a centered structure; and reason makes the world a world, namely, a structured whole."[13] Although being is the fundamental category of the unity of the whole reality, it would be chaos without reason. Thus, reason is the dynamic source that enables humans to grasp and shape reality.

However, in Chu Hsi's thought, the source is not reason but the heart-mind. Mencius has depicted this heart-mind as the greatest part of humanity. The heart-mind is the main difference between humans and things and also the source of bodily movements, emotions, and feelings.

What do reason and the heart-mind have in common? First, both of them are the source of humanity and enable human beings to grasp and shape reality. In other words, they are the dynamic source of humanity. Reason links us to the world. In this linkage, the self-world structure becomes the subject-object structure of reason. On the subjective side, the self is a structure of centeredness, while in the objective side, the world is a structured whole, the grasped-and-shaped reality. In grasping and shaping the world as an object, humans are aware of themselves as subjects in a world of objects.

According to Chu Hsi, the heart-mind is the source of all movement with a creative or generative function. It stores, holds, and manifests principle.[14] Thus, Chung–ying Cheng employs a common tool of contemporary philosophical hermeneutics to argue that the heart-mind needs a pre-understanding of things in order to have a deeper understanding of itself. And due to this deeper understanding of itself, the heart-mind can be further engaged with things and acquire a deeper understanding of things.[15] In other words, the heart-mind has the same ontological principle that the myriad things have. But the activity of the heart-mind "gives rise to knowledge of things and therefore realizes the objective principle of things." That is to say, the activity of the heart-mind grasps and shapes the objective principle of reality.

Second, both reason and the heart-mind act as the commander of the whole human being. Reason is the creative power of human beings that creates, shapes, and reshapes cultural life in all its aspects. Reason characterizes every aspect of any cultural activity that is creative,[16] and reunites the subject and object sides of human reality. In this respect, reason reunites the participation and detachment of the objective world. Thus, in order to understand the world, humans cannot only detach from the objective world, but also participate in the world. Without the participation in the objective world, humans can never know the objective world. Reason here presents an important role to drive us toward a deep level of unity between subject and object.[17]

Correspondingly, the heart-mind, for Chu Hsi, means the master of the body.[18] That is to say, the heart-mind is the source of the movement of the four limbs and the feelings of human desires, such as being hungry and thirsty. In addition, the heart-mind is the master of the myriad things. Since the heart-mind embraces all principle, people then can enter into all things in the world if they enlarge their heart-mind. In other words, people can know the world if they participate in the world through investigating things. In addition, the heart-mind commands human nature and feelings, and includes both of them. For nature is the principle of the heart-mind while feelings are the function of the heart-mind.

Finally, both reason and the heart-mind have the characteristic of transcendence. For Tillich, in relation to the world, humans realize that not only does the self belong to and participate in the world, but also it can transcend the world. By grasping and shaping its reality, the self is not bounded by reality, and even transcends it in accordance with universal norms and ideas. As the creative power of humans, reason provides humans with the ability to transcend all environments.

In Chu Hsi's thought, nature is principle, while the heart-mind is that which stocks, holds, implements and manifests principle.[19] However, the heart-mind is not principle; rather, it is vital force (*ch'i*), and even the refined vital force. Not only does the heart-mind unite the different faculties of humans, but also links all things together in the unity of the whole reality. Most importantly, the heart-mind unites principle and vital force within itself. Since the heart-mind stores, holds, and manifests principle, if it is activated, it transcends itself and integrates all principles together. The heart-mind is always in a state of consciousness. As the refined vital force, the heart-mind is the power of consciousness of other things.

Even though both the heart-mind and reason are similar in several ways, it is worth noting that both of them basically represent two different streams of thought. In Tillich's thought, reason is the foundation of all meaning and the source of principles and norms pointing to goods and goals in the Western tradition from Plato to Hegel.[20] Tillich makes the distinction between technical reason and ontological reason. Most importantly, in relation to the conception of revelation, he advocates ecstatic reason. According to Tillich, revelation is the depth of reason and the fulfillment of reason, while ecstatic reason is used to depict the receptive side of humans by the experience of ultimate concern. Given that, Tillich's reason is basically theocentric.

On the contrary, Chu Hsi's heart-mind is the most refined aspect of vital force (*ch'i*); and stores, holds, and manifests principle. Before the heart-mind is activated, it is nature; after it is activated, it is feelings. Thus, the heart-mind includes nature and feelings as well as commanding or controlling them. As the most refined aspect of vital force, the heart-mind is the pivotal element of human beings. Unlike Tillich's ecstatic reason, although Heaven endows humans with the heart-mind, the heart-mind is not the receptive side of humans mediated by the experience of ultimate concern. Rather, the heart-mind is the dynamic element of human beings, and embraces all human faculties. It links not only them, but also Heaven, Earth, and humans together. Thus, the heart-mind is anthropocosmic.

Individuality

In the self-world structure, human self and the world are interrelated. One cannot exist without the other. The world is a place in which the self belongs, and is always a projection or construction of the self. If this is the case, what does the individual mean in both Christian and Confucian traditions? How similar is the concept of individuality in the thought of Chu Hsi and Tillich? According to Tillich, "individualization is not a characteristic of a special sphere of beings; it is an ontological element and therefore a quality of everything. It is implied in and constitutive of every being."[21] That is to say, humans have individuality, and so do other things. However, the difference between the individuality of human beings and of other things is that humans can experience their individuality. Human awareness is due to the fact that human beings are completely self-centered. "Centeredness is a quality of individualization"[22] and a universal phenomenon.[23] What makes the centeredness of human beings differs from that of other things is that humans realize "the definiteness of the center, on the one hand, and the amount of content united by it, on the other."[24] Because of their self-centeredness, human beings realize that they are endowed with a more definite center and also are capable of incorporating their environment or world more completely.

Correspondingly, Chu Hsi has the concept of self-centeredness as well. For him, human nature is called principle because it is received from Heaven and is possessed by the self,[25] while the heart-mind stores, holds, and manifests principle. With this understanding, for Chu Hsi, if one can fulfill one's nature, then one can reach an ultimate unity with the principle of Heaven and Earth. Thus, fulfilling one's nature is similar to Tillich's idea of self-centeredness. As Tillich argues, in this process of self-centeredness, humans realize the definiteness of the center. In Chu Hsi's thought this definiteness of the center is clearly the principle received from Heaven. In addition, fulfilling one's nature, one realizes the natures of other persons and things, because all things have the same ultimate principle. In this regard, "to fulfill one's nature is to know in clarity and act in propriety in reference to all aspects of one's nature."[26] In fulfilling one's nature, one knows one's environment or world more completely.

Furthermore, an individual person is also a communal or social person because every individual person participates in this objective world. Participation is then correlative with individualization. People relate to each other in the world. Every individual person is merely a potential person without any relationship to others. Thus, in Tillich's thought, to be an individual is to enter into communion with others. This is the way to avoid being objectified through the dynamic of ego-ego confrontation in the human encounter, and the only process of human growth. In this communion with others, humans realize not only their selfhood, but also their association in the relational structure of their world.

In Chu Hsi's thought, there is no idea that an individual can be defined without a community. The method of the development of the self is never separated from a community. In his commentary on the *Great Learning*, Chu Hsi argues that to investigate the principles of all things that we contact daily is the way to extend human knowledge to the utmost; and human heart-mind is designed to know.[27] Because nature is principle, and the heart-mind is that which stocks, holds, implements, and manifests principle, human beings have to preserve the heart-mind. Otherwise human beings will not be able to investigate principle to the utmost. If humans cannot investigate the principle, then they cannot extend their knowledge to the utmost. That is, they cannot exert their heart-mind to the utmost.[28] In this circular argument, the motion of the heart-mind is from the heart-mind to things and then back to the heart-mind. In this respect, one cannot isolate one's self from the world according to the thought of Chu Hsi. Besides, one has to fully participate in one's environment in order to development oneself. That is to say, for Chu Hsi, individuality is also correlated with participation.

Creativity

Human beings are creative beings. In the second ontological element of Tillich's thought, human beings can experience the polar structure of form and dynamics. What Tillich means by form is that it makes a thing what it is, while dynamics is the potentiality of being, the becoming of being. Tillich relates the polarity of form and dynamics with the polarity of being and nonbeing, and also with the polarity of vitality and intentionality. In this regard, Tillich indicates that vitality is the creative power of humans that pushes them towards new forms. Thus, human vitality is not limited to certain environments, and is open in all directions. This would also be the case for Chu Hsi. For human beings "are not only vital individuality, dynamically realizing themselves as a natural process, but they are spirit, creating in unity with the eternal forms and norms of being."[29]

However, for Tillich human vitality is conditioned by human intentionality. What Tillich means by intentionality is movement towards the fulfillment of existential meaning. In this polar structure of vitality and intentionality, human dynamics or creative vitality is directed. Human vitality is directed and formed, and transcends itself toward meaning. In other words, human creativity is moving towards the fulfillment of meaning in human beings.

Chu Hsi's basic ontological elements are principle and vital force. In human beings, there are nature, heart-mind, and feelings. What principle gives to humans is human nature, whereas the heart-mind and feelings are the manifestation of vital forces. Using the polarity of form and dynamics, nature as principle can be described as form, while heart-mind and feelings can be described as dynamics. Regarding the relation of nature, heart-mind, and feelings, "the dynamics heart-mind mediates the formal side of human nature and the dynamic drive of emotion and passion."[30] As the source of human beings, heart-mind is the director of feelings and nature, while nature is the principle of heart-mind, and feeling is the function of the heart-mind.[31] Since nature is principle in the heart-mind, the heart-mind as vital force is conscious of having principle as nature. This power of consciousness is not only conscious of the human self, but also of other things. Thus, this consciousness directs human life towards reunion with Heaven and Earth.

Similarly, although the heart-mind is the refined vital force and ever active, it does not mean that humans should let their heart-mind be uncontrolled. Therefore, Chu Hsi urges us to preserve our heart-mind. To preserve the heart-mind, one must know the nature. To know nature is to know Heaven.[32] "To know the heart-mind is to know how it acts in the world, to understand its choices, but not to be ultimately bound or constrained by them because the process never ceases nor does creativity ever abate."[33] This heart-mind is always creative and its directive is to know Heaven. In so doing, it masters nature and feelings, that is, "unites and apprehends nature and the emotions."[34]

In order to know Heaven, one has to fulfill one's heart-mind. Through this process, one can then know one's nature and Heaven. For Chu Hsi, the creativity of human beings has both inward and outward dimensions. On the one hand, humans are to extend knowledge by investigating everything; on the other hand, they have to nourish their heart-mind so that they can fulfill their nature. However, in Tillich's thought, the creativity of human beings moves towards unity with the eternal forms and norms of being. That is to say, there is no inward dimension of nourishing the heart-mind. Here, Tillich does not urge us to preserve our reason in order to fulfill our nature.

Destiny

As an individual with creative power, every human being can be defined as a free being. However, humans are not absolutely free since they are bound by their destiny. According to Tillich's third ontological polarity, "freedom in polarity with destiny is [a] structural element which makes existence possible because it transcends the essential necessity of being without destroying it."[35] Indeed, to be human is to have freedom. However, human freedom only exists in polar interdependence with human destiny. For Tillich, human freedom is the human capacity to determine human acts, whereas human destiny is the world in which humans must interact. In this respect, human destiny is the basis of human freedom.

Humans are free to act and have the capacity of transcendence because of their centeredness. And yet due to this centeredness, humans are also constrained by it. This is described as the paradox of self-transcendence. When humans exercise their freedom, they realize that they are predicated on their finiteness. This is what Tillich calls destiny. In order to be human, one will live at a definite place, in a definite time, under definite conditions. That is to say, humans are free but they are also limited by their finitude, or by what conditions them. As Tillich contends, "destiny is not a strange power which determines what shall happen to me. It is myself as given, formed by nature, history, and myself. My destiny is the basis of my freedom; my freedom participates in shaping my destiny."[36]

In Chu Hsi's thought, the understanding of destiny differs from Tillich's meaning. According to Chu Hsi, destiny (*ming*) can mean an order. What is called destiny has an order like "a ruler ordering a person to assume a certain office and delegating him to do certain things."[37] Chu Hsi postulates a new meaning that destiny is ordering someone to do something.[38] Ch'en Ch'un also argues that "*ming* is like an order, an order from a superior or an official order."[39] Thus, *ming* "represents the forceful, ordering aspect of the power of Heaven, Earth and humanity. It is what forces us to make our choices."[40]

Further, Chu Hsi defines destiny in terms of principle and of vital force. Spoken of in terms of vital force, "there is inequality in a greater or lesser amount and in purity or impurity"[41] due to the endowment of humans. According to Thomas A. Metzger, what Chu Hsi's ideas of destiny (*ming*) mean is "what heaven has conferred."[42] First, heaven has conferred the external circumstances of each individual life, that is, the individual's economic position, social status, and longevity.[43] Second, heaven has conferred the internal capacity or talent of each individual to respond to external events.[44] These external circumstances and the internal capacity of each individual are determined by the in particular portion of vital force (*ch'i*). Finally, heaven has conferred true principle to each individual.[45] Spoken of in terms of principle, "what is endowed in humans becomes the nature of humanity, righteousness, propriety, and wisdom."[46] "Both principle and vital force are endowed by Heaven and it is therefore called *ming*."[47] Since principle and vital force are not separated, destiny then can be spoken of either in terms of principle or in terms of vital force. Yet, for Chu Hsi, principle is fundamental. Humans receive destiny from Heaven when they are born. After being born, human destiny is to follow the evolution of human vital force.

In addition, Ch'en Ch'un also defines *ming* as principle. In this respect, "*ming* is clearly identified with human nature, which is the normative aspect of a person in Chu and Ch'en's moral anthropology."[48] Since destiny is principle and nature is also principle, Chu Hsi contends that destiny refers to Heaven whereas nature refers to humans. "Destiny is what Heaven bestows on things that Heaven cannot refrain from doing, and nature is what I have received from this destiny in its totality to be born."[49] In this regard, is Chu Hsi's concept of destiny a form of blind fate? The answer, of course, is no. Many times Chu Hsi stresses the necessity of human effort. There are many places where human effort and destiny or fate are interrelated with each other in the Confucian tradition, for instance in obeying fate, waiting for destiny, establishing destiny, and correcting destiny.[50] What Chu Hsi emphasizes is that destiny is like the emperor ordering a person to take a certain office. The duties of that office are the fate of that person because they can be easy or difficult, and some can be done and some cannot be done.[51] Therefore, human effort is necessary in fulfilling human duties that are assigned by Heaven. Human beings make efforts to comprehend the fate that Heaven has imparted to them in order to fulfill their destiny. Moreover, *ming* "is not merely an element of blind compulsion, but takes on an element of the lure for perfection which is best represented by the life of the sage."[52]

Although Chu Hsi and Tillich have different views of "destiny," they still agree that people are bound by their conditions in the self-world structure. In other words, people have no choice at what place, in what time, under what conditions they are born. Both Tillich and Chu Hsi realize that although human beings are free and have the capacity of transcendence, they are conditioned by their ontological structure because they are finite beings. Human beings have to live at a definite place, in a definite time, and under definite conditions. They have to comprehend their finiteness or their own fates so that they can fully develop their nature and fulfil their destiny. Thus, both Chu Hsi and Tillich agree that, due to their destiny, human beings are given the self, which is formed by nature and history. In the self-world ontological structure, destiny as the condition or limitation of humans is the commonality of the thought of Chu Hsi and Tillich.

Experiencing the Transcendent

After discussing the ontological structure of human beings, we turn to the relation of humans and the Transcendent. Surely, there are divergences between Chu Hsi's and Tillich's concept of religiosity. General speaking, Tillich's religiosity is theistic, while Chu Hsi's is humanistic and naturalistic. Here we will not discuss the concept of their religiosity. Rather, we will deal with the way human beings can experience the Transcendent. In this respect, we realize that for both of them the way people experience the Transcendent is through the human capacity for self-transcendence. To reiterate his concept of being, Tillich argues that being manifests itself in and through all dimensions of our reality. Regarding humanity, being manifests itself in human awareness of human beings from the inside. Thus, being actualizes the meaning of human existence. In other words, humans realize that they are finite beings. They are conscious of their finitude through encountering nonbeing, through encountering infinity, or through both. Only in the relationship between humans and nonbeing, and between humans and the Transcendent can humans understand human finitude.[53]

To be human is to be finite. What finitude means is that our being is limited by nonbeing. Here Tillich indicates dialectical nonbeing (*me on*). Thus, "finitude is the basis of Tillich's assertion of the ontological dependence of the creature upon God."[54] Moreover, humans have the capacity for infinity. Tillich refers to infinity as the dynamic and free self-transcendence of finite being.[55] Humans can transcend their finite state towards their infinitude. Indeed, humans continuously experience their finitude. This infinity in the self-transcendence of humans has two results. "First, infinity becomes the negation of finitude or finite being and thus an expression of dialectical nonbeing."[56] And second, infinity as the unlimited self-transcendence of human finitude indicates that humans are rooted in the Transcendent, or Being-itself, which is beyond the polarity of finitude and infinity. The infinite self-transcendence of humans indicates that humans belong to that which is beyond nonbeing, namely, to being-itself. Not only is infinity the source of the negation of the negative element of finitude, but it indicates the source of the negation of nonbeing, namely, being-itself.[57] With this understanding, the relation of humans to the Transcendent, for Tillich, is through the self-transcendence of humans, namely, infinity. In other words, through human infinitude, humans can experience their dependence or divine ground.

In Chu Hsi's thought there are two kinds of human nature, the nature of Heaven and Earth or original nature, and the nature of vital force and matter or physical nature. The former is the nature endowed by Heaven, while the latter is the natural endowment of vital force. The former can be called incorporeal, while the latter can be called corporeal. Moreover, with respect to Heaven, there are origination, flourishing, advantage, and correctness. Correspondingly, with respect to the original nature of humans, there are humanity, righteousness, propriety, and wisdom.[58] These are the principle of human morality.

In addition, Chu Hsi relates nature to the heart-mind and feelings and develops his innovating concept that the heart-mind controls nature and feelings. Nature as principle is the heart-mind before it is activated, whereas feelings are the heart-mind after it is activated. That is to say, the principles of human morality, humanity, righteousness, propriety, and wisdom, are all rooted in the heart-mind before it is aroused. After being aroused, there are feelings of commiseration, of shame and dislike, of respect and reverence, and of right and wrong. Corresponding to the two natures of humans, there are also two heart-minds, namely, Tao heart-mind and human heart-mind. The former is the principle of Heaven, while the latter is human desires.[59] This does not mean that humans have two heart-minds. Rather, there is one heart-mind with two kinds of perception.

Human nature is principle as endowed by Heaven and called the nature of Heaven and Earth. Also, Tao heart-mind is the heart-mind of Heaven and Earth because it produces things. That is to say, at the time of their birth, humans possess this heart-mind of Heaven and Earth. Moreover, Chu Hsi tries to relate the heart-mind of Heaven and Earth with the heart-mind of humans. Chu Hsi contends that origination, flourishing, advantages, and firmness are the cosmic moral qualities of the heart-mind of Heaven and Earth, whereas humanity, righteousness, propriety, and wisdom are the Four Virtues of humans. As the heart-mind of Heaven and Earth creates things unceasingly, the heart-mind of humans extends love to people and benefits all things.[60] Clearly, the capacity for human self-transcendence is the nature and heart-mind of humans that embraces the principle of Heaven and Earth. In order to comprehend this principle, Chu Hsi urges us to investigate things to the utmost so that we can probe the principles of things and unify knowledge of things. In so doing, we can fulfil our nature and nourish our heart-mind. Only then can we know Heaven. On the one hand, we have to investigate the principles of things outwardly; on the other hand, we have to nourish our heart-mind inwardly. Both of these are ways to exhaust principle and to know Heaven.

Despite the difference between Tillich's theistic view and Chu Hsi's humanistic and naturalistic view of religiosity, both Chu Hsi and Tillich have a similar view in that humans can experience the Transcendent by the innate human capacity of self-transcendence. Through this experience, not only do humans know the Transcendent, but also themselves. In Tillich's thought, one way understand human finitude is to know the relation of human finitude to infinitude. While in Chu Hsi's thought, one must extend knowledge to develop the heart-mind to the utmost, and then one can fulfil one's nature and know Heaven. In this process, knowing Heaven is possible through fulfilling one's nature.

In the fundamental structure of the whole human reality, we realize that both Chu Hsi and Tillich have their fundamental categories for this structure, principle and being respectively. These categories are the common structure and common ground of human reality. They penetrate into all things and are what things emerge from. Thus, both Chu Hsi and Tillich agree that human reality has its essential order. In addition, Chu Hsi's and Tillich's human sources for the ontological structure are heart-mind and reason respectively. Both sources make humans different from other things and enable humans to grasp and shape reality. Moreover, they are the commander of the whole human being and have the characteristic of transcendence. In the self-world, humans are defined in relation to world; the objective world cannot be self-sufficient because it is always a projection or construct of the self. In this respect, the human self and the world are interrelated. One cannot exist without the other. Thus, within this ordered world, every particular thing has its own place and its role in relation to the others.

Moreover, to be an individual person is to be a communal person, to participate in the objective world. Moreover, humans are creative beings due to their vitality. As an individual with creative power, every human being can be defined as a free being. However, on the other hand, humans are not absolutely free in the sense that they are bounded by their destiny. Finally, this ontological structure of the human being includes the experience of the Transcendent. Both Chu Hsi and Tillich have a similar view of experiencing the Transcendent. In this fundamental structure, humans exist not merely in relation to other things immanently, but also in relation to the ground of the whole reality transcendently. Thus, both Chu Hsi and Tillich agree that the whole human reality is the order of things in which things exist not merely in relation to themselves, but also in relation to the foundation or basis of this order, that is, the infinite ground of this structure. The whole reality then is united in a harmonious state. Thus, unity is understood as the essential structure of the whole. All of the above points indicate that Chu Hsi and Tillich have similarities pertaining to the ontological structure of humans even though they come from different cultural worlds.

Notes

1. In their book *Anticipating China*, David L. Hall and Roger T. Ames argue that the idea of Chinese thought concerning the beginning of the universe is chaos and the ordered or harmonious world comes out of chaos. Here in this study, the ordered world refers to the human reality. Unity refers to the whole human reality, not the beginning of the universe. Thus, we have no conflict with the argument of Hall and Ames. See *Anticipating China*, 3-11.

2. Gilkey, *Gilkey on Tillich*, 28.

3. Chan, *A Source Book in Chinese Philosophy*, 636.

4. Chan, *Chu Hsi: Life and Thought*, 111-2.

5. Tillich, *Systematic Theology, vol. 1*, 168-9.

6. Ibid.

7. Ibid., 170.

8. Chung-ying Cheng, "Methodology and Theory of Understanding," 170.

9. Gilkey, *Gilkey on Tillich*, 86.

10. Tillich, *Systematic Theology, vol. 1*, 170.

11. Gilkey, *Gilkey on Tillich*, 87.

12. Tillich, *Systematic Theology,* vol. 1, 169-170.

13. Ibid.,172.

14. *Yü-lei*, ch 16, sec. 51, 515.

15. Chung-ying Cheng, "Methodology and Theory of Understanding," 172.

16. Gilkey, *Gilkey on Tillich*, 36-37.

17. Ibid., 38.

18. As noted already, the concept of the heart-mind as the master of the body comes from Chang Tsai's doctrine that the heart-mind commands human nature and feelings. See the previous section of Chu Hsi's concept of human nature.

19. *Yü-lei*, ch 16, sec. 51, 515.

20. John E. Smith, "The Impact of Tillich's Interpretation of Religion," in *The Thought of Paul Tillich*, eds. James Luther Adams, Wilhelm Pauck, and Roger Lincoln Shinn (San Francisco: Harper & Row, Publishers, 1985), 252.

21. Tillich, *Systematic Theology, vol. 1*, 174-5.

22. Tillich, *Systematic Theology, vol. 3*, 32.

23. Ibid.,34.

24. Ibid., 36.

25. Ch'en Ch'un, *Neo-Confucian Terms Explained*, 46-7.

26. Chung-ying Cheng, *New Dimensions of Confucian and Neo-Confucian Philosophy*, 378.

27. Julia Ching, "Chu Hsi on Personal Cultivation," 285.

28. Chan, *A Source Book in Chinese Philosophy*, 606.

29. Tillich, "The Conception of Man in Existential Philosophy," 206.

30. John Berthrong, *All Under Heaven*, 86.

31. Ch'en Ch'un, *Neo-Confucian Terms Explained*, 60.

32. *Yü-lei*, ch. 60, sec.15, 1424. *Book of Mencius*, 7A:1.

33. John Berthrong, *All Under Heaven*, 93.

34. Chan, *A Source Book in Chinese Philosophy*, 631.

35. Tillich, *Systematic Theology*, vol. 1, 182.

36. Ibid., 184-5.

37. Chan, *Chu His: New Studies*, 213.

38. Ibid., 214.

39. Ch'en Ch'un, *Neo-Confucian Terms Explained*, 37.

40. Berthrong, *All Under Heaven*, 97.

41. Chan, *Chu His: New Studies*, 214.

42. Thomas A. Metzger, *Escape from Predicament: Neo-Confucianism and China's Evolving Political Culture* (New York: Columbia University Press, 1977), 129.

43. Ibid., 129.

44. Ibid.,130.

45. Ibid.

46. Chan, *Chu His: New Studies*, 214.

47. Ibid.

48. Berthrong, *All Under Heaven*, 97.

49. Chan, *Chu His: New Studies*, 216.

50. Ibid., 216-7.

51. Ibid., 217.

52. Berthrong, *All Under Heaven*, 98.

53. Gilkey, *Gilkey on Tillich*, 91.

54. Ferrell, *Logos and Existence*, 55.

55. Tillich, *Systematic Theology*, vol. 1, 190.

56. Ferrell, *Logos and Existence*, 56.

57. Ibid., 57.

58. Chan, *A Source Book of Chinese Philosophy*, 594.

59. *Yü-lei*, ch. 78, sec, 110, 2014.

60. Chan, *A Source Book of Chinese Philosophy*, 594-5.

CHAPTER ELEVEN
Activity

Unity is the essential structure of the whole human reality. Human reality is the order of things in which things exist not merely in relation to themselves, but also in relation to the foundation or basis of this order, that is, the infinite ground of the whole structure. However, once this structure is activated, things may move in different directions. Thus, once human beings are activated from their statically fundamental structure, their original nature will be distorted. In other words, human original nature is good, and yet it is merely human potential nature. It is prior to the actualization of human beings and refers to the nature that precedes actual existence. Once humans actualize their original nature in existence, they have broken with the original status of their fundamental structure, and the perversion of the principle in human life will have occurred. If the principle of human fundamental structure is being violated, then the original nature will be distorted and the selfishness of human desires will be uncontrollable. Selfishness will prevent humans from doing what they ought to do. This is the problem of human existence. In this chapter, we discuss the similar understanding the problem of human existence in Chu Hsi's and Tillich's thought.

Original Human Nature

Although Chu Hsi and Tillich are representatives of two radically different traditions, they still share a common view of the origin of human nature. First, both Chu Hsi and Tillich agree that the original human nature exists in the potential sense. In Tillich's thought, the essence of human beings is the potential aspect of human beings. Original human nature, or essential nature, refers to the nature that precedes actual existence. It has mere potentiality, but not actuality. Thus, Tillich uses the imagery of "dreaming innocence" to delineate it.[1] It is the state of undecided potentialities.[2] Furthermore, Tillich indicates that there are two types of essence. One is understood as the nature of a thing or as the quality or a universal in which things participate. This is the empirical or logical sense of essence. The other is understood as the undistorted nature of things. What Tillich refers to as the essential nature of humans means the potentialities of human nature. This essential nature is the original human nature before it is activated, or before the act of existing.

The original human nature was one of the controversial issues for classical Confucianism and Neo-Confucianism. To resolve this controversial issue, Chu Hsi divides human nature analytically into the nature of Heaven and Earth or original nature and the vital force and matter of nature or physical nature. What he means by original nature is human nature before its physical form. This nature is merely principle because the nature of Heaven and Earth is principle without any vital force (*ch'i*). However, this original nature has no appearance because it does not have any form. Therefore, Chu Hsi avers that if there is merely the original human nature, there will be no human beings. For without the physical nature, the original nature has no place in which to inhere.

Correspondingly, Chu Hsi divides the heart-mind analytically into Tao heart-mind and human heart-mind. What Chu His means by Tao heart-mind is the Principle of Heaven or the perfection of endowed nature and destiny. As Chu Hsi claims, "it is the Principle of Heaven, and is subtle."[3] Or in other words, it embraces all principles in itself.[4] In addition, Chu Hsi avers that Tao heart-mind emerges from principle and righteousness, and is the heart-mind of humanity, righteousness, propriety, and wisdom.[5] That is to say, the heart-mind, which is conscious of principle and righteousness, is Tao heart-mind.[6] In order for Tao heart-mind to conform thoroughly to principle and righteousness, it must be perfectly good. Therefore, Chu Hsi argues that the original nature with Tao heart-mind is the Principle of Heaven, but it does not have any form or shape. In this respect, the original human nature is merely the potential nature of human beings. It is the nature before the existence of human beings.

Second, both Chu Hsi and Tillich agree that the original human nature is good. According to Tillich, the notion of essence has both an empirical and a valuational meaning. When it is used to describe "the nature of a thing, or as the quality in which a thing participates,"[7] then essence is used in its empirical sense. It also means the ontological structure of things. Speaking in terms of humans, "essence (essential humanity) here stands for the ontological structure of human being: its structure as finite, as self and world, as composed of the polarities. . . . It is this essential structure that makes a human human."[8] The other meaning is a valuational meaning. When essence is understood as that from which being has "fallen," the true and undistorted nature of things, then essence is used in its valuational sense. No matter whether the essential nature of human being refers to the ontological structure or the true and undistorted nature, the essential nature of human being is good.

In the development of Confucianism, the goodness or badness of human nature is also one of the controversial issues. Chu Hsi tries to integrate two classical Confucian theories of human nature, namely, the Mencian idealistic concept of human nature and Hsün Tzu's realistic concept of human nature. In so doing, he reinterprets traditional concepts of human nature by two ontological elements, principle and vital force. Chu Hsi discerns the original nature as well as the physical nature of humans. The former is merely principle and the latter is principle and vital force combined. In this respect, the original nature of a human being is basically principle and is endowed by Heaven. Since the original nature is principle, it is good and does not have any defect. This original human nature is what Mencius means by the original nature of humans. In this original human nature, there is no obscurity or obstruction which would be due to the impurity of the physical nature.[9]

Selfishness

If the original human nature is good, it should follow that the human situation is good. However, in reality, that is not the case. There are many problems in this world, individually and socially. And the fundamental religious problem is selfishness.[10] However, selfishness is not merely a problem of moral misdirection. It is also "an ontological problem of perversion of divine principle that is supposed to be expressed in human life, a perversion of creative love."[11] Although the metaphors used to express selfishness differ greatly in the two traditions, the underlying principle is the same. That is, selfishness is aroused after humans have broken from the original status of their ontological structure. Consequently, humans are estranged from their original nature and selfishness prevents them from doing what they ought to do.

If selfishness is ubiquitous at both the individual and the social level of human reality, we must discuss the causes of the ontologically crippling selfishness in both Chu Hsi's and Tillich's thought. Since both of them claim that the original human nature is merely the potential nature and is good, then it means that humans are not originally selfish. Both Chu Hsi and Tillich assert that humans have one nature with two perceptions. One is the original nature and the other is the actual nature, which has form and shape and appears in human reality. In both Chu Hsi's and Tillich's thought, the polarity of the potential nature and the actual nature is one of the major concepts needed to understand selfishness.

If selfishness can be described as "the breaking of an original contract that defines human life, and hence is intimately bound up with law and obedience to God who is interpreted as a personal party to the contract,"[12] then selfishness for Tillich can be understood by his concept of sin. In Tillich's theological system, the polarity of essential and existential nature is used to construct an ontological interpretation of the biblical myth of the fall. Thus, the fall for Tillich is the transition from essence to existence. Since essence refers to potentiality, human essential nature then is merely human potential nature. What Tillich means by existence is "the actuality of what is potential in the realm of essences."[13] In other words, existence is the actualization of or standing out from potentiality. In contrast to Plato's position, Tillich argues that although existence is the loss of true essentiality, it is not a complete loss because humans still have their potential or essential nature.[14] "The essential nature of man is present in all states of his development, although existential distortion."[15]

In addition, as potentiality, essence is merely not-yet-being (*me on*) but not absolute nonbeing (*ouk on*). However, once humans actualize their potentiality, they distort their essential nature. Human actuality can be understood as standing out from the human ontological structure. Once humans move away from their ontological structure, humans are separated not only from their original nature, but from the power and ground of this structure as well. In their existence, humans realize that they are estranged from what they essentially are. However, existence is the fulfillment of creation and the actualized expression of God's creativity. Therefore, existence can be described as "fallen actuality." This is the reason why Tillich was criticized by some theologians for identifying the creation with the fall.

Humans possess their essential potentiality when they are born. However, as their self-consciousness is developed, they no longer remain in this potentiality. Rather, they are in their actual existence. In this transition from potentiality to actuality, humans are awakened from the state of dreaming innocence. This awakening is comprised of an assumption of experience, responsibility, and guilt, what Tillich called the fall, the passage from essence to existence. In other words, the fall can mean that humans actualize their potential nature, but at the same time, humans can break the original contract that defines human life. Consequently, humans turn away from their ground, and instead turn to themselves. This movement called *hubris*, is one of the categories of estrangement. Selfishness emerges and humans substitute themselves for their divine ground and make themselves the center of the world. We will discuss estrangement in more detail later.

In Chu Hsi's thought, selfishness arises from human desires, which are not derived from the original nature of humans (*t'ien-ti chih hsing*). Instead, they emerge from human physical nature (*ch'i-chih chih hsing*). The original nature of humans is merely the potential nature of humans and is principle. However, since human original nature is principle, it does not have any form and shape and needs physical nature in which to inhere. In other words, the original nature and the physical nature are interdependent. If physical nature exists without the original nature, there will be no human beings, while if original nature exists without the physical nature, there will be also no human beings.[16] One cannot exist without the other.

While the original nature is principle, the physical nature is principle and vital force combined. Using an analogy of water, original nature is like pure water and the physical nature is like water flowing in a channel, its purity and turbidity is thoroughly dependent upon the channel. That is to say, when water is in its state of tranquillity, it is pure; however, when it is activated and flows in a channel, it may be pure or turbid, dependent upon the channel. Therefore, due to the endowment of vital force, the physical nature is differentiated as good or bad. Correspondingly, Chu Hsi also divides the heart-mind into Tao heart-mind and human heart-mind. The former is the Principle of Heaven or the perfection of endowed nature and destiny; whereas the latter embraces the particularity of physical form and vital force. In this case, human heart-mind is mixed with physical endowment and human desire. Thus, it is precarious because it can be bad.

Although human heart-mind is precarious, it is not thoroughly bad. And human desires are not necessary bad either. Chu Hsi clearly indicates that when humans are hungry, they eat; when humans are thirsty, they drink. Eating and drinking are human desires that arise from hunger and thirst respectively and are not absolutely bad because these kinds of human desires are human basic needs. However, there is another kind of human desire that causes humans to go astray. This kind of human desire is called selfishness. Chu Hsi argues that in response to human desires, the human heart-mind has two choices. If the human heart-mind is conscious of the principle and righteousness, then this is the correct heart-mind. However, if the human heart-mind is conscious of human self desires regardless of the principle and righteousness, then it falls into the state of selfishness.

Like Tillich's essential nature, Chu Hsi's original nature and Tao heart-mind are still present in the state of human actuality. There is no physical nature without the original nature nor any human heart-mind without Tao heart-mind. Humans have only one nature as well as one heart-mind, not two. One cannot exist without the other. That is the reason why humans are not only finite but also infinite. Therefore, in human existence, humans, for Chu Hsi, have both original nature and Tao heart-mind as their potential essence and the physical nature and human heart-mind as their actual existence.

Based upon the polarity of the potential nature and the actual nature, both Chu Hsi and Tillich agree that selfishness is not merely a problem of moral misdirection. It is also an ontological problem of perversion of the principle that is supposed to be expressed in human life. In Tillich's thought, the myth of the fall of human beings delineates the breaking of an original contract between humans as creatures and God as the creator.

This is the movement from the original nature, which was in Adam before the fall, to the fallen nature, which is the result of Adam's legacy.

Although Chu Hsi does not have the concept of the fall, he still accepts the logic behind this concept. That is, once humans actualize their original nature in existence, they have broken with the original status of their fundamental structure, and the perversion of the principle in human life will then occur. If the principle of human fundamental structure is violated, then their original nature will be distorted and the selfishness of human desires will be uncontrollable. Selfishness will prevent humans from doing what they ought. In human reality, only the sage is thoroughly conscious of the Principle of Heaven. Most people are only conscious of their own desires. Actually, when humans manifest their human nature in their daily life, they realize that they fail to behave in accordance with their Tao heart-mind. In other words, existentially, the selfishness of human desires prevents humans from doing what they ought to do. Humans are then estranged from their essential nature, from their principle, and from Heaven. Therefore, Chu Hsi urges everyone to distinguish carefully between two heart-minds and to keep steadily to the justice of Tao heart-mind.

The Logic of Sin

Following the concept of the fall, Tillich has the concept of sin. For him, the Christian concept of sin is estrangement. It is also described as fallen actuality. "The state of existence is a state of estrangement. Man is estranged from the ground of his being, from other beings, and from himself."[17] Gilkey indicates that Tillich's idea of estrangement has four aspects. First, estrangement is the 'already there' character of dislocated existence as our situation. Second, this is the universal fact for all humans. Third, this effect impacts not only on our whole being, body, mind, spirit, but also our community, race and history. And finally, this is not a human's essential structure or what who humans really are.[18] That we are estranged means "we belong essentially to that from which we are now estranged."[19]

Although estrangement is a universal fact, Tillich reminds us that we should not overlook the element of personal responsibility in our estrangement and the personal act of turning away from that to which we belong,[20] since human estrangement is sin and sin is unnatural. Rather, sin is our personal act and is chosen by us; therefore, it expresses our personal responsibility and guilt. As Tillich avers, "sin is a universal fact before it becomes an individual act, or more precisely, sin as an individual act actualizes the universal fact of estrangement."[21] In the ontological element of freedom and destiny, humans are free to choose, but this freedom is imbedded in the universal destiny of estrangement. In this respect, the destiny of estrangement is involved in every individual act, or vice versa, the destiny of estrangement is actualized only through all human free acts.[22] Therefore, estrangement is the human situation, which is universally and already there, while sin is unnatural, that is, not part of our human essential structure. Sin refers to personal choice and participation and also to the human personal responsibility for being wrong or guilty.

Furthermore, Tillich elucidates the three faces of estrangement, namely, unbelief, hubris, and concupiscence.[23] They are not the logical consequences of existence, but rather the natural consequences of human existential being. That is to say, these categories are used to depict how humans respond to their existence. What Tillich means by unbelief is that humans turn away from God, or the ground of being. Humans separate their will from the will of God. They are estranged from God in the center of their being.[24] When humans turn away from their ground, they turn to themselves and to the world. These movements are the second and third categories of estrangement.

Hubris is a Greek word and Tillich prefers to use self-elevation; therefore, "*hubris* is the self-elevation of man into the sphere of the divine."[25] When humans turn to themselves, then humans take themselves as the substitute for their divine ground and the center of the world. This self-elevation can be described as the misappropriation of the creature treating itself as divine.

The third category, concupiscence, means the unlimited desires of the estranged self. One wants to grasp the whole world in one's self. In so doing, one "wants one's own pleasure through other beings, but it does not want other beings."[26] Not only is concupiscence an individual phenomenon, but it can also characterize a social world. It can describe "a consumerist goods-society, scrambling for money, for place, for possessions."[27]

Although Confucianism is not a theistic religion, nor does Chu Hsi share any Christian idea of sin, we can still find a resemblance between Chu Hsi's and Tilich's logical argument of the passage from human potentiality to actuality. In Chu His's thought, once humans step out of their ontological structure, that is, by not behaving in accord with their Tao heart-mind, they are estranged from their original nature. Their selfish desires emerge from their existential situation. Following this argument, Chu Hsi agrees with Tillich that human estrangement is "already there" as a character of the human existential situation, and it is a universal empirical fact as well. Because if humans do not distinguish between Tao heart-mind and human heart-mind and let the former become the master of the whole human being with the latter as servant, then humans fall into a state of estrangement. Although the difference between Tao heart-mind and human heart-mind is very small, they can lead humans to different states. In this respect, if the heart-mind is activated in the slightest degree, it will lead the whole human being into good or bad behavior. [28] Existentially, we are in this state of estrangement because we are still learning to be sages. We are still in the process of letting our Tao heart-mind be the master and escape from this situation. And we are still conscious of our sensual experience. Our human heart-mind is still the master of our whole being, regardless our ontological structure. However, this state of estrangement is not what we essentially are.

Chu Hsi would agree with Tillich that estrangement is a universal fact, but also a personal act. In Chu Hsi's thought, human desires are associated with feelings. Using the water metaphor, Chu Hsi avers that the heart-mind is like water, nature is like the tranquillity of water, feelings are flowing water, and desires are waves. Just as there are good and bad waves, so there are good and bad desires.[29] The heart-mind is the master of nature and feelings. Before the heart-mind is activated, it is nature; while it is activated, it is feelings. Since human desires are associated with the activated state of the heart-mind, it implies that human desires are aroused in human actuality. In this respect, human desires do not necessarily distort the human ontological structure. Instead, they are aroused because of a human personal act. Originally, the heart-mind is the Principle of Heaven; however, when it is activated and does not follow principle, it then becomes selfish and depraved.[30] In other words, selfishness is the misdirection or excess of human desires and is aroused when the heart-mind is conscious of the human sensual experience, regardless of the principle of Heaven. This is a universal fact, but this also occurs because of a personal human act.

In the argument of Tillich's three categories of estrangement, when humans turn away from their ground, they turn to themselves and to the world. Correspondingly, in Chu Hsi's thought, when humans turn away from the principle of Heaven, then humans follow their selfish desires and become selfish as well as depraved. That is the reason why Chu Hsi urges us to distinguish between our two heart-minds, and also to keep our heart-mind clean and pure through self-cultivation, the practice of restoring and maintaining our original purity of our heart-mind by removing all selfish desires in our heart-mind.[31] In addition, Chu Hsi argues that "the task of the investigation of things is none other than to understand that there are both the Principle of Heaven and human desires in things and to examine them in each case."[32] These two ways of knowing, to nourish the heart-mind and to extend knowledge, direct us to keep steadily to the justice of Tao heart-mind. If humans are not conscious of the Principle of Heaven, then they will be conscious of their own selfish desires. In his discussion of righteousness versus profit, Chu Hsi argues that "righteousness is what is proper according to the Principle of Heaven, whereas profit is the desire of human feelings."[33] Obviously, whenever humans do not follow their Tao heart-mind, then their human heart-mind will lead them to selfishness. Therefore, Chu Hsi warns us that the human heart-mind is precarious if it become the master instead of the servant of the whole human being.

Although both Chu Hsi and Tillich have a similar logic of human actuality, it is still worth noting that they come from two radically different traditions. There are clear differences not only between Tillich's theistic thought and Chu Hsi's naturalistic and humanistic thought, but also between their explanations of actual human existence. For Tillich, there are no ontological differences between the actualization of creation and the beginning of the fall. These coincide and yet are not identical. In his reply to Reinhold Niebuhr's criticism, Tillich contends that "the fall is the work of finite freedom, but it happened universally in everything finite, and therefore unavoidably. The universality and consequently the unavoidability of the fall is not derived from 'ontological speculation' but from a realistic observation of man, his heart, and his history."[34] On the one hand, human existence is positive because it is the fulfillment of creation. But, on the other hand, it is negative because the actualization of human potentialities is not completed and leads to the distortion of human original nature. In this respect, the fall is not necessary but inevitable.

Nevertheless, in Chu Hsi's thought, the original nature and the physical nature of humans coexist. Correspondingly, Tao heart-mind and human heart-mind cannot be separated. In human actuality, the physical nature or human heart-mind are both principle and vital force combined. That is to say, not only is it not necessary for human beings to be in the state of estrangement, but also there is no coincidence of human actuality and human estrangement. The main difference between Tillich and Chu Hsi is the coincidence of human actuality and human estrangement. For Chu Hsi, in human actuality, humans still have two natures and two heart-minds. The physical nature and human heart-mind combine both principle and vital force, although they are precarious. That is to say, humans are not estranged from their ontological structure at the beginning of their actualization. The human heart-mind is not thoroughly bad, although human desires are aroused from it, because human desires are not bad but precarious.

However, in Chu Hsi's thought, human estrangement is still inevitable, although it is not necessary. If not, there would be no reason why Chu Hsi should urge us to practice personal cultivation. Through our spiritual cultivation, the Principle of Heaven inside us may be recovered and our bad desires can be controlled. Evidently, in human actuality, human original nature is neither completely actualized nor distorted. If human physical nature is a full and total actualization of our potential nature, there would be no need to recover the Principle of Heaven. In other words, if one's life is as good as it could possibly be, why should one need to improve one's life? If our original nature is completely actualized, we then will be conscious of the Principle of Heaven whenever we act. But our reality is quite different. We are not acting in accord with the Principle of Heaven, but in accord with our desires. Those who can behave in accordance with their Tao heart-mind instead of their human heart-mind are sages.

In the Confucian tradition, Confucius is always spoken of as a sage. But in the *Analects*, Confucius seldom mentions the sage and never claims to be one or personally to have met one. Actually, the sage is merely an ultimate ideal for ordinary people. Before one becomes the sage, one has first to achieve the more realistic goal of becoming a noble person.[35] As Confucius says, "a sage it has not been mine to see, could I just see a noble man that would be enough."[36] In Neo-Confucianism, the sage then is portrayed as an ideal for humans at the end point of their cultivation and learning process. If one is in the state of sagehood, one is fully realized in the development of one's potential nature and heart-mind. [37] In this respect, although the physical nature and human heart-mind are combined with principle and vital force, people are often conscious of human sensual experience regardless of the Principle of Heaven. Their actual natures are estranged from their original nature. Thus, human personal cultivation is a way to actualize a fuller manifestation of the Principle of Heaven in human original nature.[38]

The Motive for being Selfishness

In *Behind the Masks of God*, Robert C. Neville asks why people become selfish if they are essentially unselfish. Is there any proper motive for being selfish? If selfishness itself is bad, there is no reason for people to want to ruin themselves. He comes to the conclusion that selfishness or sin is motiveless.[39] In this respect, both Chu Hsi and Tillich agree that selfishness or sin is motiveless. First of all, both of them contend that there are two sides of human nature and the distinction of the original nature and the existential nature of human beings is not derived from human choice. Rather, this distinction is ontological. However, how humans respond to their free volitional acts in their existential circumstance is the theme of morality. In Chu Hsi's and Tillich's thought, selfishness or sin emerges from the distortion of human original nature. This distortion occurs when humans actualize their potential nature. Tillich contends that this circumstance is called the fall. It is the passage from human essence to existence. But coincidentally, humans are estranged from the ground of their being, from other beings and from themselves. This is the state of human estrangement, a universal fact. Therefore, there is no pure motive for sin. Humans do not plan to sin. Rather, human existence is sin.

Similarly, in Chu Hsi's thought, selfishness comes from the perverseness of human desires, and human desires come from the physical nature and human heart-mind of human beings. They are not necessarily bad but precarious. However, selfishness is a universal fact although it is a personal act, because humans are conscious of the human sensual experience instead of the Principle of Heaven. Between Tao heart-mind and human heart-mind, people inevitably tend to take the human heart-mind as the master of their whole being. That is the reason why people have to cultivate their mind-hearts in order to manifest their nature perfectly. Thus, like Tillich, Chu Hsi argues that in human reality, people are selfish. He does not attempt to explain it, but just takes it for granted. Thus, humans do not have any proper motive for being selfish. Rather, this is our existential problem.

In this chapter, we deal with the problem of human existence. Both Chu Hsi and Tillich agree that humans are originally good. Human original nature is merely human potential nature. The essential nature of humans is in the ontological structure. As discussed in the previous chapter, human original nature is part of the ontological structure of unity. Therefore, this human original nature is prior to the actualization of human beings and refers to the nature that precedes actual existence. Second, both Chu Hsi and Tillich agree that once humans actualize their nature in existence, their original nature will be distorted. Therefore, both recognize two sides to human nature. In Tillich's thought, there are essential and existential natures. In an empirical sense, the essential nature is prior to the existential nature. And in terms of valuational sense, the existential nature is the distortion of the essential nature. Like Tillich, Chu Hsi divides human nature into the original and the physical natures. The former is the essential nature which is endowed with the Principle of Heaven, while the latter is the existential nature which is endowed with principle and vital force (*ch'i*) combined.

Third, the problem of human existence is the actualization of human beings, which is the passage from essence to existence. This is what Tillich calls human estrangement. Once human nature departs from the unity of the original human ontological structure, humans are estranged from their ground, others, and even themselves. In this respect, humans fall into existential distortion. This is a universal fact of our humanity, but also a personal act for us. Thus, human estrangement is not necessary but inevitable. Both Chu Hsi and Tillich share this view on human existence. Following this concept of estrangement, both Chu Hsi and Tillich also agree that selfishness or sin is motiveless, because it is the problem of human existence and humans have no motive for being selfish. In other words, the distinction of the original nature and the existential nature of human beings is an ontological, not a moral, issue. And yet when human nature moves from stillness to activity, then feelings will be stirred. And how humans respond with their free volitional acts raises the issue of morality. We now turn to Chu Hsi's and Tillich's idea of the resolution of the human existential problem.

Notes

1. Tillich, *Systematic Theology*, vol. 2, 33.
2. Dreisbach, *Symbols and Salvation*, 77.
3. *Yü-lei*, ch. 78, sec. 89, 2010.
4. *Yü-lei*, ch. 78, sec. 107, 2013.
5. *Yü-lei*, ch. 78, sec. 123, 2018.
6. *Yü-lei*, ch. 78, sec. 85, 2009.
7. Tillich, *Systematic Theology*, vol. 2, 33.
8. Gilkey, *Gilkey on Tillich*, 119.
9. Chan, *A Source Book in Chinese Philosophy*, 624.
10. Neville, *Behind the Masks of God*, 119.
11. Ibid., 119-120.
12. Ibid., 120.
13. Tillich, *Systematic Theology*, vol. 1, 203.
14. Tillich, *Systematic Theology*, vol. 2, 22.
15. Ibid., 33.
16. *Yü-lei*, ch. 4, sec. 50, 68.
17. Tillich, *Systematic Theology*, vol. 2, 44.
18. Gilkey, *Gilkey on Tillich*, 123.
19. Tillich, *Systematic Theology*, vol. 2, 45.
20. Ibid., 46.
21. Ibid., 56.

22. Ibid.

23. Gilkey, *Gilkey on Tillich*, 126.

24. Tillich, *Systematic Theology*, vol. 2, 48.

25. Ibid., 50.

26. Ibid., 54.

27. Gilkey, *Gilkey on Tillich*, 130.

28. *Yü-lei*, ch. 13, sec. 19, 224.

29. Chan, *A Source Book of Chinese Philosophy*, 631.

30. Chan, *Chu Hsi: New Studies*, 202.

31. Julia Ching, "Chu Hsi on Personal Cultivation," 283.

32. Chan, *Chu Hsi: New Studies*, 204.

33. Ibid., 203.

34. "Reply to Interpretation and Criticism," in *The Theology of Paul Tillich*, eds. Charles Kegley and Robert Bretall (New York: Pilgrim Press, 1982), 342-43.

35. Confucian concept of a noble person is parallel with the English gentleman. See Wm. Theodore de Bary, *The Trouble with Confucianism* (Cambridge: Harvard University Press, 1991), 5

36. Ibid.

37. Rodney L. Taylor, *The Religious Dimensions of Confucianism* (Albany: State University of New York Press, 1990), 43-44.

38. Julia Ching, "Chu Hsi on Personal Cultivation," in *Chu Hsi and Neo-Confucianism*, ed. Wing-tsit Chan (Honolulu: University of Hawaii Press), 282.

39. Neville, *Behind the Masks of God*, 121-2.

CHAPTER TWELVE
Reunification

If actual human existence is the distortion of human ontological structure, the way to resolve this existential distortion is to be reunited with the fundamental structure. Reunification here means reuniting with the ground of being, others, and even ourselves. However, reunion does not mean that humans return to where they were before. Once humans depart from their statically ontological structure, there is no way they can return to where they were before being activated. What reunification means is that human estrangement is overcome by reunifying the whole human reality. Thus, the distinction of subject and object, of matter and spirit, and of inorganic and organic and psychological reality is reunited. The whole human reality is then in a harmonious state.

We now turn to the main categories of reunion in both Chu Hsi's and Tillich's thought. For Tillich, the central category is love. Not only is it the drive towards reunion, but it also belongs to the structure of Being-itself that every being participates in it.[1] In Chu Hsi's thought, the central category of reunion category is *jen*. Traditionally, *jen* is one of the cardinal virtues. But Chu Hsi proposes the ontological meaning of *jen* such that *jen* is the principle of all cardinal virtues.[2]

Ontological Dimension

Undoubtedly, love is a kernel in Christianity paralleling *jen* in Confucianism. Traditionally, the Christian idea of love is understood in an emotional and ethical sense, while the Confucian idea of *jen* is understood as one of the cardinal virtues. This may be too simplified because these two concepts, love and *jen*, have had many meanings in different periods throughout their own traditions. However, both love and *jen* in their own traditions mainly emphasized their ethical dimension.

In the Christian sense, love is treated as the Great Commandment and it has been interpreted often from the ethical dimension. "Let us love one another, for love comes from God." (1 John 3:14) Tillich criticizes the claim that love is merely emotion. This claim misinterprets Christian love because love can be the function of the human mind.[3] In addition, the ethical dimension of love is totally dependent upon its ontological nature. "The ontological nature of love gets its qualifications by its ethical character."[4] For Tillich Christian love means "the drive towards the reunion of the separated; this is ontologically and therefore universally true."[5] This reunion is the resolution of human estrangement. That is, the separation of human beings from their ground, Being-itself, from the others, and even from themselves. Therefore, Tillich's idea of love is much more than just the ethical dimension. It has its ontological meaning such that human beings drive toward the unity of an unambiguous life.

Correspondingly, in the Confucian tradition, as Wing-tsit Chan depicts it, *jen* has been defined as benevolence, perfect virtue, or universal love, etc. All these meanings are focused upon three dimensions, namely, humanity, virtue, and love.[6] Basically, these are mainly contained within the ethical realm. However, Chu Hsi synthesizes all these meanings of *jen* creatively into two phrases, which are the character of mind and the principle of love. Here Chu Hsi develops the ontological meaning of *jen*. Not only is *jen* a moral principle or the principle of virtue, but it is also an ontological principle of creativity. Since humans receive the heart-mind of Heaven and Earth as their heart-mind and this heart-mind produces things, *jen* as the character of heart-mind has the character of productiivity. As Ch'en Ch'un argues, "*Jen* is the totality of the heart-mind's principle of production. It is always producing and reproducing without ceasing."[7] Moreover, Chu Hsi defines *jen* as the principle of the Four Virtues. As the principle of origination unites and controls the moral qualities of the heart-mind of Heaven and Earth, *jen* embraces the Four Virtues. In this respect, *jen* is the beginning of life and the principle of all virtues of human beings. Chu

Hsi's idea of *jen* goes far beyond the ethical dimension because for him *jen* is the ontological principle of human beings.

The Vertical Dimension

Following their ontological dimension, both *jen* and love are the source and path for humans to follow to reunite with their ground. As the main category of the reunion of human estrangement, both *jen* and love are the source of reunion with the ground of human beings. Although both Confucianism and Christianity agree that humans can be reunited with their ground or the ultimate, the ground of human beings or the ultimate is understood differently in these two traditions. Confucianism is an inclusive humanistic and naturalistic religion, while Christianity is a theistic religion. But, this does not negate the fact that *jen* and love have a vertical dimension directed toward the Transcendent.

In Tillich's thought, love is the nature of God because God is love. Thus, "God manifests Godself to us as love."[8] God as love implies that there must be an independent being in relation to God who is loved. For in the loving relationship, there must be a lover and a be loved. Evidently, between God and humans, God is a lover and the human being is a loved. In their existential situation, humans are estranged from the ground of their beings, namely, God. That is, once humans were essentially united with God, but now they are separated. In order to move towards reunion with what they are separated from, there is the movement of love and this movement can only be fulfilled with God as love. In this respect, love can be understood as the reunion of the estranged and manifestation of its power to overcome the separation. Thus, not only will the separation of humans and God be reunited with love, but the separation of humans from the others and even from themselves as well. Therefore, love as God's unconditional love is the source of reunion and of the other forms of human love.

Similarly, in Chu Hsi's thought, the foundation of *jen* is the heart-mind of Heaven and Earth and the heart-mind of Heaven and Earth is to produce things. First of all, Chu Hsi identifies Heaven with principle. Humans receive this principle as their nature. Therefore, the original nature of human beings is the Principle of Heaven. Second, humans receive the heart-mind of Heaven and Earth in the beginning of their birth. And "*jen* is the complete character of the original heart-mind, if the innate heart-mind of the Principle of Heaven as it naturally is has been preserved and not lost, whatever one does will be orderly and harmonious."[9] In this respect, humans and Heaven are originally united. However, once humans actualize their nature in existence, their physical nature can cause selfishness. If this happens, then humans are separated from their original ground. Finally, since the heart-mind of Heaven and Earth produces things, the heart-mind of humans is to practice *jen*. As the character of the heart-mind, *jen* is the principle of productivity in the heart-mind. It is operating and producing and reproducing ceaselessly, and remaining from the beginning to the end without interruption.[10] As the character of growth, *jen* is endowed by Heaven as the principle of human nature and is the complete character of the original heart-mind. And the heart-mind of human beings is to practice *jen* so that the nature of human beings can be fully realized. Once human nature is fully realized, then humans are in the state of sagehood. "In sagehood Heaven and humans are united as one."[11] Therefore, "the ultimate aim of *jen* is to achieve a unity with the universe through manifesting one's own virtue."[12]

Nevertheless, it is worth noting that although both *agape* and *jen* have a vertical dimension, it does not mean that there is no difference between the Christian God and Confucian Heaven. In Christianity, since God is love, Christian love is first of all a downward vertical movement from God to humans. By receiving this objective movement of God's love subjectively, humans transcend themselves in unity with God. This is what Tillich calls grace. "Grace means that the Spiritual Presence cannot be produced but is given."[13] As the movement of divine love or *agape*, grace comprises the resolution to the estrangement in human existence.

In Confucianism, Heaven is understood as transcendence and the totality of natural and human existence.[14] For Chu Hsi, Heaven can mean three things, namely, the master, principle, and the blue sky. These meanings are derived from Ch'eng I. In these meanings, Heaven can be understood collectively as well as separately.[15] Cosmologically speaking, Heaven is the source of the whole universe. But this universe consists of passive cosmic force (*yin*) and active cosmic force (*yang*). This *yin-yang* force moves circularly and ceaselessly. Thus, in this circular movement, Heaven depends on the physical shape of the Earth and the Earth depends on the vital force (*ch'i*), which is from Heaven.[16] Ontologically speaking, Heaven is identical with principle. "Everything in the world has to follow principle before it can fulfill its nature to become a thing."[17] Thus, principle in this sense is the substance of Heaven. When it functions, it becomes the destiny (*ming*) of things. And nature is what a thing receives its own share of to be born. Finally, as the master, Heaven refers to a Heavenly Lord, who is a master of this natural rotation of the universe.[18]

Despite differences between the Christian God and Confucian Heaven, there are still resemblances between love and *jen*. First of all, both *jen* and love are initiated by the Transcendent. That is to say, the vertical movement of *jen* and love moves downward from the Transcendent to human beings. Second, humans are the finite recipients. In Tillich's thought, unconditional love is the grace of God. What humans can do is to accept this grace. Correspondingly, in Chu Hsi's thought, humans "receive the heart-mind of Heaven and Earth as their heart-mind."[19] The character of this heart-mind is *jen*. *Jen*, then, is the original character of the heart-mind of human beings.

Third, both *jen* and love have the upward vertical movement from humans to the Transcendent. For Tillich to respond to God's love is to participate in it. This is what Tillich calls regeneration. In regeneration, humans are in the state of having been drawn into the new reality. Humans participate in this reality and are reborn through participation. This is what humans do in order to reunite with what they are estranged from. This also can be called the subjective side of the reunion between God and humans. In other words, humans must accept that God accepts them. They must accept acceptance.[20]

In Chu Hsi's thought, to actualize *jen* is to realize the complete character of the heart-mind. In other words, to actualize *jen* is to actualize one's own potential nature. *Jen* is neither love nor the heart-mind. Instead, it is the principle of love and the character of the heart-mind. Besides, *jen* is nature and nature is principle. It then is not only the root of love, but also the ground of things. In order to lead to *jen*, humans have to fully realize their nature. This leads to the concept of *ch'eng* (self-actualization). It is the direction of the actualization of principle in the formation of human virtue, and a participant in the creation of a just social order as well.[21] Thus, *ch'eng* is a process of self-actualization. This is the process that humans ought to follow and the normative values embedded in the person can be realized through this process.[22] In this process, humans are reunited with Heaven and human estrangement can be resolved.

Nevertheless, the difference between *jen* and love is that *jen* is certainly anthropocosmic, while love is basically theocentric.[23] What this means is that love is not only the source but also the function. Although it requires human regeneration, this self-giving love is only possible in God's love. Human love is possible only in associating with God's love. In this respect, love is theistic and centered on God's salvation. In Tillich's threefold characterization of salvation, regeneration is associated with justification. That is, humans participate in reality such that they are being accepted by God. God's love is the center of salvation, even though it does not imply that human participation is unnecessary.

On the contrary, *jen* is basically due to the activation of the responsible self. Although *jen* as the character of the heart-mind is endowed by Heaven, it can be manifested because of a human's own self-realization. This self-actualization is the dynamic process of growth through one's daily activity, with truthfulness and steadfastness as its guide. In this respect, *jen* does not embrace the theistic idea of salvation. Rather, it is directly anthropocosmic. The actualization of *jen* depends solely on humans, while human love depends on God's love. Therefore, human love arises in response to the love of God, while *jen* is activated by human self-cultivation. "To respond to God, one has to have firm faith in God; to cultivate one's self, one has to have a responsible self."[24]

The Horizontal Dimension

Not only are both *jen* and love the source of reunion with the Transcendental, they are also the source of reunion between humans, and between humans and nature. In the process, both *jen* and love embrace all other forms of love or virtue. In western classical thought, there are four traditional categories of love, namely, *libido/epithymia*, *philia*, *eros*, and *agape*. As Tillich argues, "Love as *libido* is the movement of the needy toward that which fulfils the need. Love as *philia* is the movement of the equal toward union with the equal. Love as *eros* is the movement of that which is lower in power and meaning to that which is higher."[25] These three kinds of love are dependent not only on contingent characteristics, which change and are partial, but also on repulsion and attraction, on passion and sympathy.[26]

However, *agape* is "independent of these states. It affirms the other unconditionally, apart from higher or lower, pleasant or unpleasant qualities."[27] *Agape* is universal and is a form of love that transcends the other three kinds of love. Yet it is not separated from them. Since *agape* is connected with these three forms of love, it can be characterized in terms of the libidinal, philial, and erotic energies. Actually, these three forms of love have been used in order to make the divine love concrete. Thus, these three types of love are vital elements in union with *agape*. Basically, agape is God's love, and yet it is also relevant to human love toward God and to relationships between humans, and between humans and nature. Since at our human level, God's *agape* needs to be expressed in the concrete, it embraces the other three forms of love.

Correspondingly, for Chu, the character of the heart-mind as *jen* has the character of growth (*sheng*). For "the heart-mind is comparable to seeds of grain. The nature of growth is jen."[28] This growth process is present in the heart-mind due to its potentiality. *Jen* as the principle of life lies dormant in the plant during winter or hidden in the seed before branches and leaves blossom forth.[29] Based upon Ch'eng I's idea of production and reproduction, the perpetual renewal of life (*sheng-sheng*), Chu Hsi contends that *jen* has the character of production. "It is always producing and reproducing without cease."[30]

As the nature of growth, *jen* embraces the Four Virtues of humanity, righteousness, propriety, and wisdom. Differening here with Mencius, Chu Hsi argues that *jen* is not only the feelings of commiseration, but also the origination (*yüan*) of commiseration. He identifies *jen*, one of the four moral qualities of the heart-mind of human beings, with origination (*yüan*),[31] one of the four moral qualities of the heart-mind of Heaven and Earth. Thus, as origination, *jen* is the beginning of life and the first stage in the process of growth. It unites and controls all human virtues. In addition, Chu Hsi indicates that *jen* is one of the Four Virtues if it is discussed in terms of an individual virtue. However, collectively speaking, the Four Virtues are aspects of the heart-mind but *jen* is the master of them.[32]

Second, both *jen* and love are the ultimate criterion of all kinds of virtue and love. In Tillich's thought, humans can love because God's love instills and awakens love in them. Thus, *agape* as God's acts of love is the ultimate criterion of the other types of love. It is ultimate reality that manifests itself and transforms life and love. As the ultimate criterion, *agape* permeates the other forms of love and elevates them beyond the ambiguities of their self-centredness.[33] In other words, *agape* enters, transforms, and brings the other forms of love to completion, as the ultimate criterion and corrective of every act of love.

Similarly, in Chu Hsi's thought, *jen* is the principle of love. It is the principle in the heart-mind. Love is what has been aroused by this principle in the heart-mind. Love is feeling, while *jen* is inner nature. Thus, *jen* is nature, while the feeling of commiseration as the beginning of *jen* is love. "When love is manifested externally, it is the function of humanity, but the principle of love is in it."[34] As *jen* embraces the Four Virtues before it is aroused, love is feeling and embraces the Four Beginnings after *jen* is aroused. Since "the Principle of Heaven embodied in the human heart-mind is totally *jen*," it is the master of all Four Virtues. Discussed in terms of substance, *jen* as the principle of love is the root of all virtues and the universal nature of the human heart-mind. Discussed in terms of function, *jen* as the character of the heart-mind combines and generates all the other virtues. *Jen* is the totality of all virtues and the generative force that makes virtues real, social, and dynamic.

Third, both *jen* and love are not only the ultimate criterion of all forms of love and virtue, but also have power to overcome estrangement between humans. Since love is understood from its emotional side, *agape* as the unconditional love is also often understood from the emotional side too. However, Tillich argues that "love is not weakness, not resignation of power but the perfect power of Being."[35] Thus, he identifies love with power. "Love is real only as the power of being."[36] Without power, love cannot be actualized in human reality. In our human capacity, one needs power in order to affirm oneself. On the social level, humans need power in order to conquer the separation of human beings. The more love there is to reunite the separation of human beings, the more power there is to conquer the separation. Thus, love and power cannot be separated in their manifestations. In order to destroy what is against love, love must be united with power.

In Chu Hsi's thought, *jen* as the character of the heart-mind is the master of all virtues, and *jen* as the principle of love is the root of things. In this respect, as the character of the heart-mind, *jen* is the production of things, the power of generation, and the master of all virtues. It is the heart-mind of Heaven and Earth able to produce things. Thus, not only is *jen* one of the Four Virtues, but it is the generative force of all things as well. With this generative force, *jen* can produce all virtues. As the principle of love, *jen* is the root of things, while love is the sprout reaching its maturity and completion. *Jen* is the principle in the heart-mind. When it is aroused, it generates all kinds of love, like filial piety and brotherly respect. These are feelings and the expression of the heart-mind. In this regard, the character of the heart-mind generates these forms of love. Therefore, as the Principle of Heaven embodied in the human heart-mind, *jen* is not only the totality of virtues, but also is the powerful force able to generate all forms of virtue in order to overcome human estrangement.

Fourth, both *jen* and love have a direction to perform their work. For Tillich, to reunite what is separated is the demand of love, and also is the precondition of justice. Justice here is "the form of uniting love."[37] If love is the power of reunion, justice then is the judgement of every process of self-realization and the demand for venturing self-affirmation as well as self-negation. Justice provides a direction for the actualization of love. In human reality, love as the ultimate principle reunites humans and their ground, between humans, and between humans and nature, while justice preserves what is to be united. Justice provides a direction in which love should be actualized or performed. "It is the form in which and through which love performs its word."[38]

Correspondingly, *jen*, for Chu Hsi, is not an idealistic concept. It is not merely principle and substance. Rather, it perfects human reality through the process of self-actualization (*ch'eng*). What Chu Hsi calls self-actualization is the process by which *jen* is actualized. *Ch'eng* as self-actualization is the direction of the actualization of principle in the formation of human virtue and a participant in the creation of a just social order.[39] As self-realization, *ch'eng* is the mode of self-actualized perfection, a model for how things ought to be. This is the direction in which *jen* actualizes itself forward in order to reunite separated humans. Therefore, *ch'eng* is a human normative moral principle and the self-realization of the norms of human excellence.

Fifth, there is a correspondence between Christian love and Confucian *jen* at the social level. Traditionally, love and justice are not separated. Justice is the form of reuniting love. In order to create social harmony in a human community, love must be embodied in action so that justice can be established. In justice, there is the balance between self-affirmation and self-negation. Thus, love with justice can make its contribution to human flourishing on the social level for human beings.[40] In Confucianism, *jen* and righteousness always go hand in hand just as love and justice. *Jen* is developed through self-cultivation. And yet Confucian self-cultivation is not merely an interior meditation such as Taoist and Buddhist meditation, but also is external participation in social reconstruction.[41] In so doing, *jen* as the totality of the principle of the heart-mind of production needs righteousness as the decision and judgment of the heart-mind. If the decision is in accord with principle, then it is right.[42] In Mencian thought, "*jen* is the peaceful residence of humanity, while righteousness is the proper way to its fulfillment."[43] Therefore, "to practice *jen* in the right manner is righteousness."

Due to their different transcendental orientations, *jen* and love are different even though they have some similarities. In Christianity, human love is possible because God's love pervades and awakens in us. Although *agape* is God's love, on our human level, it must be expressed in concrete forms by uniting *libido*, *philia*, and *eros*. In this respect, human love is a human response to God's *agape* and also to God's command. As a human response to God's *agape*, not only is human love manifested in accepting God's love by faith, but also is manifested in reuniting humans as well as humans and nature. However, *jen* is not merely a human response; rather, it is the principle of virtue. Although *jen* is given by Heaven in the heart-mind of human beings, it is the principle of love and the character of the heart-mind. It generates all the virtues due to its character of production and reproduction. Before it is activated, it is the principle of love. All virtues emerge from it and humans act in accord with it via the formation of human excellence. In this respect, unlike Christian love, *jen* is not a human response to God's love. Instead, it is the principle and goal of human cultivation. It is the totality of all virtues.

The Dynamic Resolution

Both Christian love and Confucian *jen* are the drive toward the reunion of separated human existential reality. They are not merely the principle of virtue, but also a unifying force. In so doing, they are correlated with the other indispensably active categories. In fact, when both *jen* and love function as unifying forces, they are no longer the principle but also the active force. Thus, both *jen* and love need another notion of the dynamic resolution of human estrangement. In Tillich's thought, in order to accept acceptance, humans must have faith. Through faith, humans can know that they are accepted. Faith is an indispensable element of love. Love needs action and both of them are implied in faith. Love and faith are one reality with two features.[44] "The concern of faith is identical with the desire of love: reunion with that to which one belongs and from which one is estranged."[45]

What Tillich means by faith is "the state of being grasped by the ultimate concern."[46] This definition of faith is basic and universal. Another definition of faith for Tillich is "the state of being grasped by the Spiritual Presence and opened to transcendent unity of unambiguous life."[47] If faith is the state of being grasped by the Spiritual Presence, then love is "the state of being taken by the Spiritual Presence into the transcendent unity of unambiguous life."[48] In the second definition of faith, Tillich expresses three characters of faith, namely, the receptive character, the paradoxical character, and the anticipatory character. Paralleling these three characters of faith is the threefold character of salvation, namely, regeneration, justification, and sanctification. Like faith, love also has these three characters. As receptive love, it accepts the object of love without restrictions. As paradoxical love, it maintains this acceptance despite the estranged, profanized, and demonized state of its objects. And as anticipatory love, it re-establishes the holiness of its object and takes its object into the transcendent unity of unambiguous life.

Faith and love are inseparable. As the state of being ultimately concerned, faith implies the desire, which is love, toward the reunion of what is separated. That is to say, if faith is understood as ultimate concern, it implies love and the expression of love is action. Thus, faith is actualized in action. "Where there is ultimate concern there is the passionate desire to actualize the content of one's concern."[49] In this respect, ontologically speaking, faith drives us toward the reunion of the separation of humans and their ground. It can transform the estranged reality and determines the kind of love and the kind of action.[50] Therefore, "faith as the state of being ultimately concerned implies love and determines action."[51] With this understanding, we realize that faith and love are two sides of a coin. One cannot exist without the other. "Being grasped by God in faith and adhering to God in love is one and the same state of creaturely life. It is participation in the transcendent unity of unambiguous life."[52]

Similarly, Chu Hsi's *jen* is the principle of all virtues. To actualize this principle in reality, another concept, *ch'eng*, is needed. *Ch'eng* is the process and the ideal foundation of all actuality. It can be defined as the self-actualization of the norms of human excellence, and as sincerity. Just as love and faith are inseparable, *ch'eng* and *jen* are also not separated. To achieve *ch'eng* is the way of *jen*. As self-actualization, *ch'eng* is a human normative moral principle. It is the real principle because it is solid and real. In this respect, Chu Hsi contends that nature is principle, while *ch'eng* is excellence. What he means is that *ch'eng* is the completely perfect nature without deficiency.

Therefore, *ch'eng* is the mode of self-actualization that humans ought to follow. As sincerity, *ch'eng* is the action of not disregarding one's conscience.[53] Thus, if one has *ch'eng*, one can actualize the normative principle of one's original nature and Tao heart-mind. If one can fully actualize one's normative principle in reality, one is on the level of the sage's moral nature, or is already a sage. However, among the common people, there is still a great distance between their real nature and the mode of self-actualized perfection. That is to say, common people are not born naturally in the state of being a sage. They require great efforts to reach this state. Therefore, the common people need faithfulness (*hsin*), which refers to human effort, in order to reach *jen*. That is, to be *hsin* is to be sincere. The difference between *ch'eng* and *hsin* is that the former describes those who are in the state of self-actualized perfection, and the latter describes those who are still working towards that perfection.

C*hung* as steadfastness is yet another notion of self-actualization in human reality. It refers to how the heart-mind responds to daily events and contacts things. What Chu Hsi means by *chung* is to exert oneself to the utmost.[54] In other words, to be *chung* is to fully actualize one's original nature and Tao heart-mind in one's daily life with nothing left undone. Actually, faithfulness and steadfastness are not sharply differentiated as two different things. Rather, steadfastness is the inner response of the human heart-mind, while faithfulness is the outer response of the heart-mind.[55] Both of them are close to sincerity (*ch'eng*) in meaning. Steadfastness and faithfulness as well as sincerity mean being real. And yet in sincerity being real comes naturally, while in steadfastness and faithfulness being real comes about in one's performance of a task.[56] Thus, *ch'eng* is the human normative moral principle and the perfection of self-actualization. It refers to the state of sagehood. Steadfastness and faithfulness refer to our daily life, such that we must exert our energy to the utmost in order to fully actualize the principle of Heaven, namely, *jen*, that dwells in us. Once human self-realization is perfectly completed, then *ch'eng* is *jen* and *jen* is *ch'eng*. At that moment, what is inherent within humans is freely expressed without an iota of insincerity. The separation between humans and their ground, between human beings, and between humans and nature will then be resolved.

Noteworthy differences between Chu Hsi's *jen* and Tillich's love characterize their respective concepts. Christian love is theocentric, whereas Confucian *jen* is anthropocosmic. This leads to the difference between the notion of faith and sincerity as well. In Tillich's thought, faith is the state of being that is manifest in the individual who has been grasped by ultimate concern. And the manifestation of this ultimate concern, for Tillich, is revelation. What Tillich means by revelation "is the manifestation of what concerns us ultimately. The mystery which is revealed is of ultimate concern to us because it is the ground of our being."[57] For Tillich, the ground of being is God as Being itself, the basic and universal symbol for what concerns us ultimately. As Being itself, God is not only ultimate reality but also the really real. Besides, God can be depicted as the power of being, the power of resisting and conquering nonbeing.

Moreover, Jesus as the Christ, for Tillich, is the symbol of the ground of being, which manifests the power of God present in a person, a person subject to all the conditions of existence. However, he overcomes human existential estrangement and brings New Being to all humanity. New Being means the new reality in which human existential estrangement is overcome. It is the reality of reconciliation and reunion, of creativity, meaning, and hope.[58] For Tillich, the New Being "can be characterized as the Being of love."[59] As the Being of Love, the New Being is "the ultimate criterion of every healing and saving process." Therefore, in relation to Jesus as the Christ as the New Being, our faith is "the state of being grasped by the New Being as it is manifest in Jesus as the Christ."[60] Humans are invited into this new reality and faith is the element of acceptance. Through the New Being, humans can experience the continuing salvation of God that is manifested in Jesus as the Christ by their faith. Obviously, in this respect, faith is theocentric and the subjective side of human participation in the new reality.

On the contrary, in the Confucian tradition, *ch'eng* is anthropocosmic even with a vertical dimension. *Ch'eng* can be defined as self-actualization and as sincerity. The former refers to its dynamic character, while the latter refers to the human normative moral principle. As principle, it is related to the nature. If nature is principle, *ch'eng* as sincerity is excellence. Chu Hsi gives an analogy that if nature is like a fan, then *ch'eng* is comparable to this fan being well made.[61] In other words, *ch'eng* can be treated as completely perfect nature. It is the beginning and the end of human beings. As the beginning, *ch'eng* is the principle endowed by Heaven. As the end, *ch'eng* is the complete perfection of self-actualization.

Although *ch'eng* is endowed by Heaven, it does not mean that it is theocentric. *Ch'eng* is mainly due to human effort. It is not the element of acceptance of God's acceptance. Rather, it is the process of self-actualization. It is sincerity, the action of not disregarding one's conscience.[62] To be sincere is to actualize our original nature to the utmost, without an iota of deficiency. As the self-realization of the norms of human excellence, not only is *ch'eng* the principle, but also the dynamic process of human self-actualization. In this self-actualization, whenever humans fully actualize their original principle endowed by Heaven in their nature, humans then become humane (*jen*). Clearly, *ch'eng* here does not correspond to the Christian idea of God. Instead, it is mainly the self-actualization of the norms of human excellence. Through this process, humans can reunite with what they are estranged from. This process is basically anthropocosmic.

In this chapter, we have surveyed the resemblance of the idea of reunification in Chu Hsi and Tillich. Basically, this reunification is the resolution of human existential estrangement. Both Chu Hsi and Tillich agree that this reunification is not a return to where human were before their departure from the ontological structure. Rather, this is the process of overcoming human estrangement and reunifying with the whole human reality. In Chu Hsi's thought, reunification is harmony. In his theory of equilibrium and harmony, Chu Hsi contends that equilibrium is the natural state of the heart-mind before it is aroused, while harmony is the function of the heart-mind as it responds to the external world in accord with moral principles.[63] In human existential estrangement, harmony is reunion with that to which one belongs and from which one is estranged.

In Tillich's thought, reunification is the process of reunion in which humans are not returning to the essential state of existence, but rather to the essential state of unity. By participating in the love of their ground, humans are able to respond to and reunite with their ground. In this return, human estrangement can be overcome and the reunion can be fulfilled. The whole human reality is then in a harmonious state.

Furthermore, both Chu Hsi and Tillich have their own pivotal categories of reunion. We have discussed how these categories mirror the ontological dimension. Both Chu Hsi and Tillich advocate new views through their categories. Traditionally, Confucianism treats *jen* as one of the cardinal virtues and Christianity treats love as an emotional and ethical concept. However, both Chu Hsi's *jen* and Tillich's love are not merely understood in the ethical dimension, but also in the ontological dimension. Both of them are the principle and the drive toward the unity of the whole human reality. Vertically speaking, Chu Hsi's *jen* and Tillich's love are the source and path for humans to reunite with their ground. That is to say, both of them have the vertical dimension toward the Transcendent, although the understandings of the Transcendent in the thought of Chu Hsi and Tillich are radically different. Following the difference between Confucian Heaven and Christian God, Chu Hsi's *jen* is anthropocosmic, whereas Tillich's love is theocentric.

Furthermore, both *jen* and love embrace all other forms of virtue or love and are the ultimate criterion of the new being. They have power to overcome estrangement between humans. *Jen* has *ch'eng* as self-actualization and love needs justice to direct their work. And finally, both *jen* and love are parallel at the social level. In addition, in order to be the dynamic resolution of human estrangement, both *jen* and love function as a unifying force. They are no longer the principle but are now the active force. Thus, *jen* needs *ch'eng* as self-actualization as much as love needs faith for their dynamic resolution of human estrangement. In fact, *jen*/*ch'eng* and love/faith are two sides of the same coin.

Notes

1. Tillich, "Being and Love," 661.
2. Chan, *A Source Book of Chinese Philosophy*, 594.
3. Tillich, *Systematic Theology*, vol .3, 135.
4. Tillich, *Love, Power, Justice*, 5
5. Tillich, *Systematic Theology*, vol. 3, 135.
6. Yao, *Confucianism and Christianity*, 94.
7. Ch'en Ch'un, *Neo-Confucian Terms Explained*, 71.
8. Tillich, "Being and Love," 662.
9. *Yü-lei*, Ch. 25, sec 22, 606. See also Chan, *Chu Hsi: New Studies*, 160.
10. Ch'en Ch'un, *Neo-Confucian Terms Explained* 75-6.
11. Chan, *Chu Hsi: New Studies*, 194.
12. Yao, *Confucianism and Christianity*, 217.
13. Tillich, *Systematic Theology*, vol. 3, 211.
14. Yao, *Confucianism and Christianity*, 217.
15. Chan, *Chu Hsi: New Studies*, 184.
16. Ibid., 185.
17. Ibid., 186.
18. Ibid., 186-7.
19. Chan, *A Source Book of Chinese Philosophy*, 593-4.
20. Tillich, *Systematic Theology*, vol. 2, 179.
21. Berthrong, *All Under Heaven*, 87.

22. Berthing, "Master Chu's Self-Realization," 43.

23. Yao, *Confucianism and Christianity*, 101.

24. Ibid., 101-2.

25. Tillich, *Systematic Theology*, vol. 1, 280.

26. Ibid.

27. Ibid.

28. Chan, *A Source Book of Chinese Philosophy*, 560.

29. Donald J. Munro, *Images of Human Nature*, 121.

30. Ch'en Ch'un, *Neo-Confucian Terms Explained*, 71.

31. This is one of the four moral qualities of the first hexagram, *ch'ien* (Heaven) in the *Book of Change*. See James Legge, *The Sacred Books of the East*, vol. 16 (Oxford: Clarendon Press, 1882), 57.

32. *Yü-lei*, ch. 20, sec. 103, 466.

33. Tillich, *Love, Power, and Justice*, 116.

34. Ch'en Ch'un, *Neo-Confucian Terms Explained*, 70.

35. Tillich, "Being and Love," 664.

36. Ibid.

37. Ibid., 665.

38. Tillich, *Love, Power, and Justice*, 71.

39. Berthrong, *All Under Heaven*, 87.

40. Yao, *Confucianism and Christianity*, 225.

41. Buddhist meditation is done for the sake of attaining unity and harmony with one's innermost self, while Taoist meditation is done for the sake of preserving health and prolonging life. See Julia Ching, "Chu Hsi on Personal Cultivation," 282. Also see Yao, *Confucianism and Christianity*, 225.

42. Ch'en Ch'un, *Neo-Confucian Terms Explained*, 71.

43. Yao, *Confucianism and Christianity*, 225.

44. Ibid., 200.

45. Tillich, *Dynamics of Faith*, 112.

46. Tillich, *Systematic Theology*, vol.3, 130.

47. Ibid., 131.

48. Tillich, *Dynamics of Faith*, 103.

49. Ibid., 116.

50. Ibid.

51. Ibid., 117.

52. Tillich, *Systematic Theology*, vol.3, 129.

53. *Yü-lie*, ch.6, sec. 33, 103. See also Berthrong, "Master Chu's Self-Realization: The Role of *Ch'eng*," 46.

54. Ch'en Ch'un, *Neo-Confucian Terms Explained*, 86.

55. Ibid.

56. Ibid., 87.

57. Tillich, *Systematic Theology*, vol. 1, 108.

58. Ibid., 49.

59. Tillich, "The Importance of New Being for Christian Theology," 174.

60. Tillich, *Systematic Theology*, vol. 3, 130.

61. *Yü-lei,* ch. 6, sec. 29, 102-3.

62. *Yü-lei,* ch. 6, sec. 29, 103.

63. Tsai-chun Chung, *The Development of the Concepts of Heaven and of Man in the Philosophy of Chu Hsi*, 127.

CONCLUSION

In conclusion, instead of rehearsing all the various conclusions of the previous sections, we would like to highlight the fact that Chu Hsi and Tillich come from two radically diverse traditions. That is to say, their philosophical perspectives, abstract categories, and cultural contexts are substantially different. As we have repeatedly argued, Confucianism is an inclusive humanistic and naturalistic tradition, while Christianity is a theistic tradition. Not only are they different types of spirituality, but also the ways of attaining or returning to their source of transcendence are different. As the central concept of Christianity, *agape* as love underlies divine love. Actually, human love emerges from divine love. On the other hand, as the fundamental principle of Confucianism, *jen* is the fulfillment of humanity. It is attained through the cultivation of the human self. This growth and progress of the human self does not depend upon anything but an extension of a person's own virtue, which dwells in human nature, to the world at large.[1]

Evidently, two different traditions have their own unique abstract categories. We cannot find any category equivalent to the Confucian concept of vital energy (*ch'i*) in Christian thought. Nor can we find any concept of grace in Confucian tradition.[2] In order to understand these two concepts, we have to understand their respective structures of thought. In Chu Hsi's thought, vital energy (*ch'i*) is one of the elements of the ontological structure. It is physical, corporeal, transitory, and changeable. But still we cannot really comprehend what vital energy means until we know another element of the ontological structure, namely, principle. Similarly, we cannot understand what grace is until we know the whole system of Christian thought. That is to say, some of their abstract categories only occur in their own framework. And those categories can only make sense within their own framework.

In terms of the social role, Confucianism is much more concerned about familial relationships than Christianity.[3] Familial relations are the first social context for enlarging the self. For Confucianism, self-cultivation is a dynamic movement within the context of the dichotomy of individual self and collective social circumstance. It is manifested concretely in the four developmental and social stages of human beings, that is, cultivating personal life, regulating familial relations, ordering the affairs of the state, and bringing peace to the world. These four stages are not understood merely in a linear progression. Thus, self-cultivation is also the unceasing process of gradual inclusion. In this unceasing process of gradual inclusion, the individual self must be taken as a starting point and the universe as a whole is the final stage. Ideally, the result of self-transformation lies in universal peace. But concretely, self-transformation cannot bypass the regulation of familial relations in the ordering of the affairs of state. Therefore, the ceaseless effort of self-cultivation is an end in itself and its primary purpose is self-realization.[4] However, on the Christian side, human social structure is based upon a covenant. To take care of the garden, to settle this land, and to love one's particular neighbors are contractual obligations, which emerge from an original contract between human beings and God.[5]

Nevertheless, despite the fact that Confucianism and Christianity are different in philosophical perspectives, abstract categories, and cultural contexts, there are still substantial resemblances in the thought of Chu Hsi and of Tillich. In the previous section, we find similarities between Chu Hsi's and Tillich's answers to three questions: What is the fundamental structure of human reality? Why do humans fail to be what they ought to be? How can humans resolve their failure? Essentially, both Chu Hsi and Tillich agree that there is a unity of the whole human reality and that a fundamental category penetrates all things. They share a similar view of the self-world structure and agree that humans have a dynamic ability to grasp and shape reality. In addition, they have similar views of human beings as an individual and communal person as well as a creative but finite being.

However, existentially, both Chu Hsi and Tillich agree that humans are estranged from their ground, their original nature, and others. Although human original nature is good, once it is actualized in the reality, it will be distorted and selfishness will emerge from this actualization. In this respect, selfishness is an ontological issue instead of a moral issue. This is our human condition. In order to resolve their existential problem, both Chu Hsi and Tillich agree that humans must not return to where they were before. Instead, they must overcome their estrangement from and reunite with the whole human reality. In so doing, both Chu Hsi and Tillich have their own pivotal categories of reunion, namely, *jen* and love respectively. These two categories have their similarities on the ontological, vertical, and horizontal dimensions.

Apparently, Confucian-Christian dialogue is a part of the modern interreligious dialogue. In view of this, the tasks of the modern interreligious dialogue are also the tasks of Confucian-Christian dialogue. Before we expound these tasks, we try to figure out why the field of the modern interreligious dialogue is growing. It is burgeoning because of the challenge of religious pluralism. The question of religious pluralism is one of the major issues that we are confronting with everyday. Therefore, in order to respond the challenge, we need to understand the diversity of many religions and wrestle with the patent and real differences among religions. In recognizing differences between the religions, we also must affirm, to a certain extent, the possible value of other religions besides ours. In interreligious dialogue, different religions must share their valuable contents among themselves. Consequentially, an authentic, fruitful interreligious dialogue might contribute to the establishment of a global community.[6] If the establishment of a global community is one of the purposes of the modern interreligious dialogue, then Confucian-Christian dialogue definitely share this goal.

In the face of such a diversity of religions, what is a common ground on which they can build a global community? Ideally speaking, if there is a global community, it seems that a common world culture is necessary. This common culture is a culture that "knits the community together and that distinguishes the world community from other potential communities."[7] Therefore, Samuel Huntington suggests that one of the rules for the world community is the "commonalities rule," that is, "people in all civilizations should search for and attempt to expand the values, institutions, and practices they have in common with peoples of other civilizations."[8] But in this pluralistic world, with so much conflict among different cultures, is it possible to have a common world culture?

Robert C. Neville answers that "the pluralism of world cultures and the internal struggles of each prohibit a unified world culture in the near future."[9] Instead of having a common world culture, Neville suggests that we can have a community of cultures. That is to say, each cultural group in this community has to not only recognize the meanings of the others, but also to respect differences from the others.[10]

In order to understand Neville's idea of a community of cultures, we need to know what he means by a community. A community, as Neville defines, "is a group of people with common patterns of social interaction who relate, at least in part, because of a common representation of themselves as bound together in a group."[11] Given that, a community of cultures then must have an inclusive sense of different cultures. Moreover, although there are different cultures in this community, in order to become a community, it must have "a minimal basic consensus on certain values, norms and attitudes."[12] In other words, if we can find a common concern of different cultures, then we are able to have a community of cultures. So what is our basic common concern today? Undoubtedly, our basic common concern today is our habitat. With the exhaustion of natural resources, the deterioration of our environment, and the endangerment of the equilibrium of our life-support system, our habitat is losing its livability. Such crises demand our responsibility not only to prevent the human community from becoming self-destructive, but also to rebuild this distorted planet. As Hans Küng says, "world society is responsible for its own future! This is [a] responsibility for our society and environment and also for the world after us."[13]

In view of such crises confronting us everyday, Han Küng argues that we need a global ethic that would provide us the ground and guideline for our response to resolve these crises. Further, he contends that the kind of global ethics for sustained global action cannot be achieved without the contribution of religion.[14] Global ethics are closely related to religion because religion can be regarded as a norm on which our values and attitudes are based. Actually, religion itself is a cultural entity and provides both public and private ritual, mythic and philosophic, and practical spiritual meanings for the world and ultimate things.[15] Thus, religion in and of itself is the fundamental element for building a community of cultures. In every cultural tradition, the most profound root is its religious elements. In this respect, religions have a valuable and irreplaceable role to play in developing global ethics. We have to search for the spiritual resource of every cultural tradition so as to establish global ethics for a global community.

According to Tu Wei-ming, there are three kinds of spiritual resources that can contribute to developing a global community. The first kind is the ethico-religious traditions of the modern West, namely, Greek philosophy, Judaism and Christianity. The second kind is derived from non-Western axial-age civilizations, which include Hinduism, Jainism, and Buddhism in South and Southeast Asia, Confucianism and Taoism in East Asia, and Islam throughout the world. And the third kind is the primal traditions, such as Native American, Hawaiian, Maori and numerous tribal indigenous religious traditions.[16] Given these three kinds of spiritual resources, the Enlightenment mentality that we are still possessing now can be enriched, transformed, and restructured for developing an ecumenical sense of a global community.[17]

Evidently, the Enlightenment mentality, as Tu says, is the most dynamic and transformative ideology in human history. All major spheres of interest characteristic of the modern age, such as science and technology, industrial capitalism, market economy, democratic polity, mass communication, and so on, are indebted to and intertwined with this mentality. With the Enlightenment faith, we think we can solve the world's major problems. In fact, the Enlightenment still remains a standard of inspiration for intellectual and spiritual leaders throughout the world. As human awakening, as the discovery of the human potential for global transformation, and as the realization of human desires to become the measure and master of all things, Enlightenment is still the most influential moral discourse in the political culture of the modern age.[18]

Nevertheless, we do not, or should not, negate the conspicuous absence of the idea of a global community in the Enlightenment project.[19] The unintended disastrous consequence of the Enlightenment mentality is the blatant anthropocentrism. In our way of thinking, knowledge is regarded as power instead of wisdom, the desirability of material progress is asserted regardless its corrosive influence on our soul, and the anthropocentric manipulation of nature is justified even at the cost of destroying the life-support system.[20] Therefore, we need to explore the three different spiritual resources, as we mentioned previously, so as to broaden the scope of the Enlightenment mentality, to deepen its moral sensitivity, and to transform its genetic constraints in order to realize fully its potential as a worldview for the human community as a whole.[21] By means of these three spiritual resources, we can reexamine the Enlightenment mentality.

In addition, whenever these three spiritual traditions exchange their resources to each other, there will be at least two consequences. First, each religious person who participates in dialogue will then learn more about not only other religions, but that person's own religious tradition as well. Second, in the process of interaction, a new language and a new kind of spirituality will emerge. With the development of a new vocabulary and a new perspective in dialogue, those who participate in the dialogue will be able to innovatively reinterpret their own religious tradition.

Needless to say, both Confucianism and Christianity are two great world religions. Despite their differences, Christianity and Confucianism, which belong to first and second kinds of spiritual resources respectively, play a significant role for rebuilding our distorted habitat. Since the primary goal of interreligious dialogue is to establish a global community and our common concern is to resolve the problem of our habitat, Confucian-Christian dialogue is definitely sharing this goal and this common concern. However, since Confucianism and Christianity are two different religious traditions, can they co-exist together and mutually respect each other as a community of cultures?

Before answering this question, we need to know at least a brief history of both Confucian and Christian traditions. Undoubtedly, both of them have their own long traditions. In his book, *Tradition*, Edward Shils suggests at least four properties in every tradition. First, tradition means a *traditum*; "it is anything which is transmitted or handed down from the past to the present."[22] For instance, material objects, beliefs about all kinds of things, images of persons and events, practices and institutions, and so on can be regarded as a *traditum*. Moreover, the duration of the existence of a tradition extends to at least three generations before it undergoes some changes.[23]

Second, every tradition has exemplars or custodians, which are regarded as paradigmatic individuals. For example, Confucianism has an ideal of a noble person (*chün-tzu*) imparting moral education. Paradigmatic individuals are the *traditum*, "that which has been and is being handed down or transmitted. It is something which was created, was performed or believed in the past."[24]. In this respect, every tradition must have some conceptions of exemplary embodiment in the lives of certain adherents.

Third, all transmitted things, such as constellations of symbols and clusters of images, "are received and modified. They change in the process of transmission as interpretations are made of the tradition presented; they change also while they are in the possession of their recipients."[25] Thus, things transmitted from the past generation do not always retain their original characteristics and are in the process of being modified. That is to say, traditions are always the objects of interpretation. They are not independently self-reproductive or self-elaborating. "Only living, knowing, desiring human beings can enact them and reenact them and modify them. ... Traditions can deteriorate in the sense of losing their adherents because their possessors cease to present them."[26] In other words, as an adherent of every tradition, one is always to enact, reenact, and even modify one's tradition.

Finally, tradition's stock and possession, such as texts, are selected. In every tradition, certain texts have been selected as having a canonical status and providing an authoritative point of reference for established standards of conduct. As Shils says, "the process of tradition is also a process of election. Parts of the traditional stock drift downward into obscurity so that they are known only to a few persons or conceivably to none at all."[27]

Needless to say, both Confucianism and Christianity have these four features and both of them have been gone through many stages of transformation. Although the first period of the development of Confucianism was in the time of three masters of Confucianism, Confucius (551-479 BCE), Mencius (371-289 BCE), and Hsün Tzu (fl. 298-238), Confucianism did not become the state-sponsored imperial orthodoxy and the civil ideology of the state until the Han dynasty (206 BCE- 220 CE) of ancient China. The Han Confucians in that period of time developed the political theory and preserved the classical Confucian tradition by writing commentaries and historical compilations. However, Taoism was revived in the Wei-Chin period (220-420) and Buddhism flourished in the T'ang dynasty (618-907). Facing the challenge of Taoism and Buddhism, there was a revival of Confucianism in the Northern and Southern Sung period (960-1279). Confucian thought was modified and a new language was developed. Further, the Four Books (*The Analects, Mencius, The Great Learning,* and *The Doctrine of the*

Mean) were selected as the major texts by Chu Hsi (1130-1200) for self-cultivation and were later made for the civil service examinations. With the challenge of the West in the modern period, Confucianism shifted paradigms again.[28] A group called New Confucianism emerged on the modern scene. As Tu Wei-ming indicates, New Confucianism can be depicted as a third epoch of the Confucian tradition and is still in the process of redefining its inherited tradition.

On the Christian side, the Christian tradition has numerous paradigm shifts throughout Western history. Hans Küng employs Thomas S. Kuhn's paradigm theory for the natural sciences to delineate the history of Christianity. Küng indicates that the early Christian apocalyptic paradigm shifted toward the ancient Hellenistic paradigm when it had encountered the Hellenistic culture. Following the disruption of the Roman Empire, there was a divide between the Eastern and Western Christian churches in the tenth century and the Christian church in the West shifted the Mediaeval Roman Catholic paradigm. After the Renaissance, the Christian church shifted again to a Reformation Protestant paradigm. With the rise of the modern era, there was a shift to the Enlightenment Modern paradigm. And with the advent of industrialization and democratization, Christianity has adopted the contemporary ecumenical paradigm.[29]

According to Shils, the transformation of traditions is based upon endogenous and exogenous factors. The former is the internal factor whereas the latter is the external factor. "A tradition does not change itself. It contains the potentiality of being changed; it instigates human beings to change."[30] That is to say, persons, who belong to the tradition, carry out endogenous changes. "The creative power of the human mind in confrontation with the potentialities resident in traditions produces changes."[31] In addition to endogenous factors, whenever the adherents of traditions contact with other traditions, traditions then will have at least four possible transformations, namely, addition, amalgamation, absorption, and fusion.[32] Regarding Confucianism and Christianity, both religious traditions were transformed whenever they encountered other religious traditions throughout their own history.

Ever since the late 1590s when Matteo Ricci put Christian ideas into Chinese idioms, two great religious traditions, Confucianism and Christianity, have been conceptually engaged in dialogue. Now the population of Christians in East Asia has increased enormously.

Confucian-Christian dialogue is more than just about ideas. If inter-religious dialogue can be divided into three different kinds,[33] then Confucian-Christian dialogue in East Asian Christians is the dialogue of life. Each day East Asian Christians face the question of how to live their Christian lives within their social context. In other words, they are facing a question whether they can be both Confucian and Christian simultaneously.

In terms of the concept of dual citizenship, which is suggested by both Hans Küng and John Berthrong, it is evident that every East Asian Christian has dual religious citizenship or even multiple religious citizenships. In answering how one can authentically be Chinese and Christian at the same time, Hans Küng quotes from Stanislaus Lokuang's words that

> An authentic Chinese must have a deep esteem for matters of the spirit. He must respect Heaven and his Ancestors. He must observe the Confucian moral code. He must cultivate the five virtues of charity, justice, temperance, fidelity, and prudence. He must have filial piety to build family. An authentic Christian must love God above all things, and his neighbor as himself. He must observe the Ten Commandments. He must put eternal life as two types of life, we find that they are not contradictory to one another. They reciprocally complete one another.[34]

Actually, East Asian Christians have no choice but to recognize the fact that once they are Christians, they already have dual religious citizenship because East Asian Christians, whether they are Korean, Japanese, Vietnamese, or Chinese, are embedded in the matrix of Confucian culture. Therefore, it is not a question, for East Asian Christians, whether or not a Confucian can be a Christian at the same time. Surely, East Asian Christians can authentically be Chinese, Korean, and Japanese and at the same time Christians although they are still struggling with their Christian faith. However, struggling to be an authentic Christian is not only the issue of East Asian Christians, but also of the western Christians. Being an American or a European does not mean that one can be an authentic Christian spontaneously. To be an authentic Christian is a process of justification and sanctification. That is to say, one has to learn, not just be born, in order to become an authentic Christian.

Saying that East Asian Christians have dual religious citizenship does not mean that there is no conflict between East Asian religions and Christianity. Surely, Confucianism and Christianity are radically different religions. And yet, they also have similarities within their differences. For instance, both Confucianism and Christianity agree that humans are inter-related with the world. One cannot exist without the other. In addition to that, humans are both individual and communal people. To be an individual person is to be communal person and to participate in our habitat. Second, both Confucianism and Christianity agree that in reality, we are not what we ought to be. In other words, essentially, our natures are good, but existentially, our original natures are distorted. Finally, both of them are concerned with resolving the problem which humankind faces. Due to these similarities, Confucianism and Christianity are not mutually exclusive. Rather, East Asian Christians can be both Confucians and Christians simultaneously in the sense that they are always in the process of integration and transformation.

In addition, dual religious citizenship is not a kind of religious cocktail. As dual religious citizens, East Asian Christians must have adequate knowledge of both religious traditions so that they can have a deeper understanding of ultimate reality as well as the fundamental ethical principles of both traditions. As noted already, both Confucianism and Christianity have been transformed many times throughout their histories. Through the dialogue within the life of East Asian Christians, the difference between Confucianism and Christianity might be integrated so as to develop a new language and new spirituality, or even a new system of thought for the Church of East Asia.

If the crises facing our habitat are a common concern of people from all religious traditions, then one of the aims of interreligious dialogue is to respond to these crises. More precisely, a concern for our problematic habitat can provide a common ground for interreligious dialogue. Therefore, the starting point of inter-religious dialogue is not to look for differences between different religious traditions; rather, religious dialogue is to affirm the value of each religious tradition. In recognizing the value of each religious tradition and respecting the differences from each other, we might build a community of cultures, that is, "the commonalities rule" of a global community, so as to resolve the problem of our distorted habitat.

Evidently, the major aim of the Confucian-Christian dialogue is not to figure out which is better, Confucianism or Christianity; rather, the dialogue is to seek for resources from each tradition so that a "distorted" habitat can be rebuilt. Then the initial step of the dialogue is to look for similarities between two radically different religious traditions. In this comparative study, we have showed that both Chu Hsi and Tillich have certain substantial resemblances in their understanding of ontological structure, human estrangement and its resolution. What do these similarities tell us? Basically, they imply that Confucianism and Christianity are not incommensurable even though they have different types of language. Their systems of thought are compatible with each other, at least in the idea of the problem of humankind, that is, we are not what we ought to be in relation to our primordial ground of being, to our human fellows, and to our habitat. And both Confucianism and Christianity share the same concern for resolving our human problems. Finally, both the Great Commission in Christianity and the unceasing process of gradual inclusion in Confucian mode of the enhancement of oneself indicate that their mission is to extend to the whole human race. That is to say, both Confucianism and Christianity share the same mission for building a global community. Therefore, Confucian-Christian dialogue becomes not only the basis for constructive theological formation, but also an ethical imperative for life in the global city of the modern world.

Regarding East Asian Christians, they are the citizens of both Confucianism and Christianity simultaneously. Therefore it is not a question of whether East Asian Christians can be both Confucians and Christians, but a matter of how they carry out their mission by having a dual citizenship. In other words, to be responsible citizens, East Asian Christians should take their own cultural tradition, i.e., Confucian tradition, as well as their Christian faith seriously by enacting, reenacting and transforming these two traditions in their mental and spiritual lives.

Notes

1. Yao, *Confucianism and Christianity*, 213.

2. Lee H. Yearley, *Mencius and Aquinas: Theories of Virtue and Conceptions of Courage* (Albany: State University of New York Press, 1990), 170.

3. Ibid.

4. Tu Wei-ming, *Humanity and Self-Cultivation: Essays in Confucian Thought*, 27-28.

5. Neville, *Behind the Masks of God*, 138-9.

6. See Paul F. Knitter, *One Earth Many Religions: Multifaith Dialogue and Global Responsibility*, (Maryknoll: Orbis Books, 1995).

7. Robert C. Neville, "World Comm unity and Religion," *Journal of Ecumenical Studies*, vol. 29, no. 3-4, (Summer-Fall) 1992: 371.

8. Samuel P. Huntington, *The Clash of Civilizations and the Remaking of World Order,* (New York: Simon and Schuster, 1996), 320.

9. Ibid.

10. Ibid., 367-8.

11. Neville, "World Community and Religion," 373.

12. Hans Küng, *Global Responsibility: In Search of a New World Ethic*, (New York: The Crossroad Publishing Company, 1991), 28.

13. Ibid., 30-31.

14. See Hans Küng, *Global Responsibility: In Search of a New World Ethic*, (New York: The Crossroad Publishing Company, 1991).

15. Neville, "World Community and Religion," 373.

16. Ibid., 42-45.

17. Ibid., 45.

18. Ibid., 41-2.

19. See Tu Wei-ming, "Global community as lived reality: exploring spiritual resources for social development,"

20. Ibid., 45.

21. Ibid., 42.

22. Edward Shils, *Tradition*, (Chicago: University of Chicago Press, 1981), 12.

23. Ibid., 13.

24. Ibid.

25. Ibid.

26. Ibid., 15.

27. Ibid., 26.

28. Berthrong, *All Under Heaven*, 81.

29. Hans Küng, *Global Responsibility*, 123.

30. Edward Shils, *Tradition*, 213.

31. Ibid..

32. See Edward Shils, *Tradition*, (Chicago: University of Chicago Press, 1981), 275-279.

33. Three kinds of dialogue are the dialogue of life, of meaning, and of the heart. See Berthrong, *All Under Heaven*, 186-7.

34. Han Küng and Julia Ching, *Christianity and Chinese Religions*, (New York: Doubleday and Collins Publishers, 1988), 277.

BIBLIOGRAPHY

Works on Chu Hsi and Confucianism

Primary Sources

Chinese Sources

Chu Hsi and Lü Tsu-ch'ien 呂祖謙. *近思錄*. [Reflections on things at hand]. 1178. TSCC ed. Taipei: Shih-chieh shu-chü, 1975.

Chu Hsi. *朱子語類*. [Classified conversations of Chu Hsi]. Ed. by Li Ching-te, 1270; 1473 ed. Rpt. in 8 vols. Taipei: Cheng-chung, 1962.

———. *朱文公文集*. [Collected writings of Chu Hsi]. 1245. SPPY ed. Entitled Chu-tzu ta-chuan [Complete writings of Chu Hsi]. Rpt. in 12 vols. Taipei: Chung Hua, 1970.

———. *四書集注*. [Collected Commentaries on the Four Books]. Taipei: Shih-chieh sh-chü, 1971.

———. *續近思錄*. [Further Reflections on Things at Hand]. Comp. by Chang Po-hsing. Taipei: Shih-chieh shu-chü, 1974.

———. *朱子全書*. [Collected works of Chu Hsi]. 1713. Yüan-chien chai ed. Rpt. in 2 vols. Taipei: Kuang-hsueh she, 1977.

Western-Language Sources

Ch'en Ch'un (115-1223). *The Pei-hsi Tzu-i*[Neo-Confucian Terms Explained]. Trans. and ed. by Wing-tsit Chan. Columbia University Press, 1986.

Chan, Wing-tist, trans. and complied. *A Sourse Book in Chinese Philosophy*. Princeton: Princeton University Press, 1963.

Chu Hsi and Lü Tsu-ch'ien. *Reflections on Things at Hand: The Neo-Confucian Anthology*. Trans. by Wing-tsit Chan. New York: Columbia University Press, 1967.

Chu Hsi. *The Philosophy of Human Nature*. Trans. by J. Percy Bruce. London: Probsthain and Company, 1922.

Gardner, Daniel K., trans. and ed. *Learning to Be a Sage: Selections from the Conversation of Master Chu, Arranged Topically*. Berkeley: University of California Press, 1990.

Wittenborn, Allen, trans. and ed. *Further Reflections on Things at Hand: A Reader*. Lanham, Md.: University Press of American, 1991.

Secondary Sources

Chinese Sources

Chan, Wing-tsit. *朱子論集*. [Collected essays on the school of Chu Hsi]. Taipei: Hsueh-sheng shu-chü, 1982.

———. *朱子新探索*. [New Investigation of Chu Hsi]. Taipei: Hsueh-sheng, 1988.

———. *宋明理學之概念與歷史*. [The Concept and History of the School of Principle in Sung and Ming]. Taiwan, Republic of China: Institute of Chinese Literature and Philosophy, Academia Sinica, 1996.

Chang, Li-wen. *朱子思想研究*. [A Study of Chu Hsi's Thought]. Peking: Chung-kuo she-hui k'o-hsueh ch'u-pan-she, 1981.

———. *宋明理學邏輯結構的演化*. [The Development of the logical structure of Sung and Ming Confucianism]. Taiwan: 萬卷樓, 1993.

Ch'en, Lai. *朱熹哲學研究*. [Research on Chu Hsi's philosophy]. Peking: Chung-kuo she-hui k'o-hsueh, 1987.

———. "朱子新學案述評." [An Introductory review of Ch'ien Mu's Chu-tzu hsin-hsueh-an]. *Chung-kuo che-hsüeh* , IX (1982): 257-269.

———. "朱熹理氣觀的形成和演變." [The formation and development of Chu Hsi's doctrine of principle and material force]. *Che-hsueh yen-chiu*, 6 (1985): 50-58.

Ch'ien, Mu . *朱子新學案*. [A new study of Chu Hsi]. 5 vols. Taipei: Sanmin shu-chü, 1971.

———. *中國近三百年學術史*. [The history of thought and scholarship in China during the past three hundred years]. Shanghai: Commercial Press, 1940.

———. *宋明理學概論*. [A general survey of the Confucian philosophers of the Sung and Ming periods]. Taipei: Chung-hua wen-hua, 1962.

Ch'iu, Han-Sheng. *四書集注簡論*. [A brief discussion of Chu His's Collected Commentaries tothe Four Books]. Peking: Chung-kuo she-hui k'o hsueh ch'u-pan-she, 1980.

Chung-kuo che-hsueh-shih hsueh-hui ed. *論宋明理學*. [Studies on Sung Ming Confucianism]. Hangchow: Che-chiang jen-min ch'u-pan-she, 1983.

Fan, Shou-k'ang. *朱子及其哲學*. [Chu Hsi and His philosophy]. Taipei: K'ai-ming shu-chü, 1964.

Fung, Yu-lan. *中國哲學史*. [A History of Chinese philosophy]. Shanghai: Commercial Press, 1935.

———. "宋明道學通論." [Introduction to Sung Ming Confucianism]. *Che-hsueh yen-chiu* 6 (1983): 61-69.

Hou, Wai-lu. et al., eds. *中國思想通史*. [A General History of Chinese thought]. 5 vols.

Peking: Jen-imn ch'u-pan-she, 1960.

———. *宋明理學史*. [History of Sung Ming Confucianism]. 2 vols. Peking: Chung-hua, 1985.

Hsiung, Wan. *宋代理學與佛學之探索*. [A Study of the Neo-Confucianism and the Buddhism of the Sung Dynasty]. Taipei: Wen-chin ch'u-pan-she, 1985.

Huang Tsung-hsi (1610-1695), Ch'uen Tsu-wang (1705-1755) et al., eds. *宋元學案*. [Records of Sung and Yuan Confucians]. Taipei: Kuang-wen shu-chü, 1971.

Jen, Chi-yü, ed. *中國哲學史*. [History of Chinese Philosophy]. Peking: Jen-min, 1963.

Kung, Tao-yün. *朱學論叢*. [Essays on the School of Chu Hsi]. Taipei: Wen-shih-che ch'u-pan-she, 1985.

Lao, Szu-kuang. *中國哲學史*. [A History of Chinese Philosophy], vol 2. Hong Kong: Chung-chi College, 1971.

Liu, Shu-hsien. *朱子哲學思想的發展與完成*. [Development and completion of Chu Hsi's philosophical thought]. Taipei: Hsüh-sheng chu-chü, 1984.

Mao, Ts'ung-hu. "朱熹和黑格爾哲學之同異簡析." [An analysis of the similarities and differences between Chu Hsi and Hegel]. *Chung-kuo che-hsueh* XIII (1985): 10-20.

Meng, P'ei-yüan. "王夫之哲學與朱熹理學." [Wang Fu-chih's philosophy and Chu Hsi's philosophy of principle]. *Chug-kuo che-hsüeh* X (1983): 211-237.

Mou, Tsung-san. *心體與性體*. [Mind and Nature]. 3 vols. Taipei: Cheng-chu chu-chu, 1968-69.

P'an Fu-en and Shih Ch'ang-tung. *中國哲學論稿*. [Studies in Chinese philosophy]. Ch'ung-ch'ing: Ch'ung-ch'ing ch'u-pan-she, 1984.

Shih-hsüeh p'ing-lun she. "*朱子思想研究專號*." [Special Issue on Chu Hsi's Thought] *Shih-hsueh p'ing-lun* 5 (1983).

T'ang, Chün-i. *中國哲學原論：導論篇*. [Fundamental Exposition of Chinese Philosophy: Introduction]. Hong Kong: New Asia Institute, 1966.

———. "朱陸異同探原." [An inquiry into the sources of the differences and similarities between Chu Hsi and Lu Hsiang-shan]. *Hsin Ya Hsüeh-pao* 8.1 (February 1967): 1-100.

———. *中國哲學原論: 原性篇*. [Fundamental Exposition of Chinese Philosophy: on human nature]. Hong Kong: New Asia Institute, 1968.

Ts'ai, Jen-hou. *宋明理學*. [Sung and Ming Confucianism]. 2 vols. Taipei: Hsüeh-sheng shu-chü, 1980.

Wang, Mao-hung (1668-1741). *朱子年譜*. [Biographical chronology of Chu Hsi]. Taipei: Commercial Press, 1971.

Western-Language Sources

Allinson, Robert E., ed. *Understanding the Chinese Mind: The Philosophical Roots*. New York: Oxford University Press, 1989.

Berthrong, John H. "The Thoughtlessness of Unexamined Things." *Journal of Chinese Philosophy* 7 (1980): 131-151.

———. "The Problem of the Mind: Mou Tsung-san's Critique of Chu Hsi." *Journal of Chinese Religion* 10 (1982): 32-55.

———. "Chu Hsi's Ethics: *Jen* and *Ch'eng*." *Journal of Chinese Philosophy* 14 (1987): 161-178.

———. "Trends in the Interpretation of Confucian Religiosity." *Ching Feng: Quarterly Notes on Christianity and Chinese Religion and Culture*. 32, no. 4 (December 1989): 224-44.

———. "To Catch a Thief: Chu Hsi (1130-1200) and the Hermeneutic Art." *Journal of Chinese Philosophy* 18 (1991): 195-212.

———. "Master Chu's Self-Realization: The Role of Ch'eng." *Philosophy East and West* 43, no. 1 (January 1993): 39-64.

———. *All Under Heaven: Transforming Paradigms in Confucian-Christian Dialogue*. Albany: State University of New York Press, 1994.

Birdwhistell, Anne D. *Transition to Neo-Confucianism: Shao Yung on Knowledge and Symbols of Reality*. Stanford: Stanford University Press, 1989.

Bol, Peter K.. *"This Culure of Ours": Intellectual Tansitions in T'ang and Sung China.* Stanford: Stanford University Press, 1992.

Bruce, J. Percy. *Chu Hsi and His Masters*. London: Probsthain, 1923.

Chan, Wing-tsit. *Neo-Confucianism, Etc. Essays by Wing-tsit Chan.* Ed. by Charles K. H. Chen. Hanover, N. H.: Oriental Society, 1969.

———. "Patterns for Neo-Confucianism: Why Chu Hsi Differed from Ch'eng I." *Journal of Chinese Philosophy* 5/2 (June 1978): 101-126.

———, ed. *Chu Hsi and Neo-Confucianism.* Honolulu: University of Hawaii Press, 1986.

———. *Chu Hsi Life and Thought*. Hong Kong: Chinese University of Hong Kong Press, 1987.

———. *Chu Hsi: New Studies.* Honolulu: University of Hawaii Press, 1989.

Chang, Carsun. *The Developmant of Neo-Confucian Thought*. 2 Vols. New York: Bookman Associates, 1957-1962.

Cheng, Chung-ying. *New Dimensions of Confucian and Neo-Confucian Philosophy.* Albany: State University of New York Press, 1991.

Ching, Julia. "The Confucian Way (Tao) and Its Transmission (Tao-t'ung)." *Journal of the History of Ideas* 35.3 (July-September 1974): 371-388.

———. "The Goose Lake Monastery Debate (1175)." *Journal of Chinese Philosophy* 1.2 (March 1974): 161-178.

———. *Chinese Religions.* Maryknoll, N.Y.: Orbis Books, 1993.

Chung, Tsai-chun. *The Develoment of the Concepts of Heaven and of Man in the Philosophy of Chu Hsi.* Taipei: Institute of Chinese Literature and Philosophy Academia Sinica, 1993.

Cohen, Paul and Merle Goldman, eds. *Ideas Across Cultures: Essays on Chinese Thought in Honor of Benjamin I. Schwartz.* Cambridge: Council on East Asia Studies, Harvard Univesity, 1990.

Cua, A. S. "The Idea of Confucian Tradition." *Review of Metaphysics* 45 (June 1992): 803-840.

de Bary, Wm. Theodore, ed. *Self and Society in Ming Thought.* New York and London: Columbia University Press, 1970.

———, ed. *The Unfolding of Neo-Confucianism.* New York and London: Columbia University Press, 1975.

———, and Irene Bloom, eds. *Principle and Practicality: Essay in Neo-Confucianism and Practical Learning.* New York: Columbia University Press, 1979.

———. *Neo-Confucian Orthodoxy and the Learning of the Mind-and-Heart.* New York: Columbia University Press, 1981.

———. *The Liberal Tradition in China.* Hong Kong and New York: The Chinese University Press and Columbia University Press, 1983.

———. *East Asian Civilizations: A Dialogue in five Stages.* Cambridge: Harvard University Press, 1988.

———. *The Message of the Mind in Neo-Confucianism.* New York: Columbia University Press, 1989.

———. "The Prophetic Voice in the Confucian Nobleman." *Ching Feng.* 33, nos. 1 & 2 (April 1990): 3-19.

———. *Learning for One's Self: Essays on the Individual in Neo-Confucian Thought.*

New York: Columbia University Press, 1991.

———. *The Trouble with Confucianism.* Cambridge, MA: Harvard University Press, 1991.

Eber, Irene, ed. *Confucianism: The Dynamics of Tradition.* New York: Macmillan, 1986.

Eno, Robert. *The Confucian Creation of Heaven.* Albany: State University of New York Press, 1990.

Fingarette, Herbert. *Confucius--the Secular as Sacred.* New York: Harper and Row, 1972.

Fu, Charles Wei-hsun. "Morality and Beyond: The Neo-Confucian Confrontation with Buddhism." *Philosophy East and West* 23.3 (1973): 375-396.

Gardner, Daniel K. "Chu Hsi's Reading of the Ta-hsüeh: a Neo-Confucian's Quest for Truth." *Journal of Chinese Philosophy* 10.3 (September 1983): 182-204.

———. *Chu Hsi and the Ta-hsüeh: Neo-Confucian Reflection on the Confucian Canon.* Cambridge: Council on East Asian Studies, Harvard University, 1986.

———. "Transmitting the Way; Chu Hsi and His Program of Learning." *Harvard Journal of Asiatic Studies* 49.1 (June 1989): 141-172.

Gedalecia, David. "Excursion into Substance and Function: The Development of the *t'i-yung* Paradigm in Chu Hsi." *Philosophy East and West* 24.4 (October 1974): 443-451.

———. "Evolution and Synthesis in Neo-Confucianism." Journal of Chinese Philosophy 6.1 (1979): 91-102.

Graham, A. C. *Two Chinese Philosophers: Ch'eng Ming-tao and Ch'eng Yi-ch'uan.* London: Lund Humphries, 1958.

———. *Disputers of the Tao.* La Salle, Il: Open Court, 1989

Hall, David L. and Roger T. Ames. *Thinking Through Confucius.* Albany: State University of New York Press, 1987.

———. *Anticipating China: Thinking Through the Narratives of Chinese and Western cultures.* Albany: State University of New York Press, 1995.

Hocking, William Ernest. "Chu Hsi's Theory of Knowledge." *Harvard Journal of Asiatic Studies* 1 (1936): 109-27.

Huang, Chun-chieh. "The Synthesis of Old Pursuits and New Knowledge: Chu Hsi's Interpretation of Mencian Morality." *New Asia Academic Bulletin* 3 (July 1982): 197-222.

Hymes, Robert and Conrad Schirokauer, eds. *Ordering the World.* Berkeley and Los Angeles: University of California Press, 1993.

Ivanhoe, Philip J. *Confucian Moral Self Cultivation.* New York: Peter Lang Publishing, Inc., 1993.

Lai, Whalen W. "How the Principle Rides on the Ether: Chu Hsi's Non-Buddhistic Resolution of Nature and Emotion." J*ournal of Chinese Philosophy* 11.1 (March 1984): 31-65.

Lee, Jig-chuen. "Wang Yang-ming, Chu Hsi, and the Investigation of Things." *Philosophy East and West* 37, no. 1 (January 1987): 24-35.

Levenson, Joseph P. *Confucian China and its Modern Fate: A Trilogy.* Berkeley: University of California Press, 1968.

Liu, Shu-hsien and Peter K. H. Lee. "A Confucian-Christian Dialogue: Liberating Life as a Commitment to Truth." *Ching Feng* 33, no. 3 (September 1990): 113-35.

Liu, Shu-hsien. "A Philosophical Analysis of the Confucian Approach to Ethics." *Philosophy East and West* 22 (October 1972): 417-25.

———. "The Confucian Approach to the Problem of Transcendence and Immanence." *Philosophy East and West* 22 (January 1972): 45-52.

———. "The Function of the Mind in Chu Hsi's Philosophy." *Journal of Chinese Philosophy* 5 (1978): 195-208.

———. "On Chu Hsi as an important source for the development of the Philosophy of Wang Yang-Ming." *Journal of Chinese Philosophy* 11 (1984): 83-107.

———. "Some Reflections on What Contemporary Neo-Confucian Philosophy Learn from Christianity." *Ching Feng* 32, no. 3 (September 1989): 145-58.

———. "Toward a New Relation Between Humanity and Nature: Reconstructing," *Zygon*, vol. 24, no. 4 (December 1989): 457-468.

———. "Some reflection on the Sung-Ming Understanding of Mind, Nature, and Reason." *The Journal of the Institute of Chinese Studies of The Chinese University of Hong Kong* 21, (1990): 331-43.

Metzger, Thomas A. *Escape from Predicament: Neo-Confucianism and China's Evolving Political Culture*. New York: Columbia University Press, 1977.

Munro, Donald J. *The Concept of Man in Early China.* Stanford: Stanford University Press, 1969.

———, ed. *Studies in Confucian and Taoist Values*. Ann Arbor: Center of Chinese Studies, University of Michigan, 1985.

———. *Images of Human Nature: A Sung Portrait.* Princeton: Princeton University Press, 1988.

Nivison, David S. and Arthur F. Wright, eds. *Confucianism in Action*. Stanford: Stanford University Press, 1959.

Rozman, Gilbert. *Confucian Heritage and Its Modern Adaptation*. Princeton: Princeton University Press, 1991.

Schirokauer, Conrad. "Chu Hsi's Political Thought." *Journal of Chinese Philosophy* 5.2 (June 1978): 127-159.

———. "Rationality in Chinese Philosophy." *Journal of Chinese Philosophy* 11.1 (March 1984): 19-29.

Schwartz, Banjamin I. *The World of Thought in Ancient China.* Cambridge, MA: The

Belknap Press of Harvard University, 1985.

Sharma, Arvind, ed. *Our Religions.* San Francisco: HarperCollins Publishers, 1993.

T'ang, Chün-i. "Chang Tsai's Theory of Mind and Its Metaphysical Basis." *Philosophy East and West* 6.2 (July 1956): 113-136.

———. "The *T'ien Ming* (Heavenly Ordinance) in pre-Ch'in China." *Philosophy East and West* 6 (1962): 113-36.

Taylor, Rodney L. *The Religious Dimensions of Confucianism.* Albany, N.Y.: State University of New York Press, 1990

———. "The Study of the Confucianism as a Religious Tradition: Notes on Some Recent Publications." *Journal of Chinese Philosophy* 18 (Fall 1990).

Tillman, Hoyt Cleveland. *Utilitarian Confucianism: Ch'en Liang's Challenge to Chu Hsi.* Cambridge, MA: Council on East Asia Studies, Harvard University Press, 1982.

———. "Consciousness of T'ien in Chu Hsi's Thought." *Harvard Journal of Asiatic Studies* 47.1 (June 1987): 31-50.

———. "A New Direction in Confucian Scholarship: Approaches to examining the differences between Neo-Confucianism and Tao-Hsüeh." *Philosophy East and West* 42, no. 3 (July 1992): 455-474.

———. *Confucian Discourse and Chu Hsi's Ascendancy.* Honolulu: University of Hawaii Press, 1992.

Tu, Wei-ming. *Humanity and Self-Cultivation: Essays in Confucian Thought.* Berkeley: Asian Humanities Press, 1979.

———. *Confucian Thought: Selfhood as Creative Transformation.* Albany, N.Y.: State University of New York Press, 1985.

———. *Centrality and Commonality: An Essay on Confucian Religiousness.* Albany: State University of New York Press, 1989.

———, Milan Hejtmanek, and Alan Wachman. *The Confucian World Observed: A Contemporary Discussion of Confucian Humanism in East Asia.* Honolulu: University of Hawaii Press, 1992.

———. "Confucianism" in Our Religions, ed. Arvind Sharma, 137-227. San Francisco: Harper and Row, 1993.

———. *Way, Learning, and Politics: Essays on the Confucian Intellectual.* Albany: State University of New York Press, 1993.

———, ed. *China in Transformation.* Cambridge, MA: Harvard University Press, 1994.

———, ed. *The Living Tree: The Changing Meaning of Being Chinese Today.* Stanford: Stanford University Press, 1994.

Weber, Max. *The Religion in China.* New York: Free Press, 1951.

Wilson, Thomas A. *Genealogy of the Way: The Construction and Uses of the Confucian Tradition in Late Imperial China.* Stanford, CA: Stanford University Press, 1995.

Wyatt, Don J. "Chu Hsi's Critique of Shao Yung: One Instance of the Stand Against Fatalism." *Harvard Journal of Asiatic Studies* 45.2 (December 1985): 649-666.

Yang, C. K. *Religion in Chinese Society.* Berkeley and Los Angeles: University of California Press, 1961.

Yearley, Lee H. *Mencius and Aquinas: Theories of Virtue and Conceptions of Courage.* Albany: State University of New York Press, 1990.

Yu, David. "The Conception of Self in Whitehead and Chu Hsi." *Journal of Chinese Philosophy* 7 (1980): 153-173.

Works on Paul Tillich

Primary Sources (Works by Paul Tillich)

Tillich, Paul. *The Interpretation of History*. New York: Scribner's Sons, 1936.

———. "Freedom in the Period of Transformation." In *Freedom: Its Meaning*, ed. by Ruth N. Anshen, 123-144. New York: Harcourt, Brace, and Co., 1940.

———. "Our disintegrating World." *Anglican Theological Review* 23, no. 2 (April 1941): 134-146.

———. "Love's strange Work." *The Protestant* 4, no. 4 (February-March, 1942): 70-75.

———. "Estrangement and Reconciliation in Modern Thought." *Review of Religion* 9, no. 1 (November, 1944): 5-19.

———. *The Shaking of the Foundations*. New York: Charles Scribner's Sons, 1948.

———. *Systematic Theology*. (Vol. 1) Chicago: The University of Chicago Press, 1951.

———. "Being and Love." In *Moral Principles of Action*. ed. by Ruth N. Anshen, 661-672. New York: Harper and Brothers, 1952.

———. *The Courage To Be*. New Haven: Yale University Press, 1952.

———. *Love, Power, and Justice*. New York: Oxford University Press, 1954.

———. *Biblical Religion and the Search for Ultimate Reality*. Chicago: The University of Chicago Press, 1955.

———. *The New Being*. New York: Charles Scribner's Sons, 1955.

———. *The Eternal Now*. New York: Charles Scribner's Sons, 1956.

———. *Systematic Theology*. (Vol. 2) Chicago: The University of Chicago Press, 1957.

———. *The Protestant Era.* (Abridged edition). Trans. by James Luther Adams. Chicago: University of Chicago Press, 1958.

———. "What is Man? A Symposium on the Individual in Modern Society." (Unpublished broadcast transcript) Yale Christian Association (January 4, 1957). Tillich Archives: 407:016.

———. "Protestant Principle and The Encounter of World Religions." (Unpublished) Matchette Lectures, Wesleyan University, (April 9-11, 1958). Tillich Archives: 411-004.

———. *The Dynamics of Faith.* New York: Harper and Row, 1958.

———. *The Theology of Culture.* ed. by Robert C. Kimball. New York: Oxford University Press, 1959.

———. "Japanese Report—August 1960: Informal Report on Lecture Trip to Japan." (Unpublished). Tillich Archives: 418:001.

———. "Christian and Non-Christian Revelation." (Unpublished) Lycoming College (October 28, 1961). Tillich Archives: 411:006.

———. *The Religious Situation.* trans. by Richard Niebuhr. New York: Meridian Books, 1962.

———. *Christianity and The Encounter of the World Religions.* New York: Columbia University Press, 1963.

———. *Morality and Beyond.* New York: Harper and Row, 1963.

———. *Systematic Theology.* (Vol. 3) Chicago: The University of Chicago Press, 1963.

———. *Ultimate Concern: Tillich in Dialogue.* Edited by D. Mackenzie Brown. New York: Harper and Row, 1965.

———. *On the Boundary.* New York: Charles Scribner's Sons, 1966.

———. *The Future of Religions.* ed. by Jerald C. Brauer. New York: Harper and Row,

1966.

———. *A History of Christian Thought*. Edited by Carl Braaten. New York: Simon and Schuster, 1967.

———. *My Search for Absolutes*. New York: Simon and Schuster, 1967.

———. *What is Religion?* Translated with an introduction by James Luther Adams. New York: Harper and Row, 1969.

———. "Christian Thought and Eastern Mysticism." (Unpublished). Tillich Archives: 411:005.

———. "Law and Love." (Unpublished). Tillich Archives: 403:018.

———. "Unity of Love and Its Healing Power." (Unpublished lectures). Tillich Archives: 407:018.

Secondary Sources

Abe, Masao. "Negation in Mahayana Buddhism and in Tillich: A Buddhist View of 'The Significance of the History of Religions for the Systematic Theologian." In *Negation and Theology*, ed. Robert P. Scharlemann, 86-99. Charlottesville and London: University Press of Virginia, 1992.

Adams, James Luther, W. Pauck and R. Shinn, eds. *The Thought of Paul Tillich.* New York: Harper, 1985.

Adams, James Luther. *Paul Tillich's Philosophy of Culture, Science, and Religion.* New York: Harper and Row, 1965.

Bulman, Raymond F. *A Blueprint for Humanity: Paul Tillich's Theology of Culture.* Lewisburg: Bucknell University Press, 1981.

———, and Frederik J. Parrella, eds. 1994. *Paul Tillich: A New Catholic Assessment.* Collegeville, Minnesota: The Liturgical Press.

Bush, Randall B. *Recent Ideas of Divine Conflict: The Influences of Psychological and Sociological Theories of Conflict upon the Trinitarian Theology of Paul Tillich and Jürgen Moltmann.* San Francisco: Mellen Research University Press, 1991.

Carey, John J., ed. *Kairos and Logos*. Cambridge, MA: North American Paul Tillich Society, 1978.

———, ed. *Theonomy and Autonomy: Studies in Paul Tillich's Engagement with Modern Culture*. Macon: Mercer University Press, 1984.

Chuck, James. "Zen Buddhism and Paul Tillich: A Comparison of Their Views of Man's Predicament and the Means of its Resolution." Th.D. diss., Pacific School of Religion, 1962.

Chun, Paul Sang-Wan. "The Christian Concept of God and Zen 'Nothingness' as Embodied in the Works of Tillich and Nishida." Ph.D. diss., Temple University, 1981.

Chun, Young Ho. "A Conceptual Analysis of Religion in Paul Tillich: with Particular Reference to his Positive Contribution towards a Theology of World Religion." Ph.D. diss., Drew University, 1981.

Clayton, John P. *The Concept of Correlation: Paul Tillich and the Possibility of a Mediating Theology.* Berlin: de Gruyter, 1980.

Davidovich, Adina. *Religion as a Province of Meaning: The Kantian Foundations of Modern Theology*. Minneapolis: Fortress Press, 1993.

Demartino, Richard, trans. and ed. "Dialogues East and West: Paul Tillich and Hisamatsu Shin'ichi." In *The Eastern Buddhist* n.s., 4 (October 1971): 98-107; 5 (October 1972): 107-128; 6 (October 1973): 87-114.

Dreisbach, Donald F. "Essence, Existence, and the Fall: Paul Tillich's Analysis of Existence." *Harvard Theological Review* 73 (July-Dec. 80): 521-538.

———. *Symbols and Salvation: Paul Tillich's Doctrine of Religious symbols and his Interpretation of Symbols of the Christian Tradition.* Lanham, MD: University Press of America, 1993.

Ferrell, Donald R. *Logos and Existence.* New York: Peter Lang, 1992.

Foester, John. "Paul Tillich and Inter-Religious Dialogue." *Modern Theology* 7/1(1990): 1-27.

Ford, Lewis S. "The Three Strands of Tillich's Theory of Religious Symbols." *The Journal of Religion* 46 (January 1966): 104-30.

———. "Tillich and Thomas." *The Journal of Religion* 44 (April 1966): 229-45.

———. "Tillich's Tergiversations Towards the Power of Being." *Scottish Journal of Theology*. 28:323-340.

Gilkey, Langdon. *Gilkey on Tillich.* New York: Crossroad Pulishing Co., 1990.

———. "Tillich and the Kyoto School." In *Negation and Theology*, ed. Robert P. Scharlemann, 72-85. Charlottesville and London: University Press of Virginia, 1992.

Grigg, Richard. *Symbol and Empowerment: Paul Tillich's Post-Theistic System.* Macon: Mercer University Press, 1985.

———. The Experiential Center of Tillich's System. *Journal of the American Academy of Religion* 53 (June 1985): 251-258.

Hammond, Guyton B. *Man in Estrangement: A Comparison of the Thought of Paul Tillich and Erich Fromm.* Nashville: Vanderbilt University Press, 1965.

Hartshorne, Charles. "Tillich's Doctrine of God" In *The Theology of Paul Tillich.* eds. Charles W. Kegley and Roobert W. Bretall. 15-27. New York: The Macmillan Co., 1964.

Hummel, Gert, ed. *God and Being / Gott und Sein: The Problem of Ontology in the Philosophical Theology of Paul Tillich.* Berlin, New York: Walter de Gruyter, 1989.

Irwin, Alexander C. *Eros Toward the World: Paul Tillich and the Theology of the Erotic.* Minneapolis: Fortress Press, 1991.

Kegley, Charles and Robert Bretall, eds. *The Theology of Paul Tillich.* New York: Pilgrim Press, 1982.

Kegley, Jacquelyn Ann K., ed. *Paul Tillich on Creativity.* Lanham, Md: University Press of America, 1989.

Kelsey, David. *The Fabric of Paul Tillich's Theology*. New Haven: Yale University Press, 1967.

Kim, Jong-Won. "Daisetz T. Suzuki and Paul Tillich: A Comparative Study of Their Thoughts of Ethics in Relation to Being." Th.D. diss., Graduate Theological Union, 1973.

Lai, Pan-Chiu. *Towards a Trinitarian Theology of Religions: a Study of Paul Tillich's Thought.* Kampen, The Netherlands: Kok Pharos Publishing House, 1994.

Liu, Shi-Hsien. "A Critique of Paul Tillich's Doctrine of God and Christology from an Oriental Perspective." In *Religious Issues and Interreligious Dialogues*, eds. by Charles Wei-Hsun Fu and Gerhard E. Spiegler, 511-532. New York, Westport: Greenwood Press, 1989.

Macleod, Alistair. *Paul Tillich: An Essay on the Role of Ontology in his Philosophical Theology.* London: George Allen and Unwin Ltd., 1973.

Mahan, Wayne W. *Tillich's System.* San Antonio, TX: Trinity University Press, 1974.

Mckelway, Alexander J. *The Systematic Theology of Paul Tillich: A Review and Analysis.* Richmond: John Knox Press, 1964.

Neville, Robert C. "A Christian Response to Shu-hsien Liu and Pei-jung Fu." In *Religious Issues and Interreligious Dialogues.* ed. Charles Wei-hsun Fu and Gerhard E. Spiegler. 555-570. New York, Westport: Greenwood Press, 1989.

Newport, John P. *Paul Tillich.* Peabody, MA: Hendrickson Publishers, 1984.

O'Meara, Thomas F. "Tillich and Heidgegger: A Structural Relationship." *Harvard Theological Review* 61 (1968): 249-261.

Olson, Carl. "Tillich's Dialogue with Buddhism." *Buddhist-Christian Studies* (1987): 183-195.

Osborne, Kenan B. *New Being: A Study on the Relationship between Conditioned and Unconditioned Being According to Paul Tillich.* The Hague: Martinus Nijhoff, 1969.

Pannenberg, Wolfhart. "Review of Systematic Theology Vol. 3 by Paul Tillich." *Dialog* 14 (1965): 229-232.

Pauck, Wilhelm and Marion. *Paul Tillich: His Life and Thought.* San Francisco: Harper and Row, 1984.

Plaskow, Judith. *Sex, Sin, and Grace: Women's Experience and the Theologies of Reinhold Niebuhr and Paul Tillich.* Lanham, Md.: University Press of America, 1980.

Ring, Nancy C. *Doctrine within the Dialectic of Subjectivity and Objectivity: a Critical Study of the Positions of Paul Tillich and Bernard Lonergan.* San Francisco: Mellen Reserch University Press, 1991.

Ross, Robert R. N. *The Non-Existence of God: Linguistic Paradox in Tillich's Thought.* New York: Edward Mellen Press, 1978.

———. "Non-Being and Being in Taoist and Western Traditions" in *Religious Tradition: A Journal in Study of Religion.* Vol 2, No. 2 (Oct. 1979): 24-38.

Rouner, Leroy S. "The Meeting of East and West: Paul Tillich's Philosophy of Religion." In *Knowing Religiously,* ed. by Leroy S. Rouner, 177-191. Notre Dame: University of Notre Dame Press.

Rowe, William L. *Religious Symbols and God: A Philosophical Study of Tillich's Theology*. Chicago: University of Chicago Press, 1968.

Sabatino, Charles J. "An Interpretation of the Significance of Theonomy within Tillich's Theology." *Encounter* Vol. 45, no. 1(1984): 23-39.

Scharlemann, Robert. "Tillich's Method of Correlation: Two Proposed Revisions."

Journal of Religion XLVI(1966): 92-103.

———. *Reflection and Doubt in the Thought of Paul Tillich.* New Haven: Yale University Press, 1969.

Schrader, Robert William. *The Nature of Theological Argument: A Study of Paul Tillich.* Missoula, MT: Scholars Press, 1975.

Schwarz, O. Douglas. "Religious Relativism: Paul Tillich's 'Last Word'." *American Journal of Theology and Philosophy* 7(1986): 106-114.

Thatcher, Adrian. *The Ontology of Paul Tillich.* Oxford: Oxford University Press, 1978.

Thomas, J. Heywood. "Tillich's Contribution to a World Theology." *Scottish Journal of Theology* 43 (1990): 350-365.

Thomas, J. Mark. *Ethics and Technoculture*. Lanham, MD: University Press of America, Inc., 1987.

Thomas, Terence. "Paul Tillich, Ontology, and Cultural Boundaries." In *God and Being/ Gott and Sein: The Problem of Ontology in the Philosophical Theology of Paul Tillich*, ed. Gert Hummel, 230-249. Berlin, New York: Walter de Gruyterr, 1989.

Thompson, Ian E. *Being and Meaning: Paul Tillich's Theory of Meaning, Truth, and Logic*. Edinburgh: Edinburgh University Press, 1981.

Westphal, Merold. "Hegel, Tillich, and the Secular." *The Journal of Religion* 52 (1972): 223-39.

Wood, Robert W. "Tillich Encounters Japan." *Japanese Religions* 2(1961): 48-71, 76-90.

Other Works

Ariarajah, S. Wesley. *The Bible and People of Other Faiths.* Geneva: The World Council of Churches, 1985.

Bellah, Robert N. *Beyond Belief: Essays on Religion in a Post-Traditional World.* New York: Harper and Row, 1970.

———. *Tokugawa Religion: The value of Pre-industrial Japan.* Boston: Beacon Press, 1970.

Berger, Peter, ed. *The Other Side of God: A Polarity in World Religions.* Garden City and New York: Doubleday, 1981.

———. *A Far Glory: The Quest for Faith in an Age of Credulity.* New York: The Free Press, 1992.

Berthrong, John H. "Tao and Logos: Confucian-Christian Dialogue." *China Notes* 15 (Winter 1986-87): 433-37.

———. "Syncretism Revisited: Multiple Religious Participation." *China Notes* 29, no. 4 (Autumn 1991): 654-55.

Braaten, Carl E. *No Other Gospel! Christianity among the World's Religions.* Minneapolis: Fortress Press, 1992.

Bryant, M. Darrol, ed. *Pluralism, Tolerance and dialogue: Six Studies.* Waterloo: University of Waterloo Press, 1989.

Ching, Julia. *Confucianism and Christianity: A Comparative Study.* Tokyo and New York: Kodansha International, 1977.

Cobb, John B. *Beyond Dialogue: Toward a Mutual Transformation of Christianity and Buddhism.* Philadelphia: Fortress Press, 1982.

Coward, Harold. *Pluralism: Challenge to World Religions.* Maryknoll, NY: Orbis Books, 1985.

Cracknell, Kenneth. *Towards a New Relationship between Christian and People of Other Faiths.* London: Epworth Press, 1986.

Cragg, Kenneth. *The Christ and the Faiths: Theology in Cross-Reference.* London: SPCK, 1986.

D'Costa, Gavin, ed. *Christian Uniqueness Reconsidered: The Myth of a Pluralistic Theology of Religions.* Maryknoll, NY: Orbis Books, 1990.

———. *Theology and Religious Pluralism: The Challenge of Other Religions.* Oxford: Basil Blackwell, 1986.

Dilworth, David A. *Philosophy in World Perspective: a Comparative Hermeneutics of the Major Theories.* New Haven: Yale University Press, 1989.

Eck, Diana. *Encountering God: A Spiritual Journey from Bozeman to Banaras.* Boston: Beacon Press, 1993.

Eliade, Mircea. *The Sacred and the Profane: The Nature of Religion.* Translated by Willard R. Trask. San Diego, CA: Harcourt Brace Jovanovich, Inc., 1959.

Griffiths, Paul J. *An Apology for Apologetics: A Study in the Logic of Interreligious Dialogue.* Maryknoll, NY: Orbis Books, 1991.

Hick, John and Brian Hebblethwaite, eds. *Christianity and Other Religions: Selected Readings.* Philadelphia: Fortress Press, 1980.

Hick, John. *God Has Many Names.* Philadelphia: The Westminster Press, 1982.

———, and Paul F. Knitter, eds. *The Myth of Christian Uniqueness: Towards a Pluralistic Theology of Religions.* Maryknoll, NY: Orbis Books, 1987.

———. *An Interpretation of Religion.* New Haven: Yale University Press, 1991.

———. *Disputed Questions in Theology and the Philosophy of Religion.* New Haven: Yale University Press, 1993.

Huntington, Samuel P. *The Clash of Civilizations and the Remaking of World Order.* New York: Simon And Schuster, 1996.

Katz, Steven T., ed. *Mysticism and Philosophical Analysis.* Oxford: Oxford University

Press, 1978.

———, ed. *Mysticism and Religious Traditions.* Oxford: Oxford University Press, 1983.

Kaufman, Gordon D. *In Face of Mystery: A Constructive Theology.* Cambridge, MA.: Harvard University Press, 1993.

Kekes, John. *The Morality of Pluralism.* Princeton: Princeton University Press, 1993.

Kitagawa, Joseph Mitsuo. *The Quest for Human Unity: a Religious History.* Minneapolis: Fortress Press, 1990.

Knitter, Paul F. *No Other Name? A Critical Survey of Christian Attitudes Toward the World Religions.* Maryknoll, NY: Orbis Books, 1985.

———. *One Earth Many Religions: Multifaith Dialogue and Global Responsibility.* Maryknoll, NY: Orbis Books, 1995.

Krieger, David J. *The New Universalism: Foundations for a Global Theology.* Maryknoll, NY: Orbis Boods, 1991.

Küng, Hans and Julia Ching. *Christianity and Chinese Religions.* New York: Doubleday, 1989.

Küng, Hans. *Theology for the Third Millennium: An Ecumenical View.* New York: Doubleday, 1988.

Larson, Gerald James and Eliot Deutsch. eds. *Interpreting Across Boundaries: New Essays in Comparative Philosophy.* Princeton: Princeton University Press, 1988.

Lee, Jung Young. *The Theology of Change: A Christian Concept of God in Eastern Perspective.* Maryknoll, NY: Orbis Books, 1979.

Lee, Peter K. H., ed. *Confucian-Christian Encounters in Historical and Contemporary Perspective.* Lewiston/Queenstown: The Edwin Mellen Press, 1991.

Lee, Thomas H. C., ed. *China and Europe: Images and Influences in Sixteenth to*

Eighteenth Centuries. Hong Kong: The Chinese University Press, 1991.

Lindbeck, George A. *The Nature of Doctrine: Religion and Theology in a Postliberal Age*. Philadelphia: The Westminster Press, 1984.

Lochhead, David. *The Dialogical Imperative: A Christian Reflection on Interfaith Encounter.* Maryknoll, NY: Orbis Books, 1988.

Loy, David. *Nonduality: A Study in Comparative Philosophy.* New Haven: Yale University Press, 1988.

Martinson, Paul Varo. *A Theology of World Religions: Interpreting God, Self, and World in Semitic, India, and Chinese Thought.* Minneapolis: Augsburg Publishing House, 1987.

Nakamura, Hajime. *Parallel Developments: A Comparative History of Ideas.* Tokyo: Kodansha, 1975.

Neville, Robert C. *Solider, Sage, Saint.* New York: Fordham University Press, 1978.

———. *The Tao and Daimon: Segments of a Religious* Inquiry. Albany: SUNY Press, 1982.

———. *The Puritan Smile*. Albany, NY: State University of New York Press, 1987.

———. *A Theology Primer*. Albany, New York: State University of New York Press, 1991.

———. *Behind the Masks of God: An Essay Toward Comparative Theology.* Albany: State University of New York Press, 1991.

———. "World Community and Religion" *Journal of Ecumenical Studies* 29:3-4 (Summer-Fall 1992): 368-382.

———. *Normative Cultures*. Albany: State University of New York Press, 1995.

O'Neill, Maura. *Women Speaking Women Listening: Women in Interreligious Dialogue*. Maryknoll, NY: Orbis Books, 1990.

Oxtoby, Willard G. *The Meaning of the Other Faiths*. Philadelphia: The Westminster Press, 1983.

Panikkar, Raimundo. *The Intra-Religious Dialogue*. New York: Paulist Press, 1978.

———. *The Cosmotheandric Experience: Emerging Religious Consciousness*. Maryknoll, N.Y.: Orbis Books, 1993.

Pieris, Aloysius. S.J. *An Asian Theology of Liberation*. Maryknoll, NY: Orbis Books, 1988.

Proudfoot, Wayne. *Religious Experience*. Berkeley: University of California Press, 1985.

Race, Alan. *Christian and Religious Pluralism: Patterns in the Christian Theology of Reigions*. London: SCM Press, 1983.

Rescher, Nicholas. *Pluralism: Against the Demand for Consensus*. Oxford: Oxford University Press, 1993.

Samartha, R. C. *One Christ--Many Religions: Toward a Revised Christology*. Maryknoll, N.Y.: Orbis Books, 1991.

Schreiter, Robert J. *Constructing Local Theologies*. Maryknoll, N.Y.: Orbis Books, 1985.

Sharpe, Eric J. *Understanding Religion*. London: Duckworth, 1983.

———. *Comparative Religion: A History*. 2d ed. La Salle, Ill: Open Court, 1986.

Shorter, Aylward. *Toward a Theology of Inculturation*. Maryknoll, N.Y.: Orbis Books, 1988.

Smith, Jonathan Z. *Imagining Religion: From Babylon to Jonestown*. Chicago: University of Chicago Press, 1982.

Smith, Wilfred Cantwell. *Faith and Belief*. Princeton: Princeton University Press, 1979.

———. *Towards a World Theology*. Philadelphia: The Westminster Press, 1981.

———. *The Meaning and End of Religion*. Minneapolis: Fortress Press, 1991.

———. *What is Scripture? A Comparative Approach.* Minneapolis: Fortress Press, 1993.

Standert, N. "Confucian-Christian Dual Citizenship: A Political Conflict?" *Ching Feng* 34, no. 2 (June 1991): 109-14.

Swidler, Leonard, ed. *Toward a Universal Theology of Religion.* Maryknoll, NY: Orbis Books, 1987.

———. *After the Absolute: The Dialogical Future of Religious Reflection.* Minneapolis: Fortress Press, 1990.

Tracy, David. *The Analogical Imagination: Christian Theology and the Culture of Pluralism.* New York: Crossroad, 1981.

———. *Plurality and Ambiguity: Hermeneutics, Religion, Hope.* San Francisco: Harper and Row, 1987.

———. *Dialogue With the Other: The Inter-religious Dialogue.* Louvain and Grand Rapids, MI: Peeters Press and William B. Eerdmans Publishing Company, 1990.

Tu, Wei-ming. "Global community as lived reality: exploring spiritual resources for social development." In *Social Policy and Social Progress: A Review Published by the United Nations.* 39-51. New York: United Nations, 1995.

Vroom, Hendrik M. *Religions and the Truth: Philosophical Reflections and Perspectives.* Grand Rapids, Mich., and Amsterdam: William B. Eerdmans Publishing Company and Editions Rodopi, 1989.

Wach, Joachim. *The Comparative Study of Religion.* N.Y.: Columbia University Press, 1958.

———. *Types of Religious Experience: Christian and Non-Christian.* Chicago: The University of Chicago Press, 1951.

Waton, Walter. *The Architectonics of Meaning: Foundations of the New Pluralism.* Albany, N.Y.: State University of New York Press, 1985.

Werblowsky, R. J. Zwi. *Beyond Tradition and Modernity: Changing Religions in a*

Changing World. London: The Athlone Press, 1976.

Yao, Xinzhong *Confucianism and Christianity: A Comparative Study of Jen and Agape.* Brighton, UK: Sussex Academic Press, 1996.

Zaeher, R. C. *Concordant Discord: The Interdependence of Faiths.* Oxford: Oxford University Press, 1970.

ASIAN THOUGHT AND CULTURE

This series is designed to cover three inter-related projects:

- *Asian Classics Translation*, including those modern Asian works that have been generally accepted as "classics"
- *Asian and Comparative Philosophy and Religion*, including excellent and publishable Ph.D. dissertations, scholarly monographs, or collected essays
- *Asian Thought and Culture in a Broader Perspective*, covering exciting and publishable works in Asian culture, history, political and social thought, education, literature, music, fine arts, performing arts, martial arts, medicine, etc.

For additional information about this series or for the submission of manuscripts, please contact:

Peter Lang Publishing, Inc.
Acquisitions Department
275 Seventh Avenue, 28th floor
New York, New York 10001

To order other books in this series, please contact our Customer Service Department at:

800-770-LANG (within the U.S.)
(212) 647-7706 (outside the U.S.)
(212) 647-7707 FAX

Or browse online by series at:

www.peterlangusa.com